THE FUTURE
OF THE
METHODIST
THEOLOGICAL
TRADITIONS

THE FUTURE
OF THE
METHODIST
THEOLOGICAL
TRADITIONS

Edited by

M. Douglas Meeks

Abingdon Press
Nashville

The Future of the Methodist Theological Traditions

Library of Congress Cataloging in Publication Data
MAIN ENTRY UNDER TITLE:
The Future of the Methodist theological traditions.
 Papers from the Seventh Oxford Institute of Method-
ist Theological Studies held July 26-Aug. 5, 1982.
 1. Methodist Church—Doctrines—Congresses.
 2. Methodist Church—Doctrines—History—
Congresses. I. Meeks, M. Douglas. II. Oxford Insti-
tute of Methodist Theological Studies (7th : 1982)
BX8331.2.F88   1985   230'.7   84-12507

ISBN 0-687-13868-X

Chapter 4, "Ecclesial Location and Ecumenical Vocation" is taken from *The
Ecumenical Movement: Crisis and Opportunity for the Church* by Geoffrey
Wainwright, William B. Eerdmans Publishing Company, 1983. Used by
permission. Scripture quotations are taken from the Revised Standard
Version of the Bible, copyrighted 1946, 1952, © 1971, 1973 by the Division of
Christian Education of the National Council of Churches of Christ in the
U.S.A., and are used by permission.

MANUFACTURED BY THE PARTHENON PRESS AT
NASHVILLE, TENNESSEE, UNITED STATES OF AMERICA

Contents

Introduction

M. Douglas Meeks

The Seventh Oxford Institute of Methodist Theological Studies was convened in the summer of 1982 at Keble College, Oxford. The Institute, as in the past, was composed of Methodist scholars, pastors, and church leaders from all over the world. This book contains the major papers given at the Institute, whose theme was "The Future of the Methodist Theological Traditions."

The overall objective of the Oxford Institute is to nurture scholarship for the ministry and mission of Methodist and Wesleyan churches, which share a common life in the World Methodist Council. The Institute thus seeks to create a community of learning that respects John Wesley's insistence on the marriage of learning and piety.

The organization of the Seventh Institute will help to explain the format of this book. The members of this Institute were divided up into working groups that dealt with issues on the cutting edge of contemporary Methodist scholarship. The five working groups were: "Wesley Studies," "Salvation, Justice, and the Theological Task," "Ecclesiology and Sacraments in an Ecumenical Context," "Evangelism in the Wesleyan Traditions," and "Wesleyan Spirituality and Faith Development." Each field of study was represented by a major lecturer who addressed the entire Institute. The results of intensive, specialized scholarly work by each working group were then shared in the plenary via a working paper. A similar structure is reflected in this book. Following an introduction of the Institute's theme in chapter one, the reader will find each chapter containing the major lecture, then the working paper of each field. The rich and complex developments within the working group on "Evangelism in the Wesleyan Traditions" have warranted the additional survey paper by David Lowes Watson. Brian E. Beck, Co-chairperson of the Institute, provides a retrospect of the Institute.

Christian scholarship in the broadest sense is the act of remembering the past and saying what it means today. Baal Shem Tov, the founder of Hasidism, said, "Forgetfulness leads to exile. Remembrance is the secret of redemption." In this sense the Old Testament prophets were scholars. They remembered the past of God's faithfulness and said what it meant for the crises of the present. Indeed many persons who are considered activists, such as Martin Luther King, Jr., are in this sense basically scholars. King remembered the promises of God and said what they meant for his time and his nation. In this respect the faith of every Christian depends on remembering the past.

The Seventh Oxford Institute began with the premise that the future of Methodist and Wesleyan churches is put in jeopardy because of a widespread forgetfulness of their traditions. They are threatened with "exile," not the physical removal to a foreign land but the slow disappearance of their distinctive calling in Jesus Christ through accommodation and enculturation in their own lands. Without remembering their past they will know neither who they are in the present nor what they should expect from the future.

Methodism throughout the world is faced with the crisis, which is also an opportunity, in which it will have to give a defense (*apologia*) of the hope that is within it (I Pet. 3:15). What hope is there, what real anticipation of the future, in a time so threatened by the nuclear apocalypse and the intensifying and deadly struggle between the rich and the poor in our world? If there is a distinctively "Methodist" Christian *apologia*, it will surely not emerge without remembering what has been passed down to us through the Methodist traditions.

But are the Methodist traditions worth remembering? The energy and courage for remembering the past come first of all from God's forgiveness of our guilt. Just as guilty persons do not have the freedom to play, neither can they remember the past. They spend too much energy repressing and forgetting a guilty past that has become loathsome to them. And thus Wesley knew there could be no learning for the sake of the gospel without the gift of the forgiveness of the learner. Prayer must ground and be conjoined with scholarship, doxology with theology. But the energy and courage of remembering the past also comes from a confidence that the past really does contain promises which open up the future and make a difference in the present. Otherwise the work of remembering and interpreting the tradition will seem sterile and unsavory. The essays collected here face the question about how the people called Methodist can be energized to remember their past in expectation of the future at a time when the future appears so threatened.

The Institute did not engage in nostalgia about the Methodist past. It is clear that we remember the Methodist traditions only because they help us to remember Jesus Christ as mediated through the scriptures. The fact that both tradition and scripture stand under the lordship of Jesus Christ means that the Methodist traditions must be retrieved critically. Thus the main theme of this book is a new assessment of the Methodist theological traditions in light of the life and death questions that world Methodism faces today.

It will be clear that these essays are the beginning of a process, not a finished edifice. On the whole they raise more questions than they give answers. They point to open vistas rather than report completed projects. They propose avenues for research in the Methodist traditions and thus invite all those who will into a worldwide community of Methodist scholarship. They offer imagination and encouragement for next steps in the journey of the Methodist/Wesleyan community of learning.

As Co-chairpersons of the Oxford Institute of Methodist Theological Studies, Brian Beck and I wish to thank the many persons who gave of their time generously in the preparation and execution of the Institute. The Reverend Donald A. Pickard served skillfully as Secretary of the Institute. Reverend Joe Hale, General Secretary of the World Methodist

Council, gave support and encouragement. Financial assistance was provided by the Overseas Division of British Methodism, the United Methodist Board of Global Ministries, and the Division of Ordained Ministry of the United Methodist Board of Higher Education and Ministry. Special gratitude is due the convenors of the working groups for their creative leadership: Professor Albert C. Outler, Professor Theodore Runyon, Professor Geoffrey Wainwright, Professor David Lowes Watson, and Professor James Fowler. Finally, these fruits of the life and work of the Seventh Oxford Institute are dedicated to four persons to whose decanal vision and perseverance the Oxford Institute owes its existence.

1

The Future of the
Methodist Theological Traditions

M. Douglas Meeks

The theme of the Seventh Oxford Institute of Methodist Theological Studies was not chosen lightly or even willingly. After all, with the exception of the two articles and the one preposition, every word is problematic: "Future," "Methodist," "Theological," "Traditions." These words have become questions to us. But it is good that we begin by acknowledging the questions before us because questions always last longer than answers and in some ways are more important. It is, to be sure, disingenious to ask questions that one cannot answer. But no theologian can control forever the questions he or she must deal with. Sooner or later, the questions of children make their way into our working context in such a way that we cannot elude them. The questions of children and of what the New Testament calls the *mikroi*, the little ones, "the least of these my brothers and sisters," are, of course, mostly unanswerable, at least in any theoretical way, for they ask questions about suffering and joy, dying and new birth, which no theoretician has ever adequately treated. It may be that here at the beginning we should raise some questions that we could not possibly answer in this fortnight. But to state the matter positively, all communities come into being through common suffering over common questions. And our common suffering, and thus our community, is likely to be shaped, at least in the first instance, around these questions: "Future," "Methodist," "Theological," and "Traditions." If we had pondered for years, we would not have been able to come up with more obdurate proposals for study. Why, then, this theme?

13

The most direct answer is that it has been forced upon us by the present historical situations of our beloved Methodist and Wesleyan churches. The last Oxford Institute made this theme especially urgent and unavoidable. The Sixth Institute, focusing on the relationship between "liberation" and "sanctification," tried to bring the present state of Methodist theology into a creative confrontation with liberation theologies.[1] Can Methodist theology contribute anything to Christian mission in the worldwide situations of injustice and oppression? If it can, what does this mean for the mission of the Methodist churches in the Northern and Southern Hemispheres? If it cannot, where does this leave Methodism? Hopelessly locked into the cultural forms and institutions of the North Atlantic community? Inevitably suffering the fate of North America and Europe, armed to the teeth as they are with horrendously destructive weapons, but increasingly impotent to envision a way for the world to survive the intensifying conflicts of injustice? Could the Methodist/Wesleyan churches make some actual contribution to the conversion of West and East, to the radical transformation of the Northern Hemisphere societies so that the world might live? These were the questions on our minds in 1977.

Behind these questions was serious wrestling with the Halévy-Thompson debates about whether eighteenth- and nineteenth-century Methodism was a positive force in bringing societal change toward justice without the abhorrent disruptions of the French Revolution or a negative force of psychological and reformist amelioration preventing the needed radical structural change in the British and American societies.[2] The Institute sought to bring these debates up to our time and to ask the same questions about the Methodism we are living.

The thesis, the main contention, the wager of the Sixth Institute was that the Wesleyan doctrine of sanctification is indeed transformationist and can relate faithfully and effectively to the radical change which the "global village" must live through in the next decades in order to survive. Theodore Runyon summarized the positive thrust in this fashion:

When Wesley is approached from the vantage point of liberation theologies, and especially from the perspective of the Marxist critique, his theology not only can be freed from the confines of pietistic individualism, it can counteract that individualism and offer resources for the responsible rethinking of theology in a time when both neo-Reformation and liberal models no longer suffice.
. . . Only a theology that is transformationist can do justice to the Christian doctrine of sanctification and to the quality of salvation which that doctrine seeks to express.[3]

It was argued that Wesley's understanding of *faith lived in love toward holiness* was intimately connected with what liberation theologies speak of as praxis, radical spirituality, and identification with the poor.

But there were serious questions raised about that contention. Argentine theologian José Míguez Bonino maintained: "The fact that Methodism was unable to disclose for them the reality of their condition as a class, but rather led them to accept their role in society and to improve their lot without challenging the rules of the game, was one element of the domestication of the working class in Britain."[4]

Third World theologians pressed very hard the project of speaking about a future of Methodism among the oppressed in the Southern Hemisphere.

For us in the third world at least, Methodism as a social force is part of history—and in some ways part of the history of our domination and exploitation. The future belongs, under God, to the people— whether Methodist or Reformed or Catholic. . . . Whatever symbols, ideas, and representations will lead them in their struggle for liberation cannot be brought from outside (least of all from a foreign history), but must be begotten in the womb of the oppressed peoples.[5]

Wesley, it was claimed, was unable to see "the structural nature" of the social problem. Wesley's "holiness was social in the narrow sense that it related to personal relations with other people, especially those in the fellowship of believers."[6] As an eighteenth-century British High Church Tory gentleman, Wesley remained within the mercantilist system of thought. He believed in the *ancient régime*, the divine order, in which monarchy offered the greatest amount of liberty. If human beings were politically free to become sanctified, no further structural change seemed necessary.[7] Wesley's anthropology seemed incurably individualistic.[8] John Kent summed it up rather pointedly:

Holiness—far from being the definable state of consciousness Wesley took it to be . . . is a constant improvisation of charity out of ignorance and against the conditioning odds. Here, liberation, understood as the kind of self-awareness that is central to both black theology and feminist theology, seems to be a more hopeful guide than are scholastic revivals of sixteenth-to-eighteenth century doctrines of sanctification.[9]

And so went the debate that has brought us thus far. The questions are acute and too conspicuous to be ignored: Are the Methodist traditions really fruitful enough to play a role in the liberation of the oppressed? Is Methodism as we have known it in the nineteenth and twentieth centuries already to be consigned to the dust bin of history? Do the Methodist theological traditions really have a future?

Do these questions represent only talismanic slogans, which themselves are evanescent? Are they fair questions? They go to the extreme in asking about the *relevance* of Methodism for the future, but do they not at the same time throw us into a deep *identity crisis?*

What is it about Methodists that makes us willing to deprecate and cashier our traditions? Do we prefer to gain our identity simply from the present actuality of our churches? Are there dangerous memories in the Methodist traditions that we want to keep from surfacing? I mean "dangerous" in the sense that if these memories were to become in any way authorizing for us, we ourselves and our life situations would have to change radically. Is it, for example, a dangerous memory that our origin is not as a church, but rather as an order, a society, a movement for the reformation of the church and the evangelization and transformation of the world? Does that memory make us unbearably uncomfortable about our denominationalism? Has the present actuality of denominationalism become the criterion of truth for us, so much so that our tradition has to be officially eclipsed? Are the memories of Wesley's solidarity

16

with the poor and of his peculiar configuration of theology, which left no easy rapprochement with the established theologies—are these memories also too dangerous for our place in the total mix of world church and world community? Why Methodist? Why be a Methodist? This is one of those children's questions that goes embarrassingly to the very heart of the matter. Sometimes I have the childlike daydream that the several million persons around the globe who call themselves after the name and legacy of John Wesley could be brought together in one place. If I had only a minute to address this body, I would ask a series of questions. *Why has the Lord put you here as Methodists? What is the reason for your being Methodists? What in actual fact do you have to contribute to the church universal? What distinctive contributions are you making to God's work to redeem the world? What are you doing for the future of the world? Whose interests do you serve?*

This scene is only an alluring chimera, but unless we can answer these questions in good faith, even though our answers will be limited by our place in history, Methodism surely will fade in terms of significance for the future. It does not much help to say that the other mainline Protestant denominations are in the same boat. Do we want to be Methodists? Are we going to remain Methodists? If we do and we are, then we have to get to work at the critical appropriation and practice of the Methodist traditions. That is what this Institute is about. To use the old Southern *bon mot*, it is time "to paint or get off the ladder."

John Wesley: "Methodist" Authority?

Let us turn first to the problematic theme "Methodist." To raise the question about Methodism is inevitably to raise the question about John Wesley. Is it not the case that those of us who will continue to call ourselves Methodist inexorably have a relationship to John Wesley? Is there anything still living in his life and thought for a faithful future of Christian mission in the world? With these questions in mind the call of this Institute has put as its initial task the critical remembrance of Wesley. For Methodist churches generally, Wesley lies buried under many decades of cult worship, ideological misuse, selective memory, and self-serving of the churches claiming his legacy. By and large, we do not even know what questions or how to ask of Wesley, much less what questions Wesley should ask of us. We have a desultory relationship with Mr. Wesley. We have discovered that the nineteenth- and twentieth-century receptions of Wesley embarrass us and, worse, mislead us. Much work needs to be done on the nineteenth century to ascertain the historical processes in Britain and the United States that gave rise to the standard views of Wesley. This work might be a candidate for a future Institute. But in light of the last Institute, we have discovered the extreme urgency of getting in touch with John Wesley himself on a broad new footing.

The fate of Methodism in the nineteenth and twentieth centuries should not determine our reading of Wesley. Nor should the hidden assumptions of our own methods. To explain the captivity of the Methodist traditions to economic interests and structures is important, but by itself it says absolutely nothing about how persons are to gain the freedom, interest, and power to change conditions in our present situation. Economic and social analysis that masquerades as theology and proceeds without the question of how persons actually are to be converted in their interests and values also contains a reactionary element and in the end serves a despairing counsel of doom.

Is it all that useful to criticize Wesley for not giving a Marxist critique of society or for not being a capitalist? Is it wise to read Wesley through post-Kantian epistemologies and philosophies of history? Is it pertinent to judge Wesley according to the standards of systematic theology since Schleiermacher or for that matter according to the Lutheran and Reformed Renaissance of our century? What intention do we have when we submit Wesley's thought and life to these methodological assumptions? Is it that we want to ask Wesley all the questions without giving him a chance to question us?

But are there other ways of reading Wesley? Should not Wesley be read in terms of his whole corpus? In terms of his time and place? And in view of the whole Christian tradition? This is the direction of the project that Albert Outler and others have been urging for several years. "Place Wesley in his own times, on his own terms—with a critical historical perspective."[10] This programme has to do with work in the primary sources of the Methodist traditions in an ecumenical style and on behalf of an ecumenical theology. It assumes that Methodist theology is congenitally and constitutionally ecumenical. That is, Wesley's theology must be set within the whole tradition in order to be able to make its own peculiar contributions. It simply cannot function without the sacramental order and universal covenant of the larger church.

This endeavor amounts, it seems, to nothing short of Wesley's liberation from two centuries and more of Methodism—all for the sake of the faithful practice of Methodist and Wesleyan churches today. Of course, there are hermeneutical questions involved in this historiographical program. It derives its hermeneutical questions from the whole tradition, including East and West. The secret is then to read Wesley the way Wesley read the tradition. It is historiography in the service of uncovering Wesley's own hermeneutic. This follows the contemporary hermeneutical principle of "the mediation of the interpretation of meaning through a subject that is itself located within a context of traditioned meaning."[11] The result is that we can be freed from narrow hermeneutic of the triumphalistic Methodist churches, the holiness movements, liberalism, Reformation theology, neo-orthodoxy, the social gospel, and colonialistic missions—while maintaining the unique contributions each might have made. Any Methodist theologian doing church theology in the context of the Methodist and Wesleyan churches, I should think, would have to come to grips with these historiographical implications.

But what about what Ricoeur calls hermeneutic "on this side of the text?" Can we simply take over Wesley's hermeneutic lock, stock, and barrel? Which elements should be taken over and why? What do the present groanings of the Holy Spirit and the sufferings of these times require that we ask of the biblical and traditional texts beyond what Wesley asked? Could we in this Institute begin to commit ourselves to the patience and care for the historiographical work necessary to encounter the real Wesley as well as to the hard work of relating Wesley's reading of the tradition to a hermeneutic that takes our solidarity in Jesus Christ with the poor as the key?

Behind the question of a new historiography and a new hermeneutic lies the more general question of Wesley's authority. By an old and widespread judgment, John Wesley does not seem to be a first-rank theologian in the mode of Augustine and Aquinas, Luther and Calvin, Schleiermacher and Barth. That judgment makes us as Methodists tend to look for Wesley's authority on other grounds. The standard notion of Wesley's authority is as founder of the Methodist churches and their offshoots. From this perspective we view Wesley as having laid the foundation stone in the eighteenth century. Great reverence can be accorded the founder, but because we can be very selective about what we remember from Wesley, invoking his name can mean not much more than sanctifying the present actuality of the church. The "Daddy," after all, would agree with anything his children would do in his name. Thinking in terms of modern historicism supports this view of authority because we are able to reduce anything we do not like about Wesley or anything that threatens our social and economic positioning to the vagaries of his eighteenth-century context. Thus, Wesley is nothing more than a faint echo whispered over the decades, while the church is free to fashion a hero figure as its immediate interests dictate.

Wesley can also be viewed as the legal founder of Methodist institutions. Authority lies in the testamentary definition, which has been fixed by the founder's intention and which determines the form of the institution's present administration. Of course, when Methodism passed over to America, it selected only parts of the "last will and testament." Wesley was seen as the founder of very successful religious movements and institutions that considered themselves the continuing action of Wesley's will. But the more the church is viewed as the continuation of Wesley's will, the more the present legal administration of this will in the church determines who the founder should and can be. The church celebrates "founders' day" but does not fully take seriously a conversation with Wesley. And over the long haul there is the suspicion, as evidenced with a vengeance in our time, of the continuing ineffective will of the founder. The result is increasing frustration.

Wesley is also sometimes viewed from a third perspective as the prototype of faith. Wesley made it possible for us to believe. There is something to this. There is something about the power of Wesley's faith as it relates to the miracle of our own faith. But there is also something highly dangerous about viewing Wesley as the origin and model of faith. And, of course, the danger is the proximity to idolatry.

In the fourth place, Wesley's authority can be seen to lie in his "holy living." He is our elder brother whose example we should follow. God occasionally gives God's people such persons whose lives embody the Pauline exhortation: "live a life worthy of the calling to which you have been called" and invite us, "Do as I do." This is not to say that ugly aspects of Wesley's life cannot be found for the looking. He was in some senses immature, boastful, authoritarian, and a compulsive neurotic.[12] But we cannot deny our fascination with certain ascetic and aesthetic dimensions of Wesley's life. Viewing the wholeness of Wesley's life as authority, however, would create by itself nothing but a personality cult.

A better way to view Wesley as our authority is as our teacher of the critical appropriation and practice of the tradition. What I wish to maintain is that Wesley's way of receiving and practicing the tradition is *his authorizing* of our peculiar Methodist/Wesleyan contribution to the ecumenical church and to the praxis of the Christian faith in the world today. Furthermore, Wesley's way of critically practicing the tradition is helpful with our struggle today over the nature and task of theology.

"Theological"

It is no news to anyone today that theology is in trouble. Some are saying that theology as the project set in motion by Thomas Aquinas is coming to an end. What will take its place? Does world Methodism even need such a creature as a *theological* institute? If our project is not to suffer abortion at its very conception, we shall have to inquire whether Wesley suggests alternative ways of understanding the nature and function of theology. Does he propose a way of viewing theology as "sound teaching" for the faithful praxis of the church? We can safely say that Wesley was neither a denominationalist nor a university theologian. He was a strategist for the renewal of the church and the evangelization of society. He had a strange relationship to the national church, never wanting to separate from its ministry and sacramental framework, but yet never becoming a theologian for the administration of the "multitudinous," the mass church.[13] University-trained in the broad humanist disciplines of philology, rhetoric, and logic, as most of us are, Wesley nevertheless was among the poor and studied communication with them in ways that some liberation theologians are only theorizing about. He did not separate biblical and doctrinal theology from the local class meeting. Despite all the obvious criticisms, which can be lodged against Wesley by liberation theologies, might it not be the case that his is after all a preeminent example of praxis theology?

For all his too facile acceptance of certain universal philosophical concepts of the eighteenth century, Wesley for the most part did not trade in the inexplicability of these great placative concepts to justify their explanatory value and thereby to cover up every conceivable contradiction in thought and society. Rather he viewed theology as a process of concrete critique of and real liberation from the godless ties in society. He did not settle for theology as a mere integration or synthesis of different positions, confessions, or cultures. He cannot be attached to a school nor did he found one. A folk theologian with no academic base, he developed no metaphysical theories. He did not have an epistemological method elaborated in advance of the first things which must be said about the gospel. He worked out no great system that lusts after the unity of being, thought, society, and church by excluding the negatives of social existence or by eclipsing the only power which can bring about unity, namely, suffering love.

Wesley is a valuable dialogue partner just at this time when we are again confronted with attempts to make theology into a *Wissenschaftstheorie* in order to justify the place of theology in the university. Theology oriented to world views and pursued as a universal science is again coming into vogue. In Europe and the United States there is a search for "the integrating meta-theological unity of theory itself," which, in my view, threatens to make theology utterly illusory. In this project the theologian overlooks his or her own conditions of existence in reference to the universal whole with the result that his or her own conditions are imperiously generalized as *the* unifying theory. Thus traditionally mediated authority is simply replaced by a new kind of subtle imperialism and totalitarianism in theology. Such theology finds it increasingly difficult to identify anything as peculiarly Christian because Christianity (in its European-North American expression) is itself viewed as the unifying theory of the West. Because for Wesley, theology is oriented to the gospel for sinners and the poor, he can authorize our struggle against the loss of the gospel's uniqueness in the dominating techniques of abstraction.

"Traditions"

In the context of the World Methodist Council we are faced with the reality of plural traditions, which name themselves after Wesley and the original Methodist movements. We increasingly sense the embarrassment that often there has been more dialogue between the various Methodist/Wesleyan traditions and other confessional traditions than among the Methodist/Wesleyan traditions themselves. But it is not only the plurality of our traditions that we have to face honestly but also the very notion of tradition itself. So deflated is the notion of tradition that in our amnesia and anesthesia our intention of considering the future of Methodist traditions could be immediately declared vain. Thus our conversation with Wesley and the Methodist traditions inevitably will take place in full acknowledgment of the crisis of tradition itself. The future of the Methodist theological traditions depends at least initially on our deciding whether the church's theological existence needs tradition. Without tradition theology has no *theo*logical given. And unless we want to contend that faith creates faith or that theological judgments fund themselves, we must be able to say how tradition is the necessary matrix and a valid criterion of theology.

The crisis of tradition in the church, as Edward Farley has shown recently, has been brought on by the fact that the "house of authority," which the early church built as its methodological home, has collapsed in the modern world.[14] The collapse of this house has been caused by suffering from evil and oppression, whether in the economic, political, cultural, natural, or personal dimensions of modern life. That is, the theodicy question has dismantled the traditional method and content of theology.

The "house of authority" was built on the "monarchical metaphor of God's relation to the world" and was expressed in the "logic of triumphalism."[15] The interconnection of the ancient Christian doctrine of God with Greek metaphysical notions of being based on political rule was demonstrated several decades ago by Erik Peterson.[16] By and large the power of God has been thought traditionally on the model of imperialism. Agamemnon's statement in preparation for the Trojan war, "Let there be one ruler only," was the background for the metaphysical and later theological connection between monotheism and monarchy. All the attributes of being itself were given to God in Christian theology: one, simple, undivided, immutable, infinite, immortal, self-sufficient, and impassible. These are the attributes one needs in order to control, to dominate, to rule an empire. Stoicism and many other traditions of political philosophy shifted these attributes in their immanent form to the anthropological sphere. Today these attributes are lusted after by the *homo Americanus* or the *homo Sovieticus* as the means of domination.

The imperial metaphor of God's relation to the world leads to one of two alternatives: Either God can but does not will to redeem creation from evil or God can and does determine everything in creation and thus is the cause of evil. Both assumptions are exploded by the theodicy question in its modern forms because both assumptions deny divine goodness and creaturely freedom. When heteronomous divine causality is denied, however, so is the notion of identity between divine and human acts, an assumption that grounds the classical conception of the authority of scripture, dogma, the magisterium, and tradition.[17]

We are then left with the products of the historian's or the sociologist's work but not with the "faith once received." Thus we get the modern and contemporary theological attempts to replace tradition with the historical study of Christianity or with phenomenology, with sociological analysis or ideology.

Could Wesley suggest to us some alternative dimensions of appropriating the tradition beyond the citation of authority based on divine causality and beyond the substitution of phenomenology or sociology? For Wesley the given matrix of theology was not dogma or feeling or experience or social analysis. It was the reality of the redemptive existence created by the grace of God—preventing, justifying, and sanctifying.[18] This was what we might call Wesley's "portraiture" of the tradition, his way of reading, comprehending, and appropriating the tradition. Wesley's writings are full of the classical genre of citation and explication of authorities, which belongs to the "house of authority." But there is also another genre at work, which we might refer to as inquiry into the tradition out of the experienced reality of the lived redemptive history. I believe we can see in Wesley the essentially catholic view that the cognitive (remembering, reflecting) dimensions of faith are founded in the corporate existence of the being-redeemed people. Tradition is an agency of the authorization (creation) of the faithful community. It is in this field that tradition comes alive. This is the context in which the *paradosis* is sought after and yearned for as is the last family member to come home at night.

Perhaps even more fruitful would be a careful investigation of the similarities between what liberation theology calls "praxis" and Wesley's relationship to faith's originative events.

How does the practice of tradition contribute to the authorization of the community? It has often been maintained that Wesley subjectivizes and privatizes the inheritance of tradition. That is not true. For Wesley, neither the content of the gospel, the narrative of Jesus Christ, nor the delivering of the gospel is subjectivized. They are objective and objectively transforming events. It is true that the evidence by which they become assured by faith seems to be for Wesley internal to the soul. But the redeeming efficacy of Jesus Christ is historically real. The "cumulative narrative bond" is found in the life and action of the person being justified and sanctified. "The crucial and indispensable continuity or linkage in the story is the journeying of the Christian person from sin through justification to sanctification. . . ."[19] God's gracious righteousness in Jesus is remembered and "storied" in the action of the believer. The redeemer is also the creator of the Christian's journey "for this is the narrative framework, the meaningful pattern within which alone the occurrence of the cross finds its applicative sense. What is real, and what therefore the Christian really lives, is his own pilgrimage: and to its pattern he looks for the assurance that he is really living it."[20]

Contemporary praxis theology speaks of the critical practice of the tradition in a similar way, except it views the righteousness/justice of God as evidence for sanctification and assurance in a much broader social, political, and economic framework. To be justified and sanctified means to become part of the history of God through the world which we see and enter into through Jesus Christ. The plot-line of the story is fixed in the cross of Jesus Christ in which we see the embodied power, freedom, and justice of God. The life of going on to maturity is the life of entering into this power, freedom, and justice by means of the gracious empowering of God the Holy Spirit.

The "Future": Power, Freedom, and Justice

We have considered the problematics "Methodist," "Theological," and "Traditions." It remains to confront the "Future." The Methodist traditions must contribute to our hope in the future in the face of increasing despair about the future, or our task of preparing for the future of the Methodist traditions will have no ground. Methodist traditions, like all other traditions, face the seemingly universal threat to the human future.

26

The future is radically questioned by a widespread sense of scarcity, on the one hand, and of satiety, at least in the developed countries, on the other hand. Both the fear of scarcity, a future not realizable, and the experience of satiety, the numbness of a future thought pretentiously to be already realized, yield a new atmosphere of insecurity. And thus as never before the future questions the Methodist theological traditions about the kind of power, freedom, and justice that can promise a future for the world.

The future confronts the tradition with this question: "Will our own power destroy us?" For the first time in history Christians are commanded to preach the gospel in a time in which the whole human race could commit suicide. The bomb, "the desolating sacrilege set up where it ought not to be" (Mark 13:14), has become the ultimate symbol of human power. It is the symbol of the power of human techné to dominate the earth and control history. The proof is in the human power to put an end to the earth. But the symbol of our greatest power is also the symbol of our greatest impotence. It is the reality of our sin's recoil. We human beings, held Wesley in agreement with Augustine, are created to be able freely to love God infinitely. The reality of original sin is that we love ourselves and our accomplishments infinitely.[21] Only this capacity for misplacing our love of God onto an infinite love of and trust in our weapons can explain the fact that the human being, a creature, could destroy the whole earth.

The bomb epitomizes the danger of this new age in which power will have to be radically transformed if we are going to survive and contribute to the future of God's creation. The existence of the power that can bring universal death to the world requires that the "age of empire" be brought to an end. It is becoming plain that we cannot continue trying to form life around the traditional conceptions of imperial power without suffering the suicidal adjudications of imperial conflicts. If it is clear that imperialistic conceptions of power must come to an end, do we not have to think of God in nonimperialistic ways and worship and love God with our lives in nonimperialistic ways? Will not the future of Methodist theological traditions depend on their fructification

27

of these attempts to worship, serve, and trust God in ways more consistent with God's character as seen in the crucified Jesus?

The basic question is how God's power is to be defined. Wesley perceived God in the passion of Christ and the passion of Christ in God. To be sure, he spoke in the traditional language of the sovereignty and omnipotence of God. But are there not many clues in Wesley for a transvaluation of God's sovereignty into nonimperialistic modes? For Wesley the power of God for redemption, for the new creation of human beings in the world, is God's power of self-giving.[22] Is it not the case that Wesley's view of the love of God as the power of the cross, the power of God's suffering love *pro nobis*, was the single most important element in the Methodist revival?

Justifying and sanctifying grace are not the action of an emperor who owns and rules the world by fiat, but the work, the grief, the suffering, the joy of the God who gives God's life away for the world. This is the God whose actions are preceded by passions. This is the God who does not coerce but invites with promises of joy in suffering; who does not glory in self-sufficiency but who suffers for our own transformation and that of the world so that we may be in God's presence of glory.

The future also questions the Methodist traditions about freedom. In the developed world, freedom and authority have been at odds at least since the Enlightenment. Reflecting the ancient theological tension between sovereignty and agency, we vascillate between *paternalism* and *autonomy*. The conflict between these two conceptions of freedom in the Northern Hemisphere in large measure contributes to the structures in which oppressed people are forced to live around the world.

Over the last several decades what Michael Walzer calls "liberal liberation" has increasingly influenced the major institutions of our societies. Liberal liberation has meant breaking all constraints on individuals due to religion, race, sex, and social ties. But the effect of this liberation without radical changes in the modern liberal ideology of progress, growth, and increase has led to the well-known "individualism with a vengeance." The autonomous individual of bourgeois moral philosophy is set loose idiosyncratically to live a life of "abolished prohibitions," as long as he or she is in search of *private satisfaction.* Freedom is identified with breaking the spell of authority. It leads to "idiocy" in the classical sense, where the "idiot" is the isolated individual.[23] The result of such freedom is best described by C. B. MacPherson's phrase "possessive individualism."[24] And the forms of autonomous authority are just as pernicious and dehumanizing as those of paternalism!

Neoconservatives, on the other hand, try to refurbish paternalistic notions of authority and property necessary to the maintenance of prevailing systems of planning and investment in the corporate economy. They think that the ideology of growth and progress is threatened by what liberal autonomy has done to traditional family and sexual life, hard work, individual freedom, and so on. Neoconservatives direct their venom against contemporary "liberal liberation," which to their minds has led to increased freedom from legal and social constraint and thus to "liberal decadence," instant gratification in a world of graceless hedonists. (And one doesn't have to be a member of the "moral majority" to appreciate their point about excesses in liberation to private satisfaction.) Both "liberal liberationist" forms of autonomous authority and neoconservatist forms of paternalistic authority depend on notions of freedom that come out of the depth ideology of growth, increase, and domination through knowledge and technology, the ideology at the heart of all existing capitalist as well as socialist societies. What neither authority as autonomy nor authority as paternalism criticizes is the notion of freedom as the control of property, work, and consumption. Are there hints of a humanizing freedom beyond paternalism and autonomy in the Wesleyan tradition?

Wesley's theology of the divine compassion redefines the nature of God's freedom and of human freedom. God's freedom has traditionally been interpreted as absolute free choice, based on God's perfect, beatific self-sufficiency within the closed life of the immanent Trinity and on God's *apatheia,* inability to suffer. God's sovereign freedom meant God's groundless decision or decree, on which everything else, including God's love, was based. The view of freedom as absolute free choice has its philosophical origins in the absolute power of disposing property found in Roman law (and modernized by John Locke). Freedom then means ability to control property and people.

Wesley's theology, then, makes a radical departure from this concept of freedom.[25] For Wesley, God's freedom is grounded in God's love. And here is an important difference from the Calvinist tradition. To put a point on it: The notion of God's lordly freedom as "free choice" denies God's nature as love. But because God cannot deny Godself, God does not have the choice between mutually exclusive possibilities: being love or not being love. "If God is love, then in loving the world he is entirely free because he is entirely himself. If he is the highest good, then his liberty cannot consist of having to choose between good and evil. On the contrary, it lies in doing the good which he himself is, which means communicating himself."[26] Thus a concept of freedom, which would be appropriate to God, cannot be derived from the language of domination. Wesley did not search the tradition for concepts of freedom that describe laws applying to property, but rather for the language of freedom that describes personal and communal relationships, fellowship, and friendship. It is for this reason that Wesley has trouble with *laissez faire* notions of freedom in relation to work, property, and consumption.

If God's eternal freedom is God's love, suffering, patience, and self-giving, then this determines the quality of the synergistic relationship with the believer. Preventing, justifying, and sanctifying grace create a new human being with freedom to enter into God's history of redeeming righteousness with the world. The freedom of the will is not yet the freedom of the gospel. Justifying grace turns freedom under good and evil into conversion of the believer's being, into liberation from guilt, liberation from the fear of death, from self-possession, from idols, from personality cults, from our compulsion to dominate our environment, and from our dependence on necrophiliac security systems. Only persons thus freed can do God's justice. Liberation theology, at least in the North American context, is nothing but a new moralism if it does not treat how the gospel's justifying grace can liberate us from sin.

Finally, the future questions the Methodist theological traditions about justice. What contribution can these traditions make to the deadly worldwide struggle over the meaning of justice? Here the greatest challenge facing the critical appropriation of the Methodist traditions is still, as Wesley himself claimed, demonstrating the reality of sanctifying grace to the ecumene.[27] Reading the tradition with Wesley on this side of the biblical and Wesleyan texts, we should say that sanctification is the practice of God's justice through the power of God's righteousness given by the Holy Spirit. It leads to a life of correspondence with Christ. It makes of Christians artisans of a new humanity with their own lives serving as the material.

The doctrine of sanctification has a future insofar as we allow its biblical heart, God's justice for the world, to be taught and practiced. The logic of Jesus' understanding of the grace of God's justice cannot be assimilated to justice as equality, equity, dessert for effort, for accomplishment, or for usefulness to society. These are the prevailing concepts of justice in our societies based on the ideology of scarcity, the presupposition that there is not enough to go around. The logic of Jesus is the "how much more," the "more than enough," the abundance and superabundance and the "second mile" of God's grace. Indeed the New Testament witnesses that God the Holy Spirit obliterates the ideology of scarcity, on which the prevailing concepts of justice in our societies are based.[28] The Holy Spirit obliterates scarcity by providing enough, more than enough, wherever God's righteousness reigns in the lives of those who are choosing the life of the gospel. Sanctifying grace makes it possible to do God's justice in the sharing of the rights of life. Sanctifying grace works by offering every human being the rights of home, the rights, as Wesley so often loved to say, of being a child of God, the rights of the inheritance of what it takes to be truly human. The process of grace in Jesus Christ gives us the rights of an obedient slave, then of a beloved child, and finally of a respected friend.

The third great revival for which Methodists, I should think, are constitutionally required to be looking, will be qualitatively different from the first two because sanctifying grace in our time will have to be connected with economic and social structures in a way never dreamed of by the generations before us. But should we not admit that there will be no significant reformation of the church for the transformation of the world without sanctifying grace? If so, we are on the way to the future of the Methodist theological traditions.

Notes

1. The papers of the Sixth Oxford Institute are published in *Sanctification and Liberation: Liberation Theologies in Light of the Wesleyan Tradition*, ed. Theodore Runyon (Nashville: Abingdon Press, 1981).

2. See Elie Halévy, *The Birth of Methodism in England*, trans. Bernard Semmel (Chicago: University of Chicago Press, 1971); E. P. Thompson, *The Making of the English Working Class* (New York: Vintage Books, 1966); Bernard Semmel, *The Methodist Revolution* (New York: Basic Books, 1973).

3. Theodore Runyon, "Wesley and the Theologies of Liberation," in *Sanctification and Liberation*, pp. 47-48.

4. José Míguez Bonino, "Wesley's Doctrine of Sanctification from a Liberationist Perspective," in *Sanctification and Liberation*, p. 59.

5. Míguez Bonino, p. 60.

6. Rupert E. Davies, "Justification, Sanctification, and the Liberation of the Person," in *Sanctification and Liberation*, p. 80.

7. Davies, p. 89.

8. The Third World analysis continued with an examination of the patterns of evangelism employed in the early days of Methodist missions in Ghana. See Kwesi A. Dickson, "The Methodist Witness and the African Situation," in *Sanctification and Liberation*, pp. 193-208. Pinpointed was the tendency to link the Christian message of the new life to the necessity that the converts separate themselves from their traditional life. Contributions from Black and feminist theologians pointed to Methodism's tendency to isolate the experience of holiness from the "spiritual empowerment to change the existing social arrangements." See James H. Cone, "Sanctification and Liberation in the Black Religious Tradition," in *Sanctification and Liberation*, pp. 188-89; see also Nancy A. Hardesty, "The Wesleyan Movement and Women's Liberation," in *Sanctification and Liberation*, pp. 164-73.

9. John Kent, "Methodism and Social Change in Britain," in *Sanctification and Liberation*, pp. 100-101.

10. See Albert C. Outler, "The Place of Wesley in the Christian Tradition," in *The Place of Wesley in the Christian Tradition*, ed. Kenneth E. Rowe (Metuchen, N.J.: Scarecrow Press, 1976), pp. 11-38; see also "Methodism's Theological Heritage: A Study in Perspective," in *Methodism's Destiny in an Ecumenical Age*, ed. Paul M. Minus, Jr. (Nashville: Abingdon Press, 1969), pp. 44-70; "Do Methodists Have a Doctrine of the Church?" in *The Doctrine of the Church*, ed. Dow Kirkpatrick (Nashville: Abingdon Press, 1964); "Toward a Re-Appraisal of John Wesley as a Theologian," *Perkins Journal* (Winter, 1961), pp. 5-14; "Introduction," *John Wesley*, ed. Albert C. Outler (New York:

Oxford University Press, 1964), pp. 3-33; *Theology in the Wesleyan Spirit* (Nashville: Tidings, 1975).

11. Josef Bleicher, *Contemporary Hermeneutics: Hermeneutics as Method, Philosophy and Critique* (London: Routledge & Kegan Paul, 1980), p. 216.

12. See Robert L. Moore, *John Wesley and Authority: A Psychological Perspective* (Chico, Calif.: Scholars Press, 1979).

13. J. L. Segundo, *The Liberation of Theology* (Maryknoll, N.Y.: Orbis Books, 1978) for a criticism of contemporary theology's captivity to the notion of the "mass church."

14. Edward Farley, *Ecclesial Reflection: Anatomy of Theological Method* (Philadelphia: Fortress Press, 1982).

15. Farley, pp. 154 ff.

16. Eric Peterson, "Monotheismus als politishes Problem," in *Theologische Traktate* (Munich: Chr. Kaiser, 1951).

17. Farley, pp. 157 ff.

18. Outler, *John Wesley*, pp. 167-72, 272 ff., 365 ff.

19. Hans W. Frei, *The Eclipse of Biblical Narrative: A Study in Eighteenth and Nineteenth Century Hermeneutics* (New Haven: Yale University Press, 1974), p. 153.

20. Frei, pp. 153-54.

21. *The Works of John Wesley*, ed. Thomas Jackson, IX, p. 456.

22. *The Standard Sermons of John Wesley*, annotated by Edward H. Sugden (London: Epworth Press, 1956), I, p. 121. Cf. John Wesley, *Explanatory Notes Upon the New Testament* (London: Epworth Press, 1948), p. 835.

23. John R. Wikse, *About Possession: The Self as Private Property* (University Park: Pennsylvania State University Press, 1977).

24. See C. B. MacPherson, *The Political Theory of Possessive Individualism* (New York: Oxford University Press, 1962).

25. See Outler, *John Wesley*, pp. 425-91, especially pp. 478 ff. In his excellent essay, "Human Liberty as Divine Right: A Study in the Political Maturation of John Wesley," Leon O. Hynson argues that regarding authority, freedom, and rights, "the issue at rock bottom is Wesley's theological persuasion that *God* is the fount of authority" (p. 18). The nature of God's authority and power (as love) is the constant principle in the maturation of Wesley's thought on rights and freedom. "The evidence disclosed from a careful reading of Wesley suggests that he moved from an early emphasis on 'divine, indefeasible, hereditary rights' of the monarchy to an emphasis on the divine right of human rights. His dedication to the monarchy is real, but becomes in his mature years the political instrument of his profound effort to preserve liberty for the people and the nation" (p. 28). In the process of this maturation in his political thought Wesley had to rethink the American Revolution, for example, in his letter to "Our Brethren in America." It may be that in terms of what is happening in God's authorizing of rights and freedom today, Northern Hemisphere Methodists will have to rethink some "revolutions" in our own time.

26. Jürgen Moltmann, *The Trinity and the Kingdom of God* (New York: Harper & Row, 1981), pp. 54-55.

27. "This doctrine is the grand depositum which God has lodged with the people called Methodists; and for the sake of propagating this chiefly He appeared to have raised us up." *The Letters of John Wesley*, ed. John Telford (London: Epworth Press, 1931), VIII, p. 238.

28. Cf. M. Douglas Meeks, "The Holy Spirit and Human Needs: Toward a Trinitarian View of Economics," *Christianity and Crisis*, 40 (Nov. 10, 1980).

2

A New Future for Wesley Studies: An Agenda for "Phase III"

Albert C. Outler

In his presentation, President Norwyn Denny warned us against pedantry and dalliance in our undertakings for this fortnight. It crossed my mind, as he was speaking, that *Wesley redivivus* might also have given us a similar admonition—even if, as I think, with a rather different nuance. Once he had alienated himself from this university, Wesley rarely commended that special sort of "leisure" that we have planned for ourselves in this Institute (*scholē*, in its original sense). Besides, his scorn for pedantry, dalliance—*and trendiness!*—was about equal. We remember how both Dr. Johnson and the Countess of Huntingdon used to complain of his busy-ness. Even so, he clung to his academic title as "Fellow of Lincoln College" long after it was appropriate, and he was subject to occasional twinges of nostalgia for "the groves of Academe." For example, in 1772, he could share with his brother a wistful backward glance (*Redde me vitae priori*) and pose a curious question: "What have I been doing these thirty years past?" Moreover he had invented a quasi-collegial device of his own (calling it a "conference"); it was designed to function as a sort of "institute of theological studies." We would not wish to imitate its format; we would do well to adopt its basic concerns.

On the one side, Wesley was a very public person, accustomed to nearly constant exposure—both to admiring followers who often failed to understand him and to disdainful critics who rarely tried. By stages, he eased into a complex leadership role—founder, patriarch, cult hero of "the people called Methodists"—with effortless aplomb.

Meanwhile, he continued to shrug off his critics with at least a slight whiff of self-righteousness. In his old age, he was the best known "private person" in England; he recounts his last visit to Falmouth (at age eighty-six), where "the people, high and low, lined the street from one end of town to the other, out of stark love and kindness, gaping and staring as if the King were going by" (*Journal*, Aug. 18, 1789; cf. other triumphal processions cited in Richard Watson, *Life of John Wesley*, (1831, p. 168). Popular reverence had also generated an astonishing iconography along with a mass of relics and portraitures (unaccountably diverse!). I think, though, that even he might have winced, as I did, at the poster (preserved in The Morley Collection, Wesley College, Bristol) that depicts his bodily assumption into heaven, with a full complement of adoring cherubs and angels!

On the other side, he was indefatigable author, editor, publisher—and he meant for his writings to be read. For his "plain people," he cultivated a "plain style" (with Glanvil and Tillotson as models) and had become rather smug on this point (cf. his preface to *Sermons on Several Occasions*, 1787). His quotations were copious and careless; his citations were negligent. He oversimplified complex issues with never a qualm. At the same time, he had out a weather eye for more sophisticated readers as well ("men of reason and religion" who shared his own taste for *The Spectator* and *The Gentlemen's Magazine*). Even for his "plain people" he would drop casual classical tags and allusions, as if to remind them of his academic credentials! But note that he rarely left them untranslated.

It seems to me unlikely, therefore, that he ever expected to be pored over by succeeding generations of scholars or ever to have his sources checked out by nitpicking editors. Why should he have? His own self-understood vocation was that of heralding an updated, simplified version of "the faith once for all delivered to the saints"—in and for his own time and place. His self-chosen role as mentor to the Methodists was geared to their immediate needs and focused on the near future as it unfolded. He was aware of the radical challenges to Christian orthodoxy by the deists and freethinkers, but he died with no more than a dim inkling of the drastic transvaluations that were even then reshaping the European mind. He was more deeply influenced by Enlightenment views than has generally been recognized; he was catholic-spirited long before his time. But he was no more the prototype of modernism (as in Umphrey Lee's retrojection) than he was the Calvinist whom George Croft Cell "rediscovered."

Thus it was that the vast bulk of his writings were produced for his own people, with other readers only incidentally in view. This clearly is the case with his *Explanatory Notes* and *A Collection of Hymns for the Use of the People Called Methodists* (1780). It seems also true of *The Arminian Magazine* (1778 et seq.), that marvelous montage of jewels and junk. *The Works* (1771–74) and the *Sermons* (1787–88) may have had a wider audience in mind, as did the *Journal* (from 1735). *A Christian Library* (1749–55) was aimed at a theologically sophisticated public (which throws some light on the fact that it had no more than a single edition in Wesley's lifetime; it was obviously an editorial miscalculation).

The point here is that, in nearly two centuries since his death, the study and interpretation of his writings has been largely a business of the Methodists alone: by them and for them. This self-enclosed pattern helps us identify what we might label "Wesley Studies, Phase I." In it, the chief stress was on the intimate links between Wesley and Methodism. Wesley Studies, Phase I began with a disgraceful contention over Wesley's literary remains between John Whitehead, Thomas Coke, and Henry Moore; it was followed by John Pawson's feckless handling of the surviving manuscripts. We can only guess as to what we may have lost from the original legacy. Much was salvaged by Thomas Jackson, whose editions of *The Sermons* in 1825 (two volumes) and *The Works* (1829–32) are still our chief reliance for more than half the Wesley corpus. The Zondervan reprint's claim (in 1958–59) of being based on "the authorized edition . . . of 1872" is off by a full forty years. Wesley Studies, Phase I, therefore, has been largely dependent on bare texts (some incomplete, some extracted from other authors, some even spurious). It has been staunchly denominationalistic in temper, ardently triumphalist in tone.

The first notable exception here was a biography of Wesley by Robert Southey in 1820. This is still a very interesting essay and certainly the best written of all the Wesley biographies. Its appendix, with its collection of Alexander Knox's comments on Wesley's character and theology is still valuable (and of more than passing interest to a Methodist Institute meeting at Keble College, since Knox was a spiritual mentor to Keble and Pusey and, as such, something of a link between the Evangelical and the Anglo-Catholic Revivals). Southey's unexpected venture (which criticized Wesley's personality but admired his complex contributions to British Christianity) was promptly denounced by John Gibson Lockhart (in *The Quarterly Review*) on the ground that its subject was unworthy of the labors of England's Poet Laureate. Most cultivated Britons were inclined to agree. But the controversy outraged the Methodists and called forth a counterattack in Richard Watson's *Life;* this helped stabilize the Wesley hero cult already flourishing, and which still survives. This cultic aspect has been yet another characteristic feature of Wesley Studies, Phase I—from the great days of Jabez Bunting on down to our time.

Left with Wesley to themselves, the Methodists proceeded to evolve a cluster of stereotypes that we know so well and which have shaped our own images of him: the hide-bound father, the peerless mother, young Jacky marked off as a special "brand plucked out of the burning," the Holy Club, "Aldersgate," the great evangelist taking the whole world for his parish, the invincible debater—and of course, above all, the founder of METHODISM. Given Methodist triumphalism and their own biases, *non*-Methodists were content to acknowledge Wesley's remarkable zeal and practical gifts but otherwise to ignore or denigrate him as a theologian. I grew up with encyclopedias and textbooks that were satisfied to link Wesley with Methodism and let it go at that. In the old *Religion in Geschichte und Gegenwart*, there was a short pithy identification of Wesley that still sticks in my mind: *"energisch, herb, und fanatisch"* ("vigorous, sharp-tongued and fanatical").

Methodists, by and large, were content with their patriarch on his pedestal. A pragmatic warrant for this was that, meanwhile, they were enjoying one of the really great success stories in the whole history of the expansion of Christianity. Their triumphalism had much to sustain it. Luke Tyerman said what most Methodists took for granted: "Methodism is the greatest fact in the history of the church" (*Life and Times* [1870], vol. I, p. 1). The anonymous reviewer of Curnock's first volume in the new edition of Wesley's *Journal* (in the *Times Literary Supplement*, Nov. 18, 1909) held the same view: "Methodism is, perhaps, the most extensive religious system, outside of Islam, among those who owe their origin to, and still derive an impetus from, the life of one man."

Wesley Studies, Phase I was, therefore, the scholarly aspect of a denominationalism preoccupied with itself and its founder. Such narcissism still continues; it accounts for an important fraction of Britain's tourist business every year. One is forever hearing Methodists recount their gratification at having walked where Wesley walked, at having stood in pulpits where he preached, at having been in the room where he died—at having had a special showing of those "digs" of his at Lincoln (misidentified as they are). Wesley "relics" are scattered over the world in museums and homes. Indeed, it would be interesting to know how many in this company have no Wesley relics of their own. For myself, I do not reckon eighteenth-century literary Wesleyana as "relics," but, if you think I should, then even I am something of an iconodule.

In living memory, however, triumphalism has fallen out of fashion (partly because there have been fewer and fewer recent triumphs!). A new ecumenical spirit has spread through the Christian community at large. At the same time, the rise and fall of "Enlightenment Christianity" has brought us to a new postmodern era in which nineteenth-century liberalism seems less and less robust. Thus, with the faltering fortunes of Methodism generally (with welcome exceptions here and there) and with the waxing of ecumenical historiography, Wesley Studies, Phase I have come to be more and more outmoded. Denominational church history has been demoted; triumphalism has been muted by sophisticated historians as bad form and bad history. The great issues that wracked the sixteenth and seventeenth centuries have been refocused. The Second Vatican Council marked an ending of the Roman Catholic Counter-Reformation. The presuppositions of nineteenth-century liberalism have called for thoroughgoing reevaluation—despite the persistence of old memories and old labels.

One of the effects of this basic shift in historical perspective has been a representation of the eighteenth century in a new light. This in its turn has prompted a second phase in Wesley Studies with less emphasis on the Wesley-Methodist symbiosis and more emphasis on one or more angles of interest in Wesley as a theologian in his own right. Motivations in Phase II have been varied: "ecumenical," as in the studies of R. Newton Flew (*The Idea of Perfection*) and Father Maximin Piette (*John Wesley in the Evolution of Protestantism*, 1937); and "antiecumenical," in the sparkling contempt in Ronald Knox's chapters on Wesley (*Enthusiasm*, 1980). In G. C. Cell and Franz Hildebrandt the concern was to link Wesley more closely with Calvin and Luther; in E. P. Thompson, there was a passion to indict Wesley for his social views; in Bernard Semmel, there has been a more credible effort to describe *The Methodist Revolution* as a different sort of social transformation. The shared twin features of Phase II—however diverse otherwise—have been: (1) the concern to rescue Wesley from his Methodist cocoon, and (2) to probe more deeply into one or another basic aspect of his thought and praxis. Here one thinks of John Deschner, Harald Lindström, Ole Borgen, John Walsh, and especially of Martin Schmidt.

One of the negative effects of the weakening of the Wesley-Methodist symbiosis has been the emergence of a full generation (or more) of Methodist theologians whose thought has been touched quite lightly by Wesley himself (save for the purposes of occasional incantation). The list here is long; the easier way to make the same point is to count off the number of contemporary Methodist theologians and ethicists of real stature, who reflect an identifiable debt to Wesley as decisive mentor. How many fingers would such a counting call for? Moreover, there are more and more trendy

Methodists who, having helped topple Wesley from his pedestal, now propose to pack him off to history's limbo. Non-Methodists find this a mite baffling. They remember the Wesley hero cult, and they wonder what will happen to a movement that lacks the wit and will to transvaluate its chief legacy.

There is a third subgroup in Wesley Studies, Phase II. These are the Methodist theological partisans of one or another of the current coterie-theologies; their interest in Wesley is confined to his possible use of them as "authority" for their own convictions, rooted in other traditions. This is not to argue for or against this coterie-theology or that, nor even to question the legitimacy of selective appeals to a selected authority. There is a crucial prior question involved and it is a methodological one. How far are these various appellants really interested in Wesley's theology itself? How competently are their appeals grounded in the primary texts taken as a whole? Eisegesis, even in a good cause, is still bad hermeneutics!

One of the distinctive achievements of Wesley Studies, Phase II has been to lift Wesley out of his Methodist matrix. And yet the question of the reassignment of his place in church history (and in contemporary Christianity) has been largely left open. This suggests two inherent weaknesses in the model (with some notable exceptions, of course). The first is its general indifference to the history of Christian thought as a whole. The other is a partial or biased reading of Wesley so that their separated parts do not quite match his whole. There is a special problem about Wesley's relevance for postcolonial Christianity in Latin America, Asia, and Africa. In these contexts today, he is bound to appear as overlaid by the thick crust of his British provincialism and thus in urgent need of artful and responsible indigenization. But if such a thing can be done with John Bunyan, why not with John Wesley? Besides, there are Charles' hymns to help!

In any case, the question of Wesley's proper place in church history, on the one hand, and in current ecumenical theology, on the other, remains open and a problem. The proposal that Wesley belongs among the really great doctors of the church is preposterous on its face. We know of other figures in Christian history who, in their times and places, were great and shining lights—and yet who now languish in oblivion—save in the most sophisticated summations of Christian memory. One thinks of men like Johann Gerhard, Martin Chemmitz, Johann Heidegger, Francis Turretin, Richard Baxter, and Horace Bushnell—great ones all and now forgotten, to our loss. Will Wesley join them presently—and should he? But if he is not a theological supernova, nor yet ready for limbo, what then? How much has he still to contribute to the issues with which we are struggling and those we are passing on to generations yet to come? Questions like these have not yet been fully formulated nor rightly answered to the satisfaction of critical historians or devoted ecumenists. But they have opened up a new horizon of inquiry that might properly be labelled Wesley Studies, Phase III.

Such a third phase would not propose to repudiate the positive residues of Phases I and II—although such a phase would be less interested in the Wesley-Methodist symbiosis and more concerned with ecumenical theology and praxis. Its first goal is that of basic reorientation—the repositioning of Wesley in his own time and place, against his larger background, and in as wide a historical context as possible. But all of this is still in order to enable an application of Wesley's relevance to issues in *our* times and *our* futures. Phase III is the effort to get beyond Wesley as Methodist patriarch toward a more fruitful place for him in the larger scene, historical and ecumenical.

For me, such a notion of yet a third phase of Wesley Studies was changed from a vision to a programme on a summer's day in 1957—in Frank Baker's parsonage in Hull. Two decades before, I had taken a doctorate in patristics and had been engaged in the fruitful absurdity of trying to master the history of Christian thought as a whole (in support of a still more grandiose project: viz., the modern dialogue between Christianity and current secular wisdom, as focused in the human sciences). The point, however, was that nowhere in my education or career had Wesley ever been regarded as other than a great evangelist and denominational founder. For example, my cherished friend and colleague, H. Richard

Niebuhr had come by his image of Wesley as a defective Calvinist, largely on the basis of Professor Cell's book, without a firsthand examination of the Wesley corpus itself, so far as I ever knew: "Wesley's essential Calvinism has recently been described by Professor Cell, though it may be that the great Methodist's limitation lay at the point of his frequent unawareness of this [Calvinistic] presupposition of his gospel" (*The Kingdom of God in America*, 1937, p. 101).

Over the years, I had read Wesley on my own, partly out of loyalty (he was a hero to my father), but more out of a historian's curiosity as to where he rightly fitted into the development of Protestant thought between the Puritans and Schleiermacher. My general impression was of a creative mind in fustian; an antidote to both moralism *and* solifidian-ism—but not one comparable in theological stature, say, to Jonathan Edwards. When, therefore, in the editorial board of *A Library of Protestant Thought*, we were threshing out a format for that collection of readings, it crossed my mind that Wesley might very well have a volume of his own—just as we had planned for Richard Baxter, Horace Bushnell *et al*. Jonathan Edwards was already being published by the Yale Press—a project that has now stretched out for more than thirty years.

My proposal drew scoffs from my non-Methodist colleagues, who reminded me that it was I who had proposed the original title for the library: viz., "Protestant *Thought*." Later, when an outside group of specialists in Reformation and post-Reformation history was polled about inclusions and allowable omissions, the project least supported by them was a solo volume for John Wesley. How Wesley got his volume is another story, but it turned out that I got the assignment to edit it. It was then that the real shocks began—especially to a generalist like me, long since accustomed to working on critical editions already prepared by specialists, together with the usual pile of sophisticated secondary literature in which the essential spadework has already been done by my elders and betters. My naïve questions about holographs and sources met with unedifying answers and led to the discovery of how tightly Wesley had been cocooned by the Methodists and how easily ignored by others. The Curnock *Journal* is almost wholly preoccupied with Methodist affairs and not very critical of Wesley's self-serving reportage. Besides, who then could check out the deficiencies in his claims of having decoded the *Diaries*? Sugden's *Standard Sermons* had a few critical comments on Wesley's theology but within a Methodist ambiance that is nearly total. Besides, what Sugden was really interested in was the question of "doctrinal standards" *for Methodists*; this allowed him to ignore the last two-thirds of the sermon corpus.

The secondary literature was dominated by the familiar stereotypes. Critical questions went unasked—or were answered stereotypically. I discovered, in England, that such primary texts as had survived were in safe enough hands but not then in safe quarters. The contrast between the Wesley archives and the Baxter archives in the Doctor Williams Library was embarrassing. There was no reliable inventory of what Wesley had read, nor any convenient collection of his sources. In short, what I had supposed would be a fairly straightforward task turned into a bafflement—and the conviction came readily that Phase III would never unfold if other Wesley scholars had to replicate my experience. Meanwhile, my colleagues nodded smugly at my complaints and hinted broadly that this was a fitting comeuppance for so ill-starred a venture. One of them (a Pascal specialist) mumbled something about silk purses and sow's ears.

In Frank Baker, however, I had finally found a Wesley specialist such as I could never be but who was ready and able to help with my project. He, too, had discovered the limited usefulness of Wesley Studies, Phase I—although he has always been more preoccupied with the man himself and less inclined than I to speak of a "Methodist cocoon." But he had conceived of a new, critical edition a decade earlier and had begun work on a proper bibliography to supersede Greene. Baker's expertise got me over many a hurdle that had balked me up to that point. Thus, with his aid and that of many others (historians, classicists, specialists in English literature) Wesley got his volume in the *Library*—and, for all its flaws (plainer now after twenty years more study), it has continued to outsell the other volumes by a ratio of ten to one and remains the only volume of the eighteen still in print. Many people (including those at the Oxford University Press) have found this unaccountable.

Actually, though, it was I who profited most from this project, because in the process, muddled as it was, I had discovered a more interesting theological resource than even I had expected. Here was valuable light shed on many of my other queries: about eighteenth-century linkages between "orthodoxy," "pietism" and "Enlightenment." The project has gone on enriching my own theological understanding of contemporary issues. Wesley's rhetoric takes a bit of getting used to, but there *is* "plain truth for plain people" in it. There is also a sort of catalytic theology there, designed to interact with other theologies (earlier and later) without losing its own integrity, and without forcing Christian doctrines into a rigid mold. It is a theology less interested in the order of Christian *truth* (as in school theologies generally) than in the Christian *life*. Its specific focus is the order of salvation as an eventful process that stretches across the whole horizon of Christian existence. Its axial theme is *grace*, which makes it Christocentric and yet also pre-eminently pneumatological. For Wesley the Holy Spirit is the Lord and Giver of *Grace* as well as the Lord and Giver of Life. Thus, "prevenience" is not a stage of grace but the crucial aspect of grace in all its manifestations. It signifies the divine initiative in *all* spirituality, in all Christian experience. Wesley's theology is intensely evangelical but it looks also toward the ethical transformation of society. It is concerned with "third alternatives" to all the barren polarities generated by centuries of polemics. It is a linkage theology between historic orthodoxy and the Enlightenment, between radical Protestantism and ecumenical Christianity. In short, what I had found in Wesley was a theologian who looked better without his halo—who was, on principle, in dialogue with Christians in many different traditions in his own day precisely because he had been in such fruitful dialogue with so much of the Christian tradition before him. He has, therefore, become an important theological teacher for me, and I am convinced that this could happen in other cases. This is why I have kept looking beyond Phases I and II. It has been the warrant for investing two extra decades of drudgery and excitement in the task of making his sermons available in fuller context.

I hope I am not misconstrued as claiming that Dr. Baker, or even Dr. Baker and I, *invented* Phase III. Historiographical perspectives have natural histories of their own. What has happened over the past three decades is the rise of a new sort of interest in the field and folk theology. Other scholars of diverse backgrounds have also discovered Wesley in new dimensions—one thinks of Timothy Smith, Robert Cushman, W. R. Cannon, Richard Heitzenrater, Bernard Semmel *et al.* One can go on from them to rejoice over the promising crop of younger scholars on whom any new future for Wesley Studies really depends.

But it must also be said, however, that Phase III is, up to now, more a vision than an achievement, more of a beginning than a full-fledged movement. This would illuminate Ronald Gibbins' instinctive reflex, in his review of the paperback reprint of the Wesley volume in *A Library of Protestant Thought:* "So much has been written about the life and work of John Wesley that one is always suspicious of *any* new treatment." He could have added, "just as we have grown suspicious of all the old ones."

And yet all of this should help explain my excitement and earnest hopes for this particular session of this Institute and the inclusion in it of a separate working group on Wesley Studies. Despite the gains of the past two decades, I am not yet wholly confident that Phase III is here to stay. There are still low moments when I have this sinking feeling of having been playing Sisyphus—the right rock up the wrong hill! On the other hand, the signs multiply that a more favorable reappraisal of Wesley as an ecumenical theologian is taking place. I know of two Methodist universities that have designed special programs in Wesley and Methodist studies— and most of our seminaries are taking this more seriously. Professors Kretschmar and Friess have allotted him a chapter in their new series on classical theologians. There is a respectful footnote in Hendrikus Berkhof's *Christian Faith* (pp. 426-27). Topical seminars have begun to appear on the programs of the American Academy of Religion; one is planned for the next session of the American Historical

Association. Conferences on Wesley as a theological resource have been held in Australia; others are planned for in Latin America and elsewhere. A private foundation in the United States is helping to underwrite the graduate education of a score or more of so-called "Wesley Fellows." Last year, a quite discerning question about Wesley *as theologian* appeared in the Oxford Honors Exam in Theology—the first one of its kind that I have noticed since I began to take those examinations as a private hobby in 1939.

Even so, a consensus as to the requisite scholarly definitions of the state of the question in Phase III has yet to be formulated—its agenda is not yet firmly in place. Wesley's impact in contemporary theology is still in the process of being tested. Our work in this Institute could, therefore, make a real difference in opening up a real future in Wesley Studies, if indeed there is to be one.

As I see it, there are at least three crucial issues in any such future:

The *first* is methodological; all theologies claiming to be Wesleyan must be based on the whole Wesley as he was (and not on this aspect or accent in his thought and praxis). Like every other enterprise in historical interpretation, he must be investigated on his own grounds and in accordance with his own theological intentions—which were not, in the first instance, denominational nor sectarian. This would enable us to begin to transcend the tragic polarizations in the Wesleyan traditions in the nineteenth century that still haunt us and hobble our mission in the world. We need to clarify the grounds on which Wesley still stands as an authority for us, insofar as he does. This cannot refer to Wesley's authority in himself; it can only point us to that authoritative complex to which he gave his own allegiance and to which we may give ours: Scripture, "Christian Antiquity," reason, and experience.

An inference from this will make a *second* point: Wesley must be read in light of his sources—and therefore within the larger ecumenical perspectives of historic Christianity. He worked in and from scripture—and so must we—but also the classics, the Fathers, the Reformation and Counter-Reformation, and the contemporary worlds he lived in. He was no antiquarian;

more than once I have thought I could hear a few ghostly snorts while I was struggling with an intricate footnote. But he was a man of tradition—and as his way of gathering up and weaving together so much of the Christian tradition is better understood, his theological oversimplifications will be less readily misconstrued. Reading Wesley calls for trifocals: one part of the lens focused on his own background, another on the seventeenth century, and a third on possible projections into the nineteenth and twentieth centuries—in that order. To move from our concerns to his and back again and to call this "Wesley Studies" is to miss the richness of the heritage he left us, and to diminish the contributions which we might share with other Christians—and other humans— in our times and in those to come.

Third, however, the justification for the drudgeries entailed in serious Wesley Studies must be sought in their perspective relevance for contemporary Christians (and not Methodists alone) in our current commitments to evangelism, renewal, and social transformation. Here, two fruitful ideas emerge as obvious: contemporary theology must be ecumenical and Wesley's is just that. Again, the idea of *development* is central in contemporary historical study (as one can see in Professor Pelikan's magisterial survey, *The Christian Tradition*). We must not claim too much for Wesley's historical consciousness, but we may claim he was more of a pioneer in grasping the idea of development than most of his contemporaries—and felt freer than most to develop his own ideas, as the revival unfolded.

In any future for Phase III, Wesley's role as a folk theologian (or people's theologian) will have to be plumbed more carefully and the secrets of his success in communicating complex notions to simple folk must be sought out. Here was a man who dedicated a competent theological training to the tasks of pastoral leadership of plain people, and who drew much of his own developing understandings from their responses. In such a perspective, his distinctiveness would be more apparent: the Anglican evangelist as devoted to the sacramental means of grace as if he were a rector; the eighteenth-century reformer with conscious ties to both the church Fathers and the radical Protestants, and who may be laid alongside other pastoral theologians like Henry Scougal. The result would be a richer sense of theology as *scientia practica* ("faith in order to action"). This would make it possible, as Wesley comes to be better known, that the traditional Methodist emphasis upon sanctification and perfection could be seen as integrated in a more comprehensive view of grace in the order of salvation. This would then recognize how comprehensive Wesley's view of salvation really was—a continuum of God's gracious acts that reaches from the first stirrings of conscience to the fullness of faith and to the full restoration of the divine image.

The problem of a credible hermeneutics for Wesley is, as I know, a vexed one. Its nub, or so it seems to me, is whether the fact that Wesley never produced a systematic exposition of his theology (and never intended to) is to be reckoned as a weakness to be remedied or as a strength to be exploited. Here, much depends on whether one sets the notion of "systematics" over against its simple antithesis, "unsystematic" and whether one uses the term "eclectic" as pejorative (a synonym for "haphazard"). There is, however, another possibility: viz., to think of theology as coherent reflection upon Christian living, with all its natural divagations. Wesley knew the history of systematic theology, from Peter Lombard's *Sentences* to Philip Melancthtons's *Loci* and in the heroic labors of the Protestant dogmaticians. He himself relied heavily on John Pearson's *Exposition of the Creed* (which comes as near to a "systematics" as seventeeth-century Anglicanism can show). But Wesley also knew that the bulk of significant Christian literature, from the Scriptures, to the Fathers, to the classics of devotion, to the liturgies, had focused on Christian *life* and the intimations of Christian truth that could be drawn therefrom.

For better or for worse, then, Wesley *chose* to formulate his teaching in unsystematic forms: sermons, tracts, letters, hymns. He could claim that "every serious man who peruses these sermons will therefore see *in the clearest manner* what those doctrines are which I embrace and teach, as the essentials of true religion" ("Preface" to *Sermons on Several Occasions*, 1746). He could speak of his collection of hymns (1780) as "a little body of *practical divinity*." His axial theme, which organizes all else in his thought, is grace, and the focus of all his thinking about grace is on the order of *salvation*. The real measure of Wesley's mind is the consistency and clarity with which he managed the connections between this axial theme and all the other facets of his thought.

It goes without saying that Methodists and other Christians are, and must be, free to do their theologizing in any genre that they find edifying. This allows for responsible efforts to produce a Wesleyan "systematics" (in the tradition of Watson and Pope), just as it also allows for other organizing principles (for example, in Professor Geoffrey Wainwright's thoroughly Wesleyan *Doxology*). What matters in any case is that all such theologies should bear the marks of careful basic homework in the Wesley texts. This is an equal prerequisite in any other efforts to update Wesley and make him relevant. Thus, I propose a slogan for Methodist theologies (comparable to current trends in other traditions we know): Back to Wesley and his sources, and then forward—with his sense of heritage and openness to the future as one of our models.

In whatever patterns Methodist theologies may continue to develop, it will be crucial for them to strike for new balances between faith and life. It *is* our task "to spread Scriptural holiness over these lands." But *scriptural* holiness has always had the whole trajectory of grace in view—and Methodism has been ill-served by those who have minimized this wholeness for whatever reason. For surely what is most interesting and truly creative in Wesley was his comprehensive vision of the Christian life: life in and from the Spirit (from repentance to justifying faith, to reconciliation, assurance, and regeneration, to sanctification); and life in and under grace as an eventful process punctuated by conversions, disciplined by the moral imperatives of holiness (personal and social).

The future of Wesley Studies so conceived depends, more than we may have realized, on a new edition that will enable such studies to go forward more expeditiously than is possible at present. We know how studies in other traditions have been spurred and sustained by critical editions; it is even more crucial in our case. But you should also know that the Wesley Works Project has just now suffered a severely damaging blow. Three volumes have been published by the Oxford University Press and a fourth, now in page proof (i.e., the 1780 "Collection of Hymns"), will be published. But the Oxford Press has now abandoned the project, leaving us with no assured alternatives. It may well be that this Institute could offer counsel and guidance in this crisis—if there is, in fact, an honest consensus among us as to its importance.

New edition or not, however, the future of Wesley Studies, Phase III really depends upon an agreed agenda that could serve all interested scholars in all traditions as a baseline for their own investigations and commitments. Each of us must already have some such agenda in mind, and it is the specific business of Group One to hammer out some such programme as part of its *report*. (The report, as agreed to by our group, appears on page 53.) The point to be stressed here is that such an agenda is not the business of antiquarians only but of all men and women who are interested in testing the possible significance of Wesley less as *patriarch* than as *mentor* (along with many others) so that those who seek such a future can bring to it an added richness from the Christian tradition to which Wesley stands as a crucial witness.

Methodists and other Christians have still much to learn about the possible role and function in Christian theologizing of what we have called "the Wesleyan Quadrilateral"—his four-fold guidelines: of Scripture as primal font of Christian revelation, of tradition (Christian Antiquity) as the sum of the collective Christian wisdom in response to the truth revealed in Scripture; of reason as the Godgiven discipline of ordering our conceptions as cogently as ever we can; of experience as the assurance of God's reconciling love in Christ, received as a special assurance of God's unmerited favor. We have much to gain from a reconsideration of Wesley's correlation of soteriology and pneumatology, the person and work of the Holy Spirit in the Mystery of Salvation.

The way beyond the schisms that still disrupt our oneness in Christ is not a backward step to some older (nineteenth century) notion of holiness of the social gospel (especially as if these were antithetical!). The way forward will come clearer as we recover the Wesleyan vision of Christian existence and all that it entails for faithful Christians in a world where justice must be served or the gospel will not get a hearing. Such a conspectus would provide a fruitful context for all our other concerns in this Institute: for the correlation of salvation and justice conceived in an evangelical mode, for effectual evangelism aimed at social transformation as urgently as personal conversions (and yet not more so!), faith development without a rigid scheme of entelechies, a substantive sacramentalism without sacerdotalism.

No one has yet refuted the validity of Robert Chiles' evaluation of *The Theological Transition in American Methodism* (1965) from its original (i.e., Wesleyan) orientations—in the late nineteenth century and thereafter: (1) from revelation to a rationalistic hermeneutics; (2) from original sin to moral man; (3) from free grace to free will—and I would add (4) from Montanism to Pelagianism. It would also seem that what has happened in mainline American Methodism has its counterparts in other branches of the Methodist movement. It may be that, for some of us, there is no strong will to reverse these deformations, no earnest urgency to recover the form and power of historic Christianity for our times and for our futures. But to desist in these endeavors would be to cut the taproot of our Wesleyan heritage and to foreclose our future as evangelical Christians. On the other hand, if and when such an urgency returns, anywhere in the Christian community, Wesley ought to be accessible as a fruitful resource for Christian self-understanding and hope. If, however, he is to be appropriated as such a resource, he must become better known by more adequate methods of analysis and interpretation. For him to be better known, he must be studied more carefully, in his context and in the light of his sources. Wesley Studies, Phase III is, therefore, aimed at making Wesley credible once again to *our* own "plain people" and yet also to the whole of the Christian community. This, of course, is no end in itself. The virtue of our heritage must be sought in its power to open a new future where catalytic theologies will do more than polemical ones to enliven the chemistries of Christian thought and action—a new future under the rule of grace.

51

If any such prospect as this is viable, I cannot think of a likelier place for it to be affirmed than by *this* company, in *this* place, in *this* fortnight. For what, pray tell, are our real alternatives? It is because I see our times as in deep crisis and because I believe that Wesley Studies have a positive contribution to make in such times, that I regard this conference as a possible landmark occasion that will call us and others to an even firmer commitment to the recovery of the heritage—as a hopeful prologue to a really new future. Who amongst us would wish for less?

Wesley Studies

Working Group Paper

Part I: "The Horizon of Inquiry"

Where two or three informed Methodists are gathered together, a reference to John Wesley can be counted on sooner or later. It need not always be germane or accurate but it signifies his unique place in Methodist hearts and minds. In our Working Group on Wesley Studies, we were steadily aware of this place and thus would begin our report with a grateful acknowledgment of our debts to all who have helped to fashion the traditions of Wesley Studies thus far.

We are also eager to disavow any notion of a Methodist monopoly of Wesley Studies; such a thing would be contrary to any of his own intentions. He was at home in the Christian tradition at large and in the whole of the Christian community. His sermon on "Catholic Spirit" was a conscious bid for mutual recognition, between separated Christians, of their oneness in Christ and in love. One of our chief concerns, therefore, is that Wesley might now be exhibited as the ecumenical churchman he understood himself to be. Contrary to the denominational engrossments that have tended hitherto to obscure Wesley from non-Methodists, we are eager for Wesley to be shared by all (and not by church folk only) as an important resource for contemporary theology, ethics, and human culture.

We are equally eager to disavow any notion that the field of Wesley Studies be regarded as a preserve for scholars only. This, too, would be a gross distortion of his intentions. As he said so firmly, his concern was for "plain truth for plain people." The least that this can mean is that the essence of his message still stands available in his bare texts—open to all who will give him a fair reading. It also means, however, that he must be read and pondered rather than reverenced at a distance, or cited from hearsay—or ignored. By the same token, he deserves as open a mind as one may bring to him: always with a special awareness of his practical concerns for Christian faith and praxis, in his actual times and circumstances. The rudiments of his teachings, and something of their applicability in other times and situations, may be grasped by serious readers of all sorts, without the benefit of editors and interpreters. This is as it should be.

Even so, Wesley's bare texts conceal much that is greatly significant, both for an understanding of his thought and for perspectives on his place in the history of Christian thought and in contemporary ecumenical theology. His deliberate oversimplifications have helped many of his readers to miss the range and richness of his theological learning. In this way, though, they also miss the scope and aptness of his quotations and allusions (biblical, classical, historical), as well as his grasp of the tangled web of the controversies which he was inclined to resolve without exposing his readers to their complexities. A consequence of this has been an obscuration of his theological sophistication and originality, which remain largely unacknowledged. Methodists and non-Methodists alike have been left unaware of the clashing traditions that converged in him, of his passion for transcending barren polarizations (theoretical and practical), of his distinctiveness as a people's theologian. It has been all too easy—both for Methodists and the others—to leave him in his traditional Methodist cocoon.

It is, therefore, the hope—and proposal—of our group that Wesley Studies be freshly reoriented toward new levels of methodological sophistication, critical rigor, and ecumenical outreach. The aims of such a move would be a clearer view of Wesley as a contemporary resource: his evangelical gospel linked to an active concern for Christian nurture and discipline; the depth and breadth of his theological and secular culture realized; his skills in the arts of communication and organization; his genius for gathering Christians into effective networks of mutual aid and welfare; and his passion for transformation—of persons and society. The resulting perspective would position Wesley more credibly within the Christian tradition as one of a special breed of servant-pastor-evangelist-teacher-reformers who have sought and found their ministerial vocations among the disadvantaged and alienated. It would also make him a far richer and more relevant resource for contemporary Christians and our perplexities.

The time is ripe, we believe, for fresh studies of Wesley in the contexts of cultural history as well as church history. Such a new phase of Wesley Studies would be self-consciously critical, historical, and ecumenical. And yet it would also aim at making him available as a fruitful teacher of Christians in *our* times. It would seek to discover the confluence in Wesley's thought of a variety of Christian traditions, the emergence of a distinctive view of salvation (focused on the doctrine of grace and the order of salvation), together with a consistent emphasis upon discipline in the Christian life, in our love both of God and of neighbor. It would recognize in him the tradition of meditative piety that stretches back to the medieval mystics, and beyond them, to the spirituality of the ancient Fathers, with their stress upon human participation in the divine life revealed in Christ by the power of the Spirit. It would see his constant emphasis on salvation by grace through faith—life in grace, life under grace, from grace to grace—from the first stirrings of conscience on to the fullness of grace in holiness. It would seek to analyze Wesley's inheritance from the Reformations of the sixteenth century (Lutheran, Calvinist, Anglican, "Radical," *and* Catholic) and his heroic effort to select the best from each. It would recognize his avoidance of all extremes: solifidianism, antinomianism, moralism, sacerdotalism. It would seek to appreciate his social and political interests, his multiple ministries to the needy and oppressed, his interest in physical and mental well-being, his concerns about health, nutrition, and effectual health services. It would recognize his interests and involvements in the issues of economic justice and human rights.

Any such approach to Wesley and his times obviously calls for critical and interdisciplinary scholarship at the highest level. It would, on principle, look toward both historical reconstruction and constructive efforts to update the Wesleyan legacy in current situations, whatever they may turn out to be. There would also be ample room here for the specialist, in selected areas of research, and for the generalist as well. The future of Wesley Studies lies in many hands, in many countries—in a responsible pluralism of interests.

There is, of course, no thought of exalting Wesley's authority as anybody's court of last resort in matters of doctrine or praxis. We would, in fact, reject any such notion, just as we reject prooftexting from Wesley as a mode of appealing to his authority. Methodists (and other Christians) have no other final authority in doctrine or praxis beyond or besides the Word of God in Scripture—"read, marked, learned and inwardly digested"—under the guidance of the Spirit. But all Christian groups (and individuals) have influential mentors and teachers whom they ought gladly to share with others. In this sense Wesley is, or ought to be, such a mentor to the people called Methodists—and not to Methodists only, since there are many others who can profit from him greatly.

Our interest in Wesley's authority, therefore, is less in the man himself than in the complex of authorities by which he chose so willingly to be guided. This complex has been identified as the so-called "Wesleyan Quadrilateral" (which may or may not be a wholly apt metaphor, since one of its sides is much more than equal to the other three). What the Quadrilateral means to point to, in its first instance, is the primacy and sufficiency of Holy Scripture in the general sense of the Anglican Article VI, entitled, "Of the Sufficiency of the Holy Scriptures for Salvation: Holy Scripture containeth all things necessary to salvation. . . ." (In Wesley's revision in the *Sunday Service*, it appears as Article V.) The Scriptures are, in this view, the primal font of Christian truth. But since they must be interpreted in every succeeding age and in each new cultural context, there is also a need for the positive aid of Tradition, understood as the collective wisdom of the Christian community in all centuries and all communions. Such interpretations, however, must also be guided by *reason*. Wesley expressly excludes interpretations that lead either to logical absurdities or to indictments of God's goodness. This is a demand for clarity and cogency in all Christian formulations. None of this, however, will suffice until all are given life and power by "the inner witness of the Spirit that we are children of God." This is the Christian *experience* that turns sound doctrine into living faith. (Wesley's experience at Aldersgate stands as the most familiar instance of this in Methodist memories.)

This four-fold complex of guidelines, with Scripture understood as their fundament, stands as an ample and applicable authority for Christians in every age and situation. As a theological base, such a set of authoritative norms deserves more careful analysis and evaluation than it has had thus far, in Methodism or elsewhere, and a careful pondering of it would prove a useful exercise for other Christians as well.

As a group, then, we are eager to encourage this new era of Wesley Studies that we envisage. It would help provide a more adequate hermeneutic for reading Wesley in the light of his sources and for the updating of his most distinctive ideas for use in new contexts. In it, Wesley's own preferences will be appreciated: for plain truth over speculation, for pluralism over dogmatism, for doctrine normed by coherence rather than ordered topically into a system. And, again on principle, such a new era will make room for a variety of interests, exposed to dialogue and fruitful interaction.

A very high level of biblical expertise will be needed in the study and evaluation of Wesley's ways with Scripture, since Scripture was for him not only the unique and sufficient source of revelation but also a sort of second language in which he thought and prayed as well. But this would open a way toward wider and deeper probes into the problems of biblical hermeneutics in general—most especially the universal relevance of biblical revelation in other times and other worldviews. Thus the Bible would become a deeper bond of shared faith than any other source for Christian self-understanding.

Competent church historians will be indispensable in the setting of background. They need to notice and evaluate his knowledge and use of the Fathers of the church, his awareness of the chief options in historic Christian teaching, East and West, his selective inheritance from his more English background: Anglicanism from Cranmer (the *Homilies*) to Pearson *(On the Creed)*, the traditions of Puritan devotion, and the inchoate movement called "Christian Platonism" (from Malebranche to Norris to Law). Another set of historical problems arise from his role as a transitional figure between historic orthodoxy and pietism, on the one hand, and between pietism and Enlightenment, on the other. This would be a necessary background for questions about historical continuities and discontinuities in Methodism *after* Wesley. Where in Wesley, if at all, is the corrective to our subsequent Methodist histories of separated and rival churches, all claiming him as founder, but with so little of his catholic spirit?

Constructive theologians of many different interests are needed to assess the continuing visibility of Wesley's doctrinal and ethical outlook—on human selfhood and its true potential; on the paradoxes of free grace and free will, on the crucial point of the divine initiative (its *pre*-venience) and all human responses. His doctrine of salvation needs pondering—his combination of a Protestant doctine of sin and a catholic doctrine of grace. There may also be guidance for modern Christian thinkers in Wesley's catalytic way of theologizing—viz., firm and funded theological views open to interaction with others without loss of integrity, evangelical in their grounding *and* catholic in their intention, whose deeply humane concern for human fulfillment grounds all hope in God's grace.

If any such new future in Wesley Studies is to unfold, it seems obvious to us that it must be supported by more ample scholarly resources than those currently available. We are, therefore, agreed that the new critical and annotated edition of Wesley's *Works* begun at the Oxford University Press some years ago is an urgent priority. We are eager to see that edition carried through to completion, at the highest level of quality and distributed at the lowerst possible cost to students. We have been reminded by Professor John Leith of the positive correlations between successive new editions of

Calvin's works and significant advances in Calvin Studies; we recognize similar correlations in such cases as Martin Luther, Jonathan Edwards, and the early Fathers. The dismaying news that Oxford University Press has abandoned its commitment to the Wesley *Works* project makes it appropriate, we believe, that this Institute express to the appropriate authorities our shared deep concern that alternative ways and means be found for its completion.

(Apropos this issue the plenary of the Oxford Institute unanimously adopted the following resolution—Ed.)

The Oxford Institute of Methodist Theological Studies, after careful study and discussion, endorses the fundamental importance of a critical text of John Wesley's writings. The publication of the Wesley corpus is one of the most important contributions we can make to ecumenical Christianity. These texts are important in the history of Christian thought and are essential to a more adequate understanding of John Wesley, of the influences upon his life and thought, of his role in his era and in the Methodist societies, and in the resources he bequeathed to the ensuing Methodist traditions. This publication effort must be completed and to this end we not only offer our endorsement but also commit ourselves to help build that base of support which will move this project to completion.

Part II: "A Provisional Agenda"

Given an adequate edition as a prospective resource (and even in advance of its appearance in toto), we were able to agree on a partial and provisional agenda for the future in Wesley Studies. We are aware that none of the following twelve items is new; the list is neither prescriptive nor exhaustive. We offer it as an outline of examples of what would be involved in a more complete and fruitful phase of Wesley Studies. Our aim is less to define the field with any finality than to open it up.

1. We would begin with an obvious and commonplace generalization: the need for more adequate basic skills in Wesley Studies and in their cognate fields: linguistic, historical, theological, psychological, liturgical. If Wesley Studies are to be taken seriously by others, their standards of historiographical rigor must be equal to those in other subdisciplines of careful scholarship.

2. We see an equally pressing need for a range of research tools, which would provide basic information truly useful (and convenient) for many readers and for Wesley specialists in particular. These would include: (a) a concordance of main terms; (b) a cross-referenced index of names, topics quotations, and their sources; (c) a dictionary of aphorisms and familiar sayings; (d) an ampler "Sermon Register" with places, dates, texts, summary charts, and graphs. Finally, (e) we need an annotated bibliography of Wesley's readings, with cross-references to his use of them. In each case, such "helps" should be keyed to all available editions, as well as the new one, if and as it becomes available. Such a set of resources would facilitate the work of the upcoming generation and their successors.

3. This, in turn, requires a comment on one of the more ironic aspects of the current state of Wesley *biography*. Much of our understanding of Wesley's thought and continued relevance depends upon the testimonies of the man himself and the impression he left upon his contemporaries who knew him or knew about him. And yet, in Wesley's case, much of the primary source-data for a fully credible biography are not available to scholars generally (and much more of it is extant than is presently accessible). This lamentable state of affairs cannot be remedied without more adequate editions of the *Diaries*, the *Journal*, and the *Letters—and* without more comprehensive studies than we have now of the Methodist people in the eighteenth century. We gratefully acknowledge the unique contribution of Professor Martin Schmidt (especially his "new" data from the Moravian archives) even as we also wonder at his judgment that Wesley's theological development virtually ceased in 1738. We recognize both the promise and perils of psycho-history; yet we would stress the need for sufficient history to support whatever psychological generalizations that are proposed. There can, of course, be no thought of an embargo on biographical research and interpretations. For the time being, however, we would urge more reserve in the credulous use of existing biographies, more caution in our own biographical hypotheses, and more modesty in our conclusions. What is

crucial, in all instances, is careful documentation, tested evidence, and credible narration.

4. We heartily commend the extension of the field of Wesley Studies to include the partnership in ministry of the two Wesley brothers, John and Charles. We recognize the mirror images of the same basic theological perspective in John's prose and Charles' poetry. But given the heavy overlay of long-standing stereotypes in this field, we would emphasize how much further work is needed here: e.g., a *new* "Osborn" at the level already established by Frank Baker in *Representative Verse of Charles Wesley*, together with a new critical edition of Charles' prose: his *Journal*, *Sermons*, and *Letters*. This will, of course, require collaboration between historians, literary critics, and hymnologists. From still another angle, we need more light shed on the tensions between the two brothers (and between Charles and the Methodist preachers), with special reference to their irreconcilable differences about "churchmanship." The bonus from such efforts would be new perspectives on the ecclesiological confusions that have been endemic in Methodism ever since, especially with respect to the meaning of ordination and the nature of the ministerial office.

5. Another hopeful horizon of inquiry is defined by the problem of growth and development in John Wesley's thought and self-understanding. His development falls naturally into three distinct periods: (1) from childhood through the end of the Georgia mission; (2) from 1738 to 1765; and (3) from 1765 to 1791. We have been intrigued by Professor Fowler's pioneering probes into the question of stages in Wesley's own faith, and would be eager to have them supplemented by extended correlations between developments in Wesley's *faith* and of his *theology*. We are especially interested in the continued reshaping of Wesley's emphases (e.g., a more paranetic theology and a theology of culture) during his last decades. The Revival in its second generation (from 1760s to the 1790s) was decisive in its own way—its history has yet to be explored in depth. Consequently, a cluster of problems has been ignored, or obscured, by the conventional Methodist historical stereotypes.

6. The study of Wesley in the light of his sources will require more interdisciplinary training and collaboration than we have been accustomed to. His sources were drawn from a wide range of disparate fields: the Bible, the classics, Christian Antiquity and its extensions in church history, the Anglican Reformation, the subsequent controversies between the Puritans and the Arminians, and, finally, the world of contemporary culture in which he was so deeply immersed. Disciplined curiosity here would turn up a full budget of interesting projects: topical monographs (for example, on "Wesley and the Fathers"); collations and analyses of *A Christian Library* and *The Arminian* Magazine; fresh interpretations of the so-called "Puritan" and "Anglican" traditions in Wesley—and in Methodism after Wesley. Moreover, given Wesley's wide-ranging use of sources, we also need a more careful study of his so-called "eclecticism" and its theological import. We would also welcome further reflection on the distinctive character of Wesley as folk-theologian (or peoples theologian). We need to see the crucial differences between religious leaders who are able to accommodate their academic competence to the higher ends of more direct communication with uncultivated hearers and readers, and those popular preachers who have no special academic competence to conceal.

7. Wesley professed himself *homo unius libri* ("a man of one book")—a curiously unbiblical phrase. This flaunting of the flag of *sola Scriptura* ("Scripture alone") poses a cluster of crucial and unresolved questions about Wesley's principles for the interpretation of Scripture. What were his rules in this crucial theological task? What is the import of his special stress on "the analogy of faith" (by which he meant "the general sense of Scripture," governing our exegesis of its parts)? Biblical scholars, knowledgeable in the history of interpretation, must be enlisted here. But they must be willing to learn from a precritical man who lived in the Scriptures and saw the world through the eyes of its writers rather than the other way around. It would be a crucial gain if we who live now in a postmodern world could recover a sense of the revelatory power of Scripture that could match

Wesley's precritical (and yet rational) confidence in the Scriptures as "the oracles of God."

8. There has always been a subtle symbiosis between great leaders and their people; to know either requires a knowledge of both. In Wesley's case, much information about his plain people has yet to be utilized properly. If part of his genius was his ability to move at will among various strata of British society and to function effectually in each, this fact must be correlated with his self-understanding of ministry. For all his passion for the poor and their acceptance of him as one with them (a topic now being fruitfully studied by John Walsh and others), he also worked with people in the "artisan class," with "people of the middling sort," and with some numbered among "the high and the mighty." What, if anything, is implied here as to the possibilities of ministries that may transcend classes and castes in one measure or another? What are we to make of Wesley's chosen role as mediator between high culture and the sensibilities of the poor? Whence his interest in health and health services, for those without physicians? What can we learn from *Primitive Physick* besides the obvious fact that it was, indeed, primitive? What, moreover, are the theological and ethical grounds for Wesley's concerns about justice and human dignity, poverty and its relief, slavery and oppression. How do we reconcile his commitments to social reform with his abhorrence of violent revolution? What are we to make of his thoughts about the use of money and his lifelong denunciations of riches (which is to say, the accumulation of wealth beyond the limits of one's morally justified needs)?

9. Another frontier still largely unexplored in collaborative study is the complex phenomenon of the interdependence of the Evangelical Revivals in America and Britain in the eighteenth century, and afterwards. Those who know the Wesleys and their work seem only rarely to recognize that George Whitefield's greatest impact may have been in America and that Jonathan Edwards was eagerly read in Britain. Clearly, we have here a network of connections that needs to be seen as a whole—in even a larger picture than the one drawn by Michael R. Watts in his pioneering work, *The Dissenters* (chapter 5). With the American context in mind, we

also see the need for a more credible analysis of Wesley's bitter controversies with the British Calvinists after 1765 than the available accounts from the contending parties afford us. This would throw welcome light on the rise of the Anglican Evangelicals (e.g., Charles Simeon)—and some light on Wesley's influence upon Alexander Knox, and through him, on the Anglo-Catholic Revival.

10. It has always been easier to claim that Wesley was "a great communicator" than to explain it convincingly, on the basis of his printed sermons and essays. But such an explanation is needed and would require at least three sorts of background studies: (1) specialist analyses of Wesley's rhetoric, as we find it in his written prose and as we have it reported by those who heard his oral preaching; (2) a historian's detailed account of how Wesley appeared to the common people; (3) a Christian educator's interpretation of Wesley's own images of the well-furnished minister, and of his special ministry as tutor to his own preachers. Beyond all this, we might be well-served if some great modern preachers would reflect aloud on the secret of Wesley's effectiveness as a preacher—to throw more light on that lifetime record of some two hundred thousand miles and four thousand sermons.

11. Contextual studies of this sort would lend foundation to a wide range of useful thematic studies in Wesleyan theology and ethics. Here the list is endless. Toward the top of it, though, would be a careful testing of the thesis that Wesley's theology is best understood as organized around the axial themes of grace and of the *ordo salutis* as the entire work of grace. Beyond this lie beckoning "systematic" questions about his pneumatology, anthropology, epistemology, and eschatology. None of these diminishes the urgency of special studies in such topical issues as liberation theology, black theology, feminist theology, political theology, and the like. Such inquiries, within the brackets of Wesley's fidelity to evangelical Christianity and subject to the rigorous standards of method and interpretation already specified, would extend and enrich the sort of Wesley Studies we hope to see develop.

12. Finally, the new phase of Wesley Studies requires much work also in the sprawling, cognate field of *Methodist* studies. These are important in their own right, even as they also must rest upon an adequate background. The nub of this problem, methodologically, is the provision of credible accounts of the sectarian divisions among "the people called Methodists" after Wesley's death, which have clearly contradicted Wesley's overconfident word to Ezekiel Cooper about "Methodists" in all the world being "one people." We need to know more about the rise and stabilization of rival denominational lines, about the invocation of Wesley's sanctions upon irreconcilable derivations from his theology. How are we to understand the controversies that did arise and their respective institutionalizations? For if, as we hope and pray, a new ecumenical day is dawning within the Methodist family as well as in the larger Christian community, these separate histories offer important insights into Wesleyan theology that should not be lost. Is there a fissiparous tendency inherent in Methodism as such, and, if so, why should it be and what, if anything, is there to be done about it?

All of this leaves us with the relatively new and unavoidably sensitive problem of how Wesley's theology and praxis can be transplanted and indigenized (if indeed it can) within those modern cultures that have developed outside Methodism's original European and North American provenance, in regions displaying many old problems in many new forms, among peoples emerging from a repudiated colonial past, and who have chosen new roads to freedom and their futures. There can be few guidelines here, and need not be—"guidance" is a singularly inappropriate notion in the circumstances. But their situation may evoke a fresh understanding of Wesley's famous letter to "Our Brethren in North America" (1784)—affirming *their* "full liberty simply to follow the Scriptures and the Primitive Church." North America did this—with a more or less grateful debt to Wesley as their chief teacher. Is this possible in radically different situations?

If some such new phase of scholarship does, in fact, unfold, it will need some kind of ongoing network of scholarly comrades such as we in this working group have found among ourselves. We hope that all who are, or may be, interested in this undertaking will act on their own initiatives to develop new programs of collaboration. Such networks could be greatly aided by the encouragement and support of the World Methodist Council, and the involvement of as many of the various denominations in the Wesleyan tradition as might be interested.

The new future of Wesley Studies must not be constrained within narrow boundaries or prescriptions. Given the perspective we have tried to define and given adequate editions of Wesley's works together with an ampler supply of high quality secondary sources, the enterprise may be trusted to find its own way, quite possibly along unforeseen lines.

What remains to be expressed is our hope that, in a time when the several worlds we live in are as hungry and needful for Wesley's vision of "the holy and happy life" as his world was, the residues of his ministry among us may become the source of a renewal that is as awakening, as humanizing, as renewing in our futures as it was in those of his immediate followers. This would be faithful to his own hopes, since he never tired of insisting that his message offered no novelties but only the plain, old religion of Scripture and the Apostles—the good news that God was in Christ—reconciling the world to himself by the gracious power of the hallowing Spirit.

3

Wesley as Read by the Poor

Elsa Tamez

It were to be wished, that none but heathens had practiced such gross, palpable works of the devil. But we dare not say so. Even in cruelty and bloodshed how little have the Christians come behind them! And not the Spaniards or Portuguese alone, butchering thousands in South America; not the Dutch alone in the East Indies, or the French in North America, following the Spaniards step by step; our own countrymen, too have wantoned in blood, and exterminated whole nations; plainly proving thereby what spirit it is that dwells and works in the children of disobedience.

John Wesley, "A Caution Against Bigotry."[1]

Rereading Wesley from a Latin American perspective is not an easy thing to do. Above all, it is not easy on this international occasion where the wounds left by British Colonialism have recently been reopened and the distancing and even actual war conditions between North and South (First World and Third World countries) are becoming more obvious and more difficult to overlook.

This situation weighs heavily on our consciences as we approach Wesley and attempt to know the Methodist tradition better. This is true especially in relationship to the theme of "justice and salvation." Knowing something about the ambiguous path followed by Wesley, our first impulse is to force the issue, that is, either to reject him completely or to "force" him to be on the side of the poor countries.

It seems to us that neither of the two attitudes is valid for Latin American Methodists. In the first place, if we are Methodists, we cannot reject our ties with the tradition that considers John Wesley its founder. In the second place, we cannot attribute to Wesley something that cannot be found in his context regardless of whether this is due to limitations of historical conditions or to his particular view of class.

As is clear, there are opposing opinions about Wesley's theology and political behavior. As far as his theology is concerned, he has been labeled "conservative," but it has also been proposed that some of his attitudes are similar to the theology of liberation. In regard to his political views, he has been classified as a reformist, a revolutionary, and even a counterrevolutionary. He has been depicted as having some similarities with Marx, but his thinking also has been seen as consonant with the underlying ideology of Adam Smith. Analyzing the young Wesley in contrast to the mature Wesley has also been proposed, and so on.[2] We recognize that many of these studies were serious attempts to account for Wesley's ambiguity and to advance along some guidelines that his theology projects.

These differences of opinion present us with a hermeneutical problem, as Theodore Runyon indicates.[3] It is precisely on this point that we wish to focus our presentation—approaching Wesley and interpreting him from a Latin American, Third World perspective—from the perspective of the poor who are struggling for their liberation. For this purpose we shall offer some hermeneutical pointers and finally shall try to reread some aspects of Wesley's theology of salvation.

Three points should be clarified in the beginning: (1) For us, it is extremely important to consider *who* reads the Methodist tradition, *from what concrete situation* they read it, and *for whom* they read it.[4] In a Latin American reading the point of view from which Christian writings (the Bible and tradition) are read becomes more important than the specific text read. *By whom* and *for whom* become more important than *what* (the theme dealt with). So we see that this reading implies a choice of perspective, and, not only this, it also implies a potentially transformative reading because the *reason why* the reading is done is also of concern. Bible reading as it is practiced by poor churches with a certain degree of political consciousness shows this quite clearly. The results of this spontaneous reading are new and promising.

(2) We believe that Wesley, even with all his ambiguities, may appropriately be reread in our times and in our situations. There is historical evidence that shows us the participation of many Methodists in the social process both today and in the past. The fact that the greatest number of persons so involved are Methodists, and not another denomination, is not an accident. We believe that this is due to certain roots of the tradition which, reread from a liberation perspective, invite one to participate actively in the liberation of the oppressed. Alan D. Gilbert, quoting E. J. Hobsbawm, states that:

[The latter] disagreed with Halévy about the significance of Methodism as a conservative force. Conservatism, he agreed, was its dominant political characteristic, but not in the all-pervasive sense of the Halévy analysis. For at a grass-roots level, even Wesleyanism, the largest and most conservative of the Methodist connections, contained significant elements of social protest and radical sympathy which could only have weakened the conservative impulse of the movement as a whole.[5]

It seems to us, then, that there is a dimension of the Methodist tradition which permits us to be sensitive to the demands of history, even when we consider ourselves conservative. Obviously, the sensitivity will be greater or smaller depending on the injustice that we have suffered. Concerning the situation of our Methodist churches in Latin America, the most thought-provoking theological interpretations are those of believers, both pastors and laity, who have suffered economic and political problems firsthand.

This sensitivity to historical conflicts must in some way be attributable to Wesley and his original movement. This is what made him attractive to the masses of workers, artisans, and farmers who filled the Methodist chapels and simultaneously struggled for their rights. The interpretation or the understanding which these oppressed groups had of Wesley is what we would like to reappropriate, vindicate, and deepen. We are dealing with the Wesley of the poor—an interpretation once popular, which will have to be rediscovered by an examination of the history of poor Methodists in England, the United States, and the Third World.

(3) Wesley's phrase "we think and let others think" authorizes us to move freely in the field of reflection. It is worth mentioning here that probably the ample freedom which a Methodist has in choosing differing theological positions is due to the fact that Wesley, or Methodism, did not develop a doctrinal creed in which "orthodox Methodism" is imprisoned.[6] The surprising thing is that Methodism gave us another kind of creed, a social creed, which, despite the obvious criticism that can be directed against it, is significant for the global outlook of the Methodist believer. This causes us to suspect the following: The believing Methodist follows the Bible, the apostolic creed, and the theological contributions of Wesley scattered in his writings. But what about this Methodist identity? Is it not more specifically given to a Methodist by his or her interpretation and practice of the social creed, which in some way reflects Wesley's pastoral practice and theological thought?

How to Read Wesley: Notes for a Hermeneutic

In order to approach Wesley we have to distance ourselves from him. That is, if we wish to grasp the meaning of Wesley's practical-theological work, we have to achieve enough distance to distinguish the different theological processes of the eighteenth and twentieth centuries and the theological contributions of both periods. We cannot deal with the theology of Wesley apart from its context; neither can we consider our own theology without its historical antecedents. Nor is it a matter of simply relating different sets of theological terminology (because this would leave us only with words) or simply relating different contexts. It is essential to search for a correlation of meaning at the level of the relationship between Wesley and his environment and of ourselves with our environment. Clodovis Boff, speaking of mediation, proposes this diagram:

writings   ourselves
↕ ⟵⟶ ↕
their context   our context

Reexamining this diagram we would say:

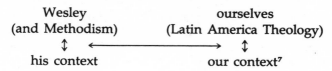

As is clear, this is a relating of relationships. We are relating the relationship between Wesley and his context and the relationship between ourselves and our context. In this "correspondence of relationships," says Boff, "we cannot expect to find formulas to copy or techniques to apply. What this can offer us is something like orientation, models, types, guidance, principles, inspirations," according to Wesley's beliefs, or better, according to the Methodist tradition.[8]

For example, everyone would agree that within this tradition, there has been a concern for our fellow human beings (for education, participation, basic needs, poverty) as part of the process of sanctification. This attitude is then taken up again today; it is reinterpreted in the light of new historical conditions and is reformulated. In this process we may discover something that was vital for Wesley in his time, but which currently is not for us. If this happens, we can relegate it to a secondary position or put it aside. It may also be the case that some of Wesley's deeds, according to our analysis, were not only reformist in their specific historical context, but hit at the heart of the system for us in Latin America today. Think, for example, about the right to live, work, eat, and study. In many Latin American countries with repressive governments, struggling for these basic needs is a matter of life and death. The masses of people who are struggling because they want to work, eat, have housing, and so on, reveal the heart of the problem in the capitalist system, which has proved incapable of satisfying the basic needs of the masses because the essence of capitalism is the maximization of profit.[9]

Was Wesley attacking the problem of structure with his reformative practices? Apparently not. Nevertheless, the same practices can be, for us, revolutionary in the sense that they point out the core of the system. Does this have anything to do with theology? Yes! For Wesley, human life was more important than anything else; it is for us today, too. Both then and now there is a theological conviction that life is a gift of God; we are created in his image, and it is his will that we have life. What we surely perceive differently is what kind of life it should be and how we can achieve it.

At this point affirmations might arise that Wesley would not make. He would perhaps even object to them. But we sense that in some way they are contained in the meaning of his words. When rereading Wesley we consider two additional facts that permit us to extract or add a new, current meaning to these writings: our interpretation of the Bible and the experience of our faith as we live it today, motivated by the Holy Spirit. Indeed, these two elements are basic to any rereading of Wesley from whatever perspective we choose.

Often we find the same words spoken by Wesley but related to different contexts. The result is that the content is different. Words do not simply have a universal meaning; they are filled and emptied and filled again with concrete historical content. The meaning of a written text, whose form remains the same, is determined at a particular moment by the meanings which it itself has engendered.[10] "Meaning comes about in the historical present by means of and beyond the letter of the written word."[11] Wesley, when he was dying, said, "The best thing of all is that God is with us."[12] This phrase, read today in the process of liberation of the exploited classes, marginal cultures, and oppressed races, contains a theological affirmation vital for the advancement of this struggle.

The Wesley of the Poor Methodists

Throughout history there have been groups of Methodists who have read Wesley and the Bible from the point of view of the oppressed. There have also been readings that have opposed this viewpoint, as for instance that of Jabez Bunting, the dominant figure of orthodox Wesleyanism and its followers. This second way of interpreting Wesley can be seen in the following two quotations from 1816 and 1819 respectively:

[It is] . . . a subject of painful and distressing concern that two of our local preachers (from North Shields) have attended the tremendous Radical Reform Meeting. . . . I hope no considerable portion of our brethren is found among the Radicals; but a small number of our leaders are among the most determined friends to their spirit and design . . . and some of the really pious, misguided sisterhood have helped to make their colours. On expostulation, I am glad to say, several members have quitted their classes (for they have adopted almost the whole Methodist economy, the terms "Class Leaders," "District Meetings," etc., etc., being perfectly current among them). If men are to be drilled at Missionary and Bible meetings to face a multitude with recollection, and acquire facilities of address, and then begin to employ the mighty moral weapon thus gained to the endangering the very existence of the Government of the country, *we* may certainly begin to tremble. . . .

The second quotation expresses:

Strong and decided disapprobation of certain tumultuous assemblies which have lately been witnessed in several parts of the country; in which large masses of people have been irregularly collected (often under banners bearing the most shocking and impious inscriptions) . . . calculated, both from the infidel principles, the wild and delusive political theories, and the violent and inflammatory declamations . . . to bring all government into contempt, and to introduce universal discontent, insubordination, and anarchy.[13]

Historian E. P. Thompson says that reading the biographies of Bunting and Bourne (founder of the Primitive Methodists) is to pass from one world to a completely different one. While Bunting viewed the workers with disdain due to their ecclesiastical-hierarchical intrigues and tried to situate Methodism to the right of the establishment, Bourne and the Primitive Methodists formed part of the working class and lived a difficult and persecuted life, similar to the situation experienced by Wesleyanism at its beginnings. The message of the Primitives "was not preached *at*, but *by*, the poor."[14]

This "militant" Methodism had already appeared before the founding of the Primitive Methodists. There is a letter in which the Methodists were accused of saying that "Corn and all other fruits of the earth, are grown and intended by Providence, as much for the poor as the rich." These Methodists "were less content with their wages and (as the letter adds) 'less ready to work extraordinary hours, as the exigencies of their masters might require.' Worse, instead of recouping themselves for the next week's labour, they exhausted themselves on Sundays walking several miles to hear a preacher."[15]

Their struggles evidently sprang from convictions of faith because their faith was a liberating one. There was no gap between their political practices and their expressions of faith. They sang, prayed, and struggled for their rights without problems of integration. For them this was the totality of their life of faith. As E. J. Hobsbawm has put it, the "characteristic attitude of the labour sectarian was this-worldly and non-mystical, or if mystical, disciplined to this-worldly activity. It is therefore not surprising that conversion indicated, reflected or stimulated the kind of unselfish activity which labour militancy implied."[16]

An interesting fact brought to light by Hobsbawm is that political awareness and political activity for many notable leaders of the working class began simultaneously with or immediately after their conversion, that is, when they experienced the "sudden emotionally overwhelming realization of sin and the finding of grace which Methodism . . . encouraged."[17]

It is important to observe how these Methodists developed their theology on the basis of their practice and how they related their political practice and their pastoral practices. Unfortunately I do not have their writings at hand; I only have the testimony of a Methodist union member from the last century and one sermon of a pastor from North Carolina dated 1929. Parts of the testimony of the Methodist union member of Lincolnshire, England, whose name was Joseph Chapman (1899), are as follows:

I was among the Primitives of the Alford Circuit for over thirty years. I worked as a local preacher for the cause of Christ. . . . When the Labourers' Union first started in Alford I took a great interest in it. . . . We don't believe in lords and ladies, priests and their wives being considered sacred and peasants being vermin. . . . I believe the time is not far distant when God will send restored apostles and prophets to his Church who will visit the aged poor and investigate how they live on three shillings a week, the annuity allowed from the Parish . . . and enter a strong protest against such cruelty and preach with much force the Gospel of God, that it will kill or cure barren and fruitless professors. . . . There is signs of the grand union that is coming when prince and peer and peasant shall combine and cooperate for the good of one and all.[18]

This same interpretation of the Bible and of the Protestant tradition is found in the labor strike of Loray, North Carolina, in 1929. H. J. Crabtree, minister of the Church of the Lord, prayed for divine guidance of the strike and then preached a sermon. These are some of his words:

"Deliver me, oh Lord, from the evil man; preserve me from the violent man." I call God to witness who has been the violent man in this strike. . . . But we must bear it. Paul and Silas had to go through with it, and today they sit a-singing around the great white throne. In a few days you'll be a singing through the streets of Loray with good wages. God's a poor man's God. Jesus Christ himself was born in an old ox-barn in Bethlehem. He was kicked about, speared about and finally nailed to a cross. And for what? For sin. It's sin that's causing this trouble. Sin of the rich man, the man who thinks he's rich. . . . All the wealthy men in this here crowd hold up their hands. I'll hold mine up for one. My father owns this whole world. He owns every hill in this world and every tater in them hills.[19]

Note the eschatological concept of the first sermon, and the christological and soteriological approach of the second one. The theological concepts are charged with concrete historical content. Sin is identified.

Justice and Salvation in Latin America: Reading Wesley

In order to reread Wesley today we first have to take into account the world view that underlies his theology and his acts. In reading his theology we are initially impressed by a lack of coordination between his thought and his pastoral disposition.[20] This is quite understandable. In his theological writings we can perceive a mercantile ideology, which fairly consistently underlies his thought and which can be seen reflected in his actions. Míguez Bonino, referring to Wesley, says:

His attempt to work with hard data, statistics, prices, and market conditions is extraordinary for a religious leader. But when he attempts to find causes and remedies, he remains totally within the premises of the mercantilist system and completely unaware of the structural causes of the crises.[21]

Wesley's view of the human being, "incurably individualistic," causes his theology of justification and sanctification to be subjectively based on the inner life of the individual.[22]

Wesley's marked emphasis on Christian perfection reminds one of the market ideal of perfect competition rather than the struggle for a just society. We recall his famous phrases: "Gain all you can. . . . Save all you can. . . . Give all you can."

Present-day Methodists, especially Latin American Methodists, live within a different framework. Through experience, we have become too familiar with that new model of production and organization of society born in the time of Wesley. We have discovered that the gods of the new order are false and diabolical because they swallow up the lives of many people. Because of this, our theology and our actions must go beyond sin and the salvation of the individual. We cannot say only, as has often been said until now, that we will change individuals in order to change society. We need to change also the heart of society itself. Society is not being governed by human beings; rather it is human beings who are being governed by a system that insists on a logic of death. We have declared war on these false gods, knowing full well that "we are not contending against flesh and blood, but against the principalities, against the powers" (Ephesians 6:12), against fetishes. The Methodist Church of Bolivia in its *Manifesto a la Nación* (1970) affirms:

Social, political, cultural, or economic structures become dehumanized when they do not serve "all men and the total man," in other words, when they are structured to perpetuate injustice.

Structures are products of men, but they assume an impersonal character, even a Satanic one, going beyond the possibility of individual action.

We must struggle against foreign powers that encircle and strangle us; we must also struggle against tendencies which undermine the inner strength of our own society and cause it to deteriorate.[23]

Theology concerning sin, salvation, and sanctification must have another meaning for us—a meaning that is historical, transforming, and liberating.

Let us then try to reinterpret Wesley from the situation of the oppressed who are struggling for liberation.

First, let us think about the Latin American situation. On the one hand, we have impoverished people, inflation, increasing living costs, incredible unemployment, exorbitant foreign debt. In the majority of countries there are repressive governments: torture, the disappearance of individuals, deaths, political prisoners, guerillas. In short, misery and struggle. On the other hand, most people are believers—many of them with a certain degree of political awareness, with a desire to discover the good news of present-day salvation, and with hope for the coming of the kingdom of God on earth.

We are engaged in a life and death struggle.

Justification and Rebirth

God has promised us life, eternal life, that is to say, life that will last forever. It is life that begins here on earth and which will be fully realized in the resurrection of the body. "Why were we sent into the world? For one sole end, and for no other, to prepare for eternity. For this alone we live."[24]

Eternity is experienced in the full and complete life, which is God: "God made man to be 'an image of his own eternity,' an incorruptible picture of the God of Glory."[25]

For this reason, the human being is called to bear the image of God. We will show forth this image; we will experience it fully, when the kingdom of God has been fully established. We are called to carry this image, and we reflect life or death depending on the degree to which we fulfill this calling. Part of this image can be perceived even now in our present movement toward complete fulfillment. In the beginning, the human being, because he or she existed in the image of God, had an innate principle of moving; he or she could move toward life. However, "by abusing his liberty," by wanting to have more than he had in Eden, man introduced evil into the world, and lost this "independent movement." So . . .

His soul died, was separated from God . . . his body, likewise, became corruptible and mortal. . . . And being already dead in spirit, dead to God, dead in sin, he hastened on to death everlasting; to the destruction both of body and soul, in the fire never to be quenched. [26]

Because of sin, the human being progressively moves away from God, who is justice itself. The farther we get from life in its fullness, the more prone we are to sin and its consequence—death, annihilation. Sin blocks and prevents salvation, the passage to life. Sin "is historical reality; it is the breach of communion among men, it is the withdrawal of man into himself." [27] With sin the process toward the fulfillment of life is suspended, and its place is taken by a project that leads to death, failure, and the wrath of God.

The document of the Methodist Church in Bolivia, previously mentioned, describes the situation of the human being in the following way:

Man . . . lives dispossessed, dehumanized. He is alienated from himself. . . . He has no clear awareness of his origin, does not understand his present state; it is difficult for him to find his mission in life; he gropes blindly in search of his destiny. . . . He is alienated from his fellow man, whom he looks upon as an enemy rather than a brother. . . . He is alienated from his society, from the moment in which he does not understand his rights and his responsibilities, and has not awakened to human solidarity and common responsibility. [28]

As human beings, if we wish to continue being human, that is to say, if we wish to recover the image of God, we must make a covenant with God—with life. Wesley calls this "the covenant of grace." This grace is free, a gift of God. [29] It is a call from God that invites us to fulfill our human vocation: to live in freedom. Without this divine intervention we cannot move because of the inertia of sin that leads to nonlife. To realize this is itself a gift of God. Wesley calls it "preventing grace."

Salvation begins with what is usually termed (and very properly) *preventing grace;* including the first wish to please God, the first dawn of light concerning his will, and the first slight transient conviction of having sinned against him. All these imply some tendency toward life; some degree of salvation; the beginning of a deliverance from a blind, unfeeling heart, quite insensible of God and the things of God.[30]

In gratitude to God we take cognizance of the reality of oppression and an effective love for others is born in us. "This earnest, steady good will to our fellow creature never flowed from any fountain but gratitude to our Creator."[31]

By the grace of God we awaken from our inertia, say *no* to everything that does not permit us to live—that is, to sin—and say *yes* to the promised life, to the good news which God presents to us by way of the reality of poverty. By "convincing grace" we become convicted not to live in sin, whether it be letting ourselves be manipulated by it and thereby causing the death of others, or by dying ourselves as a result of sin without making a sign of protest, without taking pity on our fellow human beings or on ourselves. We need to repent and change our attitude.

Salvation is carried out by convincing grace, usually in Scripture termed repentance.

And, First . . . the Son begins his work in man by enabling us to believe in him. He both opens and enlightens the eyes of our understanding. Out of darkness he commands light to shine, ... And we then see not by a chain of *reasoning,* but by a kind of *intuition,* by a direct view, that "God was in Christ, reconciling the world to himself. . . ."[32]

It is in this process of "convincing grace" that justification takes place, God's forgiveness for our having lived in sin, that is, nonlife, and the new birth to life or the renewal of fallen nature.[33] Before being born again, the human being had eyes but did not see, ears but did not hear, consciousness but did not think. Upon being born again: "He feels 'the love of God shed abroad in his heart by the Holy Ghost which is given unto him;' and all his spiritual senses are then exercised to discern spiritual good and evil."[34]

Being born again, we acquire the ability to distinguish between life and death. We can identify those who produce death, the principalities and powers that govern the earth, the anti-Christs. We become aware of the meaning of real life and realistic possibilities of achieving it. We see God as the source of life and justice who gives his life for our life. Now awakened, we are motivated to announce this good news to the poor and oppressed. We begin to fear death, and the birth of faith begins.

At the same time, we "receive the spirit of bondage unto fear;" fear of the wrath of God, fear of the punishment we have deserved; and, above all, fear of death, lest it should consign us over to eternal death. Souls that are thus convinced feel they are so fast in prison, that they cannot get forth. They feel themselves at once altogether guilty, and altogether helpless. But all this conviction implies a species of faith. . . .[35]

This belief in the full life, promise and fulfillment in our Lord Jesus Christ, is not just intellectual assent; it is a profound conviction felt in our inner person, in our conscience.

The true, living, Christian faith, which whosoever hath is born of God, is not only assent, an act of the understanding; but a disposition, which God hath wrought in his heart; "a sure trust and confidence" in God that, through the merits of Christ, his sins are forgiven, and he reconciled to the favour of God.[36]

The Christian sees Jesus Christ as the prototypical human being, the human being that God desires. The Methodist Church in Bolivia, in *Manifesto a la Nación* (page 9), declares:

The whole man is free, developed and fully realized in his vocation, his mission and his destiny. This is the man completely obedient to God and totally dedicated to mankind. To the extent that men become similar to God and give themselves to Him to be transformed, they become truly human.

Sanctification

With new birth, we have access to sanctification. It is not enough to recognize God as the one who is in favor of those who do not have life, especially the poor. It is necessary to move ahead in the historical process of salvation; sanctification is necessary, that is "renewal in the image of God in justice and true holiness."[37] New birth is not enough; it is necessary to accept the challenge and risk the struggle for the fullness of life, to make visible the kingdom of God: the kingdom of love and justice. New birth and sanctification are two different steps and both are indispensable. There cannot be sanctification without a new birth; there cannot be a struggle for life without a desire to live, just as there cannot be fullness of life without sanctification.

[The] new birth is not the same with sanctification. . . . [It] is a part of sanctification, not the whole; it is the gate to it, the entrance into it. When we are born again, then our sanctification, our inward and outward holiness begins; and thenceforward we are gradually to "grow up in Him who is our Head."[38]

That is to say, we begin to follow the example of Jesus Christ of Nazareth, the Son of God, who struggled until the end for justice here on earth. And we do this with a living hope because we know beforehand that the triumph of life over death is sure, because on the cross Jesus Christ overcame death and the principalities and powers. There is nothing more damaging than failing to emphasize holiness in the life of the believer. Wesley said:

But of all preaching, what is usually called gospel preaching is the most useless, if not the most mischievous; a dull, yea or lively, harangue on the sufferings of Christ or salvation without strongly inculcating holiness. I see more and more that this naturally tends to drive holiness out of the world.[39]

The source of all holiness is love for God, says Wesley, and one loves God only if one does his will, and his will is that man should live, that he act in liberty, that he have work, food, shelter, that he celebrate, participate, that his culture be respected—in short, that he recover the image of God.

81

"[Christian perfection] is a renewal of the heart in the whole image of God, the full likeness of Him that created it. . . . It is the loving God with all our heart, and our neighbour as ourselves." ("A Plain Account of Christian Perfection"). "Let none rest in any supposed fruit of the Spirit without the witness."[40]

The human being's affirmative response to God propels him or her on to the path of holiness. It is not a passive response. Although this "very first motion of good is from above," the person who is released from the inertia of sin by virtue of a potentially liberating faith must throw himself or herself into the search for life in his or her present circumstances in the world.[41] If we do not do this, we are condemned to failure, to death, to abandonment by God.

First, God worketh in you; therefore you *can* work: Otherwise it would be impossible. . . . Secondly, God worketh in you; therefore, you *must* work: You must be "workers together with him," (they are the very words of the Apostle) otherwise he will cease working. The general rule on which his gracious dispensations invariably proceed is this: "Unto him that hath shall be given: But from him that hath not,"—that does not improve the grace already given,—"shall be taken away what he assuredly hath."[42]

"Salvation, as an intra-historical reality,—communion of men and women with God and among themselves—guides, transforms and propels history on to its fulness."[43]

Hope impels us to move toward the kingdom of justice on this road to sanctification, in this experience of a true and liberating faith, in this struggle for life over against death. If this hope is destroyed, salvation is blocked and it decreases: "Whereas, just the contrary effects are observed whenever this expectation ceases. They are 'saved by hope,' by this hope of a total change, with a gradually increasing salvation. Destroy this hope, and that salvation stands still or, rather, decreases daily."[44]

Sanctification, as the struggle for life, gives meaning to our existence. Curiously, after rereading Wesley on sanctification, we understand more clearly how it is that the Nicaraguan priest Ernesto Cardenal was able to speak of the holiness of the revolution without any problem.

Finally, we wish to say that hope is kept alive in us because we are already experiencing in part what will come in the future. We have "anticipatory signs," the signs of the kingdom of God that are visible and tangible. Where there are signs of life, of liberation, of joy, of the sharing of bread, we feel within ourselves, we see with our eyes, we hear, we feel with our hands, the hope of life. We also announce this to the four winds so that our joy may be complete.

The suffering involved in this struggle, in the "not yet," makes us persevere, and the hope produced by the "already" makes us strong.

Notes

1. *Wesley's Standard Sermons*, ed. Edward H. Sugden, 2 vols. (London: Epworth Press, 1921), 2:110.

2. Leon O. Hynson, "Human Liberty as Divine Right: A Study in the Political Maturation of John Wesley," a paper prepared for the Seventh Oxford Institute.

3. Theodore Runyon, "Wesley and the Theologies of Liberation," in *Sanctification and Liberation* (Nashville: Abingdon Press, 1981), pp. 14ff.

4. Gustavo Gutiérrez, *La Fuerza Histórica de los Pobres* (Lima: CEP, 1979), p. 157. According to Gutiérrez, theological reflection is made within a definite process context and is hence linked to it. Theology is not atemporal but is rather the contrary. It is an effort to tell the Lord's word in everyday words, with the codes of each epoch.

5. "Methodism, Dissent and Political Stability in Early Industrial England," *Journal of Religious History*, 10 (1979), p. 382.

6. It does not seem to us that the Protestant creed which appears in *The Letters of John Wesley*, ed. John Telford, 8 vols. (London: Epworth Press, 1931), 2:18-19, is a confessional creed in the true sense of the word.

7. Clodovis Boff, *Theologia de lo Político* (Salmanca: Sígueme, 1980), p. 276.

8. Boff, p. 279.

9. CPID/CMI and Association of Third World Economists, *Tecnología y Necesidades Básicas* (San José: DEI, 1979), pp. 13-26.

10. Boff, p. 265.

11. Boff, p. 277.

12. Thomas Coke and Henry Moore, *Life of the Rev. John Wesley, A.M.*, pp. 39-40, quoted by Reginald Kissack in *Así pensaba John Wesley* (México: CUPSA, 1975), p. 51.

13. These quotations have been taken from E. P. Thompson, *The Making of the English Working Class* (New York: Vintage Books, 1966), pp. 352, 353.

14. Thompson, pp. 396-97.

15. Thompson, p. 397.

16. E. J. Hobsbawm, *Primitive Rebels: Studies in Archaic Forms of Social Movement in the 19th and 20th Centuries*, rev. ed. (Manchester: Manchester University Press, 1971), p. 141.

17. Hobsbawm, p. 140.
18. Hobsbawm, pp. 190-91.
19. Hobsbawm, p. 190.
20. See José Míguez Bonino, "Wesley's Doctrine of Sanctification from a Liberationist Perspective," in *Sanctification and Liberation*, p. 57.
21. Míguez Bonino, p. 59.
22. Míguez Bonino, p. 55.
23. *Manifesto a la Nación* (Evangelical Methodist Church in Bolivia, 1970), pp. 10, 12.
24. *The Works of John Wesley* (London: Wesleyan-Methodist Book-Room, 1872; reprint, Grand Rapids: Baker Book House, 1979), 7:229.
25. *Sermons*, 1:116.
26. *Sermons*, 1:117.
27. Gustavo Gutiérrez, *Teología de la Liberación* (Salamanca: Sígueme, 1972), p. 198.
28. *Manifesto a la Nación*, p. 10.
29. *Works*, 7:373.
30. *Works*, 6:509.
31. *Works*, 6:359.
32. *Works*, 6:509; 6:274-75.
33. *Works*, 5:56.
34. *Sermons*, 2:234.
35. *Works*, 7:235.
36. *Sermons*, 1:284-85.
37. *Works*, 8:279.
38. *Sermons*, 2:239-40.
39. *Letters*, 5:345.
40. *Works*, 11:444; *Sermons*, 2:358.
41. *Works*, 6:509.
42. *Works*, 6:511, 513.
43. Gutiérrez, *Teología de la Liberación*, p. 199.
44. *Works*, 8:329.

Salvation, Justice, and the Theological Task

Working Group Paper

We believe that those who stand in the Methodist traditions have a crucial responsibility to the present moment in world history. Through the brutal sufferings of the majority of humankind, God is calling us to reexamine our heritage to determine the resources that can speak to this situation. Within our group we have heard that Wesley is already being discovered in Latin America, Africa, and elsewhere as a significant resource for the life and mission of the church. The cries of the poor arising from all corners of the globe have opened our eyes to the special place which the marginalized and disenfranchised occupy both in the Bible and in the Wesleyan revival of the eighteenth century.

Nineteenth-century Methodism, we can argue, changed from a "religion of the poor" to a "religion *for* the poor." Twentieth-century affluent Methodism is challenged to reappraise this situation by being open to and challenged by both the Scriptures' demand for justice and what the oppressed have to teach us about the need for changes in the world socio-economic systems. Do the poor not call into question theology as we have understood and practiced it thus far? Do they not call for repentance and conversion, for a "new Aldersgate?"

We agree that the Scriptures are the criterion by which we discern the coming of God's kingdom, and the values that structure our discipleship in response to the poor and oppressed.

Not only the Scriptures but also the Eucharist challenges us. If the Eucharistic meal is really a celebration of God and humanity in the Christ of the poor, it critiques the justice of the relationships of all who share in this celebration—rich and poor. In this sense, some of us interpret the Eucharist as a justice meal. Participating in the Eucharist, are we not required to be active in the breaking in of the kingdom? Are we not here invited by the Scriptures to follow Christ into the depths of human suffering among the wretched of the earth?

For many the new situation implies a new starting point: discipleship precedes theory, so that Christian thought grows out of experience in a new way. A number of us consider philosophical analysis important for theology. We need warrants for the claims we make. But philosophies also need reevaluation in the new context.

We hope that out of this process of reflection at Oxford will come a continuing program of action and reflection. We need to develop a clearer understanding in several areas, in view of the above shift in the way in which we need to do theology, and would invite all who are willing to engage in such a research commitment to join us.

(1) *A new starting point for theology? Contextual analysis.*

Wesley and Wesleyan thought forms cannot be imposed on the contemporary situation either in the world or the church, important as the Wesleyan contribution is. This would be to make the reappropriation of Wesley a new orthodoxy, and would be untrue to Wesley's own method. Nevertheless we find in Wesley some warrant for a theological method that can begin with an analysis of the concrete situation where persons find themselves, which names the demons in that situation, and which then brings to bear the healing power of the gospel. The chief difference between Wesley's time and our own is that Wesley generally analyzed the context within which his hearers found themselves in theological terms. It must be added, however, that he also employed "empirical" analyses to make his case (see many of his occasional essays and the treatise on original sin). In keeping with Wesley, contextual analysis is an appropriate first step in Christian thought.

(2) *Variety of contexts.*

We have discovered, however, that we are rooted in a variety of contexts: the Third World, where issues of economic exploitation and poverty demand first priority; the Black church; the feminist struggle; and other contexts of people fighting for their rights in their own or their adopted land; and secularized western cultures, largely indifferent to, if not openly hostile toward, their own Christian roots and Christian forms of life and thought. Others come from affluent cultures that have often co-opted Christianity for purposes of civil religion and made too easy an identification between their national political, economic, and military policies, and biblical faith. We discover in these same affluent, nominally Christian cultures the unmistakable signs of the breakdown of meaning and purpose for large segments of the population. Many find their affluence vapid and empty, or do not participate in the fruits of the system. To these contexts is added the church contexts within which we all work: from quasi-establishment status to small minorities within indifferent or hostile environments, or environments where non-Christian religions are dominant.

(3) *The unity of our contexts.*

Notwithstanding the diversity of contexts in which we find ourselves, we also recognize common elements in all our contemporary human contexts: racism, militarism, sexism, environmental deterioration, nuclear holocaust. Moreover, as useful as distinctions between the First, Second, and Third Worlds may be for analysis, we cannot afford to divide up the world too neatly. An answer, for example, which appears to provide existential meaning to persons in the First World but leaves untouched the needs of persons in the Third World is not a Christian answer. Each of us, therefore, regardless of the variety of our individual contexts noted in point two above, will undertake reflection and action in terms of a larger context, as required by the "global village" in which we all find ourselves. Worldwide issues that have not been solved but rather exacerbated by all existing economic systems, such as ecology and energy, bind us together in a more universal concrete context. And likewise all our critiques will be subsumed under the critique exercised by the "already—but not yet" of the kingdom of God.

(4) *The individual and the social.*

The organic relation in Wesleyan thought of the individual and social dimensions of the Christian faith has proved to be an important insight for us. Methodism was born at a time when the individual was emerging as significant in political, social, and economic life; and Methodism flourished in the nineteenth century, when individualism was the dominant trend. This inevitably affected the ways in which conversion and faith were understood. We have since become aware of the real limitations of individualism, not only in terms of the critique from Scripture but in terms of the injustices which it has legitimated. We must deepen our appreciation of Wesley's understanding of the relation between the individual and the social. In Wesley there are undeniable individual and personal emphases. Genuine salvation for him involves participation in the love of God for the individual, consciously experienced in justification. But this love experienced personally has as its goal nothing less than the creation of just human communities and the reconciliation and renewal of all creation. Wesley testified that as we love God and are loved by God, our hearts are inevitably opened up to all persons. The creative love, which transforms the person and the social context, affects both the perspective from which we see the world through the eyes of Jesus and the demand for changes in our own lives and in the life of the world. Thus sanctification as a process seeks that holiness, which is the renewal of all things in the image of the Creator and the eschatological fulfillment of the Creator's purpose (a conviction transmitted to Wesley from his patristic sources).

In his eighteenth-century location, however, Wesley cannot be expected to have seen the structural interrelationships in the society that his theology addressed. His converts were able to change from passive victims into active agents in society, but they were not able to analyze critically the interwoven character of the systems in which they existed.

The concept of a "network" may show us how to link the individual and social dimensions of salvation. Wesley saw creation as a whole, all the parts being interrelated and interdependent, and in their multiplicity contributing to a unity which praises its Maker. The fall of humanity has fundamentally affected this unity and interrelationship, for the disobedience of humanity has, according to Wesley, affected the whole of creation. Although his analysis of the forms of bondage included such evils as unemployment, slavery and war—as well as the economic motivations which lie behind them—his solutions were not by today's standards sufficiently radical. He did not understand that men and women cannot be released from these bonds simply by appealing to the hearts and consciences of Christians.

Although his condemnations of slavery were consistent and thorough (cf. *Works,* vol. 11, 59-29; *Letters,* vol. 8, 265-66), he did not make sufficiently clear the demonic character of the other institutions of his day, nor did he call Christians to radical transformation of other structures. Wesley was no political revolutionary, and believed that disruptions and revolutions were more likely to serve the devil than God, although by 1784 he was reconciled to the independence of the colonies and could urge "our brethren in America" to "stand fast in that liberty wherewith God has so strangely made them free" (*Letters,* vol. 7, 239).

Today we see that individual and piecemeal approaches are not enough. Whole interrelated networks must be radically questioned and transformed if people are to be released from injustice. But the problem remains: Where do we attack the networks? What is our point of entry? Where do we take hold to effect change? Simply to preach *at* a social order only raises the ire of those who have a stake in the status quo; although it may enable some to claim to be making a prophetic witness, in itself it does not change anything.

Latin American colleagues teach us that an important first step to which the church may contribute effectively is that of "consciousness raising." As a part of our theological task we seek to make persons and societies aware of the contradictions between the intention of God for his creation and the present reality. Jesus' announcement of the kingdom of God points to an everchanging vision and calls for the transformation of relationships in this age in the light of the age to come. Every democracy (which all of our societies, east and west, north and south claim to be) depends on an informed citizenry. Our first responsibility, therefore, may be to provide information from a biblical and Wesleyan perspective about the tensions between things as they are and things as they should be under God. The purpose of this "conscientization" is to bring persons not just to an awareness of the facts but also to an acceptance of their responsibilities for effective action. The nature of this action must be dictated by the possibilities in a specific context. Always the primary responsibility is to God's justice and to God's ways of making things right. Therefore our methods are constantly to be criticized in the light of our responsibilities. We need to show the same openness as Wesley, allowing our practice to be revised in the light of experience, keeping always uppermost the ultimate context of the universal holiness of the kingdom. As Wesley wrote, "God is already renewing the face of the earth: And we have strong reason to hope that the work he hath begun, he will carry on unto the day of the Lord Jesus; that he will never intermit this blessed work of his Spirit, until he has fulfilled all his promises, until he hath put a period to sin, and misery, and infirmity and death, and re-established universal holiness and happiness, and caused all the inhabitants of the earth to sing together, 'Hallelujah, the Lord God omnipotent reigneth!' " (*Works*, vol. 7, 288).

(5) *Spirituality and social transformation.*

We have learned from the Black church in the United States that the task of liberation entails the combination of concrete social action with deep spiritual commitment. It is the power of the Spirit that sustains when human spirits grow weak and would flag in their zeal. Therefore, it is vitally important that all our efforts be undergirded by a deep conviction of divine sovereignty and a spiritual practice consistent with divine transcendence and human need.

(6) *Solidarity.*

The Wesleyan doctrine of prevenient grace enables us to recognize the presence of Christ's judging and liberating spirit not only in the church and traditionally Christian enterprises, but in other movements. This allows us to enter into solidarity with persons and movements with whom we may not agree in every respect but in whom we recognize the activity of the God we know in Jesus Christ. Solidarity implies commitment to change the system and not mere pronouncements. Yet to be discussed are the limits, if any, of this solidarity.

(7) *Holiness and intellectual challenges.*

We bring to intellectual dialogue the commitment to extend the wholeness and justice, which we have discovered in the gospel, to all aspects of human existence. This is part of our discipleship as theologians. But we need also to become aware of the ways that theology relates to or is informed by other forms of inquiry. For example, in the Latin American situation some theologians have found Marxist socio-economic analyses useful. However, there needs to be a continuing critical analysis of the relationship between Christianity and Marxism, for any system of socio-economic analysis that reduces theology to social ethics should be regarded with suspicion.

What has been presented so far is necessarily brief and inconclusive. To sharpen the edge of our theological task, we raise the following questions, which emerged in our discussions and helped shape our continuing agenda:

(1) Can we find a hermeneutic that connects:
    a. our reading of Wesley's texts;
    b. Wesley's reading of traditional texts;
    c. a socio-analytical reading of his context and our context?

(2) What are the similarities and differences in our various ways of doing biblical exegesis and relating our exegesis and our theology? In the midst of our differences is there a shared Wesleyan hermeneutic?

(3) What is the essential relation between systematic theology and ethics? How can we avoid the danger of collapsing theology into ethics? Is this a particular danger for a liberation theology?

(4) Much of our criticism has centered on the present economic order. For many of us the "option for the poor" means opting for some form of socialism. Are there values in capitalism which should be incorporated into any new economic order? What are the givens in any economic order which have to be taken into consideration by those seeking change?

(5) What is the role of Marxist social analysis in our critical theology? Is it possible to separate Marxism as an analytical tool from Marxist ideology? Are there other tools of analysis?

(6) Is poverty a critical factor for doing theology in every context? How do we relate the poor to the Wesleyan quadrilateral: Scriptures, tradition, reason, and experience? In what ways do the Scriptures require specific attention to the poor?

(7) How can we balance psychological-existential themes with social themes of liberation? What is the bridge between the personal and the social? Are there particular insights offered by Black theology and feminist theology?

(8) How are traditional theological categories, such as prevenient grace, justification, and the kingdom of God, related to salvation in a liberationist perspective?

(9) What is an adequate Christian concept of justice? How is justice related to truth, equality, and freedom? Can analytical philosophies, challenged by liberationist concerns, contribute to clearer definitions and understanding?

(10) Is violence ever a legitimate Christian option in the struggle for justice and freedom?

4

Ecclesial Location and Ecumenical Vocation

Geoffrey Wainwright

I. Schism and Pluralism

When, in the teaching of fundamental theology, I come to the church and tradition, I begin, tongue-in-cheek, with a rapid sketch of ecclesiastical history. It shows how, in the fifth century, the non-Chalcedonians split from the hitherto undivided church. Then the Byzantine East broke away in 1054. The unreformed Roman Catholics were left behind in the sixteenth century, while the continental Protestants had the misfortune of being foreigners. In the eighteenth century, even the Church of England refused Wesley's mission, so that finally only Methodists remained in the body of Christ. At this point in the recital, general laughter occurs. Closer inspection of the emotions released reveals that English Methodist students usually experience a little *Schadenfreude* at seeing the tables turned in this way, but they retain after all a certain guilt at the responsibility of their forebears in the separation from the Church of England, and while being forced by historical circumstances to reject the ecclesiological model ironically employed in the sketch, they cannot quite be content with an alternative understanding that renders all divisions innocuous. On the other hand, Roman Catholic students are sometimes shamed into awareness that their instinctively Cyprianic view is not entirely satisfactory either, when it takes all schism to be schism *from* the church and rejects the "other party" into an ecclesiological void. Anglican students are caught in the middle, marooned on their bridge. In contrast to the English, American students of all ecclesiastical stripes tend to be surprised that one should begin thus diachronically at all, rather than synchronically with the existing state of denominational pluralism; and to this contrast between the two approaches I will return in a moment.

But first a paragraph about the theological seriousness of the strictly ecclesiological question in the Christian faith, particularly with reference to recent ecumenical discussion. The decade following the 1952 Lund Conference brought a welcome christological concentration into the work of Faith and Order as well as the explicit introduction of the Holy Trinity into the membership basis of the World Council of Churches. Attention should never stray from the divine center of the message, which is being proposed for the world's belief and salvation. But it was a mistake to suppose that the earlier concerns of "comparative ecclesiology" had then been surpassed. It is no accident that the church figures among the realities confessed in the classical creeds. The official entry of the Roman Catholic Church into the modern ecumenical movement, and then the bilateral conversations that followed Vatican II, probably did most to recall the fundamental importance of the ecclesiological question for the ecumenical movement as its very *raison d'être*. At stake in the understanding of unity and schism, of continuity and discontinuity, of integrity and fragmentation, is precisely the *identity of the church* and therewith the nature and substance of *truth* and the conditions of its *authoritative expression*. To seek and confess the ecclesiological location of one's community is an act of discerning and proclaiming the gospel itself. There is no preaching and living of the gospel without at least an implicit ecclesiological claim being made.[1]

Now to return to the diachronic and synchronic approaches to the matter of Christian unity. From his observations of the United States in the 1930s Dietrich Bonhoeffer drew a contrast between a European sense of a unity once given and now sundered and an American sense of a given pluralism which might perhaps, though not certainly, call for the construction of an eschatological unity.[2] On the European side, Bonhoeffer's own preferred emphasis on the divine gift of unity may have derived as much from a

Constantinian nostalgia as from the once-and-for-all redemption recorded in the New Testament. On the American side, the varied escapes from Europe, the hard-won development of internal tolerance, and the effort of building one nation from the many peoples have all contributed to a semicompetitive, semicooperative denominationalism whose strongly voluntaristic character is seen as an acquisition not lightly to be set at risk for the sake of a unity that might mean restrictive uniformity. In the republic of God, pluralism rules O.K. Individual crossovers from one denomination to another are achieved fairly easily, while the denominational structures remain intact. To the European churchman with a diachronic sense of schism, American Christianity may appear as too ready a synchronic acquiescence in an existing fragmentation whose murkier historical and theological origins are best not inquired into. Something of this contrast underlies the well-known tension between British and American Methodists in their understandings of ecumenism; and one result which may be hoped for from the work of the Oxford Institute of Methodist Theological Studies is increased mutual understanding and correction on these issues. The contrast between the British-diachronic and the American-synchronic is not, of course, absolute. American scholars such as Albert Outler, John Deschner, and I think, William Cannon have placed their loyal investigation of Wesleyan origins and the Methodist tradition in the context and service of historic Christianity and its search for full unity; while the dearest desire of some British Methodists at present seems to be the further dilution of the Wesleyan content in the principal vehicle of our tradition (namely, the hymnbook), though they yet remain content with a denominational life thus largely deprived of its distinction.

In the final section of this essay I will return to the fundamental ecclesiological question concerning necessary unity and legitimate diversity. The intervening six sections will particularize the Methodist application. Sections II, III, and IV will be largely diachronic in method. Their purpose is to illuminate the way in which we have reached the present situation and so to help show what factors will shape our choices if we are to be recognizably Methodist in face of our synchronic options as set out in sections V, VI, and VII.

II. A Part, Not the Whole

The notion of "a part, but not the whole" was recurrently employed by Wesley in ecclesiological controversy. Thus in reply to Bishop Richard Challoner's *The Grounds of the Old Religion,* he notes: "In the first thirty pages the author heaps up scriptures concerning the privileges of the Church. But all this is beating the air till he proves the Romanists to be the Church, that is, that a part is the whole."[3] Conversely, in response to the same Roman Catholic bishop's *Caveat against Methodists,* Wesley claims that all sinners converted to God by preachers and teachers of the faith once delivered to the saints, even if they be Methodists or any other kind of Protestant, "although they are not the whole 'people of God,' yet are they an undeniable part of his people."[4] As far as Methodism is concerned, our question must be: *What kind* of part did, does, and might Methodism constitute in *what kind* of whole? Let me give one answer that is phenomenologically certain, another that is historically speculative, a third that is scripturally indefensible, and a fourth that is eschatologically possible.

1. A society within the Church of England

That Methodism began as a society within the Church of England is certain, whether we think of the Holy Club at Oxford[5] or of "the rise of the United Society, first at London [The Foundery] and then in other places."[6] A minor complication stems from the fact that some who were admitted to membership—upon the sole condition of their "desire to flee from the wrath to come, to be saved from their sins"—were not Anglicans but belonged to Dissenting bodies. Wesley no more desired them to interrupt their old allegiance than he would countenance the withdrawal of Methodists from the Church of England. Internal pressures for separation from the Church of England arose early in the Methodist movement, but Wesley resisted them at successive Conferences.[7] Neither the early violence of the mobs, nor the persistent hostility of the parochial clergy, nor the recurrent rebuffs of the bishops could weaken John Wesley's self-understanding as "a Church of England man."[8] He rejected his disappointed brother Charles' acceptance that "ordination was separation,"[9] and it is true that not even Wesley's ordination of men for America, Scotland, and finally England brought forth an official expulsion from the Church of England. Yet there is no doubt that a certain "unstitching" (the image is Wesley's own)[10] had already begun during Wesley's lifetime; and his death soon removed the final reticence from his English followers,[11] so that on the ground plan which he himself had drawn—notably in the Deed of Declaration of 1784—an ecclesiastical structure was quickly built. The process is usually called the transition "from Society to Church."[12] Certainly by 1795 the Plan of Pacification was allowing Methodist worship at the times of church services (Wesley's discouragement of this liturgical "competition" had been a key element in his resistance to separation[13]), and the Methodist people were being permitted to receive the sacrament at the hands of their own preacher-pastors. As distinct from those nineteenth-century Methodist bodies with less direct origins in Wesley's work, the Wesleyan Methodists for longer saw themselves as retaining certain links with the Church of England, such as occasional communion and the use of "Mr. Wesley's Abridgement" or even the *Book of Common Prayer* itself. But the growth of Methodist "self-confidence,"[14] coupled with a perceived Romeward drift of the Church of England,[15] had by the middle of the nineteenth century undeniably put an end to any but the most romantic idea of English Methodism's *continuing* as a society within the Established Church. That option was closed; but the sense of our partial character remains with us from our origins.

2. *A province of the Anglican Communion?*

The adaptation that sticks closest to our original position was put forward some years ago in the brilliant hypothesis of a non-Methodist historian of Methodism to a Strasbourg colloquium on "Aspects de l'Anglicanisme." Writing at the time of the Anglican-Methodist unity scheme in England,

C. J. Bertrand suggests that Methodism might be viewed and treated as a hitherto "unrecognized province of the Anglican communion."[16] Bertrand shows how Methodism was the first body—with the possible exception of the Scottish Episcopalians?—to display an ensemble of characteristics which later came to mark the various ecclesiastical "provinces" that developed beyond England but remained in communion with Canterbury and one another: a doctrinal kernel well within the limits of Anglican "comprehensiveness," an independent liturgy but with family resemblances to the Prayer Book, a spirituality and a ministry adapted to the people, an autonomous administration, and withal a certain *je ne sais quoi*, which can only be called Englishness. Interestingly, Bertrand recalls the proposal made by Fletcher of Madeley to John Wesley at the Conference of 1775, that Methodism should become an independent denomination—the Methodist Church of England—in close association with the Church of England itself: article one of his plan suggests that "the growing body of the Methodists in Great Britain, Ireland, and America be formed into a general society—a daughter church of our holy mother," with article five "asking the protection of the Church of England, begging that this step might not be considered as a schism."[17]

Bertrand's hypothesis deliberately left out of account American Methodism, which at least since the War of Independence has enjoyed little "special relationship," whether real or imagined, with Anglicanism. It remains questionable how far even English Anglicans, at least since the latter part of the nineteenth century, have viewed Methodism with any greater affection than they have the other "Free Churches." The biggest obstacle in the way of Bertrand's proposal has proved to be a very legalistic understanding by Anglicans of their claimed episcopal succession, which was shared neither by Wesley nor by many other Anglicans before the Oxford Movement.[18] British Methodism has repeatedly declared its willingness to accept an episcopal ordering of the church, but English plans for unity were blocked in 1969 and 1972 and again in 1982 by Anglican doubts concerning the generation of living Methodist or other ministers who would not have received ordination from a bishop meeting Anglican approval. It grieves me to say it, but I think that Bertrand's kind of ecclesiological interpretation and the consequent possibilities for a relatively easy (re)integration of Methodism into the Anglican communion now have been killed stone dead.

3. *A church within the church catholic?*

As early as the Christmas conference at Baltimore in 1784, American Methodism declared itself the Methodist Episcopal Church; and its nineteenth-century historian Abel Stevens had little hesitation in writing of the "catholicity of Methodism."[19] In England, Wesleyan Methodism took a century longer before officially calling itself a church—as part, no doubt, of its late nineteenth-century assimilation to the "Free Churches," but then H. B. Workman showed little doubt as to Methodism's churchliness when he wrote his celebrated essay *The Place of Methodism in the Catholic Church*.[20] In 1932, the Methodist Church in Great Britain declared at the start of the doctrinal article in its Deed of Union: "The Methodist Church claims and cherishes its place in the Holy Catholic Church which is the body of Christ."[21] The problem with such formulations is that all *denominational* claims to the word *church*, for example, "The Methodist Church," run counter to the New Testament. The 1937 British statement *The Nature of the Church according to the Teaching of the Methodists* was being a little self-sparing when it said that "The Church today is gathered for the most part in certain denominations or 'churches.' These form but a partial and imperfect embodiment of the New Testament ideal."[22] As Wesley rightly recognized in his sermon "Of the Church" (1786), the New Testament writers mean by *church* either the church universal or a local church, whether its size be that of a family, a city, or a country. The nearest things to denominations get short shrift from the apostle Paul: "Each one of you says, 'I belong to Paul,' or 'I belong to Apollos,' or 'I belong to Cephas,' or 'I belong to Christ.' Is Christ divided? Was Paul crucified for you? Or were you baptized in the name of Paul?" (I Corinthians 1:12-13). The existence of *denominations*— which so far in history always implies *divisions*—calls into question the reality of *the church*. As Howard Snyder has recently observed concerning certain paradoxes in Wesley's own ecclesiology: "The paradoxical nature of the church in a sinful world . . . makes a totally consistent, systematic theory of the church difficult, if not impossible, from a human standpoint."[23] But it is not simply a matter of theology in a pejorative sense: the very power of the gospel is at stake if it fails to unite those who claim to respond to it.[24]

The question is: What is the *Ecclesia* in which Methodist writers sometims rather too cozily claim for Methodism the status of an *ecclesiola?*[25] A befitting tentativeness in respect both of the *Ecclesia* and of the *ecclesiola* marked the words of the English Wesleyan Methodist J. E. Rattenbury in *Wesley's Legacy to the World* (1927):

> The struggle of Methodism to remain a mere Society within the Church of England, when she had no longer association with a Church of which she could be called a Society, lingered on till our days. It was one hundred years before [Wesley's] society called itself a Church. . . . Methodism seems to be standing at the crossways. Much of her distinctive denominational life has gone, and she is feeling, perhaps subconsciously, after Catholicity.

Colin Williams used that text thirty years later to illustrate his description of Methodism as "a society in search of the Church."[26] Retain the tentativeness and shift the model from "society" to "order," and I think we may even today find the direction for a dynamic self-understanding with which to share in the ecumenical task and pursue the ecumenical goal.

4. *An order within the* Una Sancta?

In his contribution "Methodism and the Catholic Tradition," made to the 1933 volume *Northern Catholicism*, R. N. Flew observed that "from Southey onward, the biographers of Wesley have compared him to the founders of great orders in the Church of Rome. His genius for organization ensured discipline in his 'societies.' "[27] But Flew himself drew no broader ecclesiological consequences from this observation. Albert Outler once described Wesley as "rather like the superior-general of an evangelical order within a regional division of the church catholic," and elsewhere he has proposed a Methodist ecclesiology consonant with his view of Methodism's founder.[28] In a paper given to the Oxford Institute of twenty years ago, Outler showed how reluctantly Methodism became a denominational church, always retaining a memory of its *ad interim* beginnings:

[Methodism] has never developed—on its own and for itself—the full panoply of bell, book, and candle that goes with being a "proper" church properly self-understood. This makes us *une église manquée*, theoretically and actually. . . . One of our difficulties, I suggest, is that Methodism's unique ecclesiological pattern was really designed to function best *within* an encompassing environment of *catholicity* (by which I mean what the word meant originally: the effectual and universal Christian *community*). . . . We need a catholic church within which to function as a proper evangelical order of witness and worship, discipline and nurture. Yet, it is plain to most of us that none of the existing unilateral options are suitable alternatives to our existing situation. The way to catholicism—i.e., Christian unity—is *forward*—toward the *renewal* of catholicity rather than in *return* to something that has lost its true status as truly catholic.[29]

As a sympathetic Roman Catholic writing before Vatican II, John M. Todd held John Wesley's inspiration and faith to be consonant with Catholic doctrine and considered that "for that very reason [they] could only find [their] proper fulfillment in the Catholic Church."[30] Much more recently, Francis Frost, author of the substantial article "Méthodisme" in the encyclopedia *Catholicisme*, recognizes the fundamental unity of Methodism in its spiritual heritage, and again the image of the religious order suggests itself: "Modern Methodism owes this heritage in the first place to John Wesley, just as a religious order or spiritual family in the Roman Catholic Church draws its spirit from its founder."[31] In a most accurate and appreciative essay, Frost treats Methodism as "une confession chrétienne autonome" and recognizes the institutional part already played by Methodism within the comprehensive ecumenical movement in which the Roman Catholic Church now also shares. But Frost's conclusion may be even more significant:

The churches' efforts to draw closer together on the doctrinal and institutional levels must be rooted in spiritual ecumenism. Division between Christians is a sin; in other words, it is produced when the divine life in us grows cold. Obedience and humility point the way to unity because they make it possible for love to expand again. Is not witness to these truths an integral part of the spiritual heritage of Methodism?

Whereas H. B. Workman regarded "experience" as the governing "Idea" of Methodism and considered "assurance," as its primary corollary, to be "the fundamental contribution of Methodism to the life and thought of the Church" (and John Todd vigorously defended Wesley against the charges brought against him in Ronald Knox's *Enthusiasm* on these scores), the more recent consensus—represented by writers as diverse as Todd, John Kent, and Reginald Kissack—has in fact returned to seeing the original inspiration, the motive force, and the abiding goal of Wesley and of Methodism as residing rather in HOLINESS. The early Methodists understood that their providential call was to "spread scriptural holiness through the land,"[32] and for this purpose Wesley was ready to "look upon all the world as [his] parish."[33] The proclamation and pursuit of holiness reached as far as "entire sanctification," "perfect love" of God and neighbor. The traditional Methodist doctrine of Christian perfection can in fact be extended into the realm of ecumenism. The prayer of Jesus was that his disciples might be "perfected into one" (John 17:23: hína ōsin teteleiōménoi eis hén), and the apostle's vision was that the church might grow into "the unity of the faith and of the knowledge of the Son of God, to mature manhood, to the measure of the stature of the fulness of Christ" (Ephesians 4:11-16). These texts were seized upon a century ago by the English Wesleyan Methodist Benjamin Gregory in his Fernley Lecture of 1873, *The Holy Catholic Church, the Communion of Saints*. Gregory recognized that "the unity of the Church and the spirituality of the Church must progress together equably"; it is encouraging that the contemporary Roman Catholic Francis Frost should think that Methodism might have a special part to play in precisely that process. Reginald Kissack, whose great merit it was to recall attention to Benjamin Gregory, comments:

The "original" unity of the Church is a logical concept, existing first in the mind of God and the will of Christ. It enters into history in the prayer of Jesus, and has had an imperative force as great as the call to holiness. . . . History has so far known only original sin among men, and original disunity in the Church. . . . The Methodist uses of Church unity the words Wesley uses of Christian Perfection. He "goes on to it." It is one of his "oughts" that is yet to be realized in history.[34]

The relation between the "already" and the "not yet" might be differently phrased, but the eschatological tension toward unity and holiness is definitely a dynamic mark of the *Una Sancta*. A Methodism true to itself would engage in the common pursuit, and if Methodist holiness has sometimes taken such problematic forms as those of revivalism, the nonconformist conscience or liberal activism, we should hope that while it may serve as a "leaven" (one of Wesley's favorite images in connection with the spread of holiness) in the ecumenical movement, a more catholic environment will in turn restore to it the sacramental dimension which the Wesleys' teaching and practice never lacked. The visibility of the church and of its unity is at stake. The alternative to visible unity is not spiritual unity but visible disunity, and that is a countertestimony to the gospel.

III. Our Own History

In one of his more triumphalist utterances, Gordon Rupp told the 1959 Oxford Institute: "What is distinctive about us is not our faith, for that we share with the whole catholic Church, but our history. The way that God has led us and what He has said and done among us—that really is our very own."[35] As to our official doctrines, I, too, would be fairly optimistic concerning their catholicity; but there is something rather divisive in this use of "our history." Even worse, Dr. Rupp went on to talk about our "painless extraction" from within the Church of England: "Call it separation, call it schism, there has never been a break as thoroughgoing and yet as undamaging on either side in the history of the Church." Can it be that our most eminent historian had forgotten Wesley's sermon "On Schism"? A "causeless separation from a body of living Christians" is "evil in itself," being "a grievous breach of the law of love" ("The pretences for separation may be innumerable but want of love is always the real cause"); such a separation is also "productive of mischievous consequences," bringing forth in ourselves and in others "unkind tempers," "bitter words," "ungodly and unrighteous actions." "The love of many will wax cold," and they will be led astray from the way of peace into everlasting perdition. And as to the effect on nonbelievers:

What a grevious stumbling-block must these things be to those who are without, to those who are strangers to religion, who have neither the form nor the power of godliness! How will they triumph over these once eminent Christians! How boldly ask, "What are they better than us?" How will they harden their hearts more and more against the truth, and bless themselves in their wickedness! from which, possibly, the example of the Christians might have reclaimed them, had they continued unblamable in their behaviour.[36]

There can be no doubt of Wesley's loyalty to what later Methodists called "the fundamental principles of the Protestant Reformation," at least as they were expressed in the Anglican *Homilies*, but Wesley chastised Luther and Calvin for some unnecessary provocativeness in their "open separation from the Church":

When the Reformation began, what mountainous offences lay in the way of even the sincere members of the Church of Rome! They saw such failings in those great men, Luther and Calvin! Their vehement tenaciousness of their own opinions; their bitterness towards all who differed from them; their impatience of contradiction, and utter want of forbearance, even with their own brethren.

But the grand stumbling-block of all was their open, avowed separation from the Church; their rejecting so many of the doctrines and practices, which the others accounted most sacred; and their continual invectives against the Church they separated from, so much sharper than Michael's reproof of Satan.

Were there fewer stumbling-blocks attending the Reformation in England? Surely no: for what was Henry the Eighth? Consider either his character, his motives to the work, or his manner of pursuing it! . . . The main stumbling-block also still remained, namely, open separation from the Church.[37]

As early as the very first Conference in 1744, Wesley and his preachers faced the question: "Do you not entail a schism in the Church? That is, Is it not probable that your hearers, after your death, will be scattered into all sects and parties, or that they will form themselves into a distinct sect?" The answer they gave was: "We do, and will do, all we can to prevent those consequences which are supposed likely to happen after our death." Yet despite Wesley's lifelong efforts, Methodism did separate from the Church of England, and worse still, the sixty or seventy years after his death witnessed, both in England and in the United States, a further fragmentation of the Methodist movement. Does Dr. Rupp believe that Methodist fissiparity in the first half of the nineteenth century did not result at least in part from our original separation from the Church of England? And was not our loss of sacramental sense at least partly due to our absence from a church whose own Tractarian revival we might have been able to moderate in such a way as to prevent the excesses and intransigencies of Anglo-Catholicism? And who can calculate the loss to Anglicanism of that Methodism which, in the judgment of such an outside observer as C. J. Bertrand, was best organized in both Britain and America to meet the needs and opportunities of evangelism?

We must face up to that nineteenth-century fissiparity. Outler describes it thus:

The British Methodists experienced five years of turmoil after Wesley's death before their first schism broke wide open. Thereafter in America and England, schism followed schism in controversy after controversy over a bewildering variety of issues: ecclesiastical authority, racial equality, lay representation, slavery, the status of the episcopacy, the doctrine of holiness, and many another. When the first "Ecumenical Methodist Conference" was held in London in 1881, there were ten separate denominations from the British side, eighteen from America—all Methodists![38]

Yet the Ecumenical Methodist Conference was positively significant, for it helped to begin that series of reunions which has brought so much of sundered Methodism together again at the national level in the twentieth century: first in Australia (1902), then in Britain and its missionary areas with the United Methodist Church of 1907, and the subsequent union of that body with the Wesleyans and the Primitives to

105

form the Methodist Church in Great Britain in 1932, and finally in the United States with the reunion of the Methodist Episcopal Church, the Methodist Episcopal Church, South, and the Methodist Protestant Church in 1939, and the formation of The United Methodist Church as a result of the merger of the Methodist Church with the Evangelical United Brethren in 1968. These reunions within the Methodist family demonstrate that, for all the early fissiparity, "fellowship" is more than an invisibilist sentiment for Methodists and is rather grounded in the

> Christ, from whom all blessings flow,
> Perfecting the saints below,

and in whom

> Love, like death, hath all destroyed,
> Rendered all distinctions void;
> Names and sects and parties fall:
> Thou, O Christ, art all in all.

It is no accident that it should be the Methodist Outler who powerfully interpreted the WCC as a recovered *koinonia* in whose ambit the members press on to fuller unity.[39] Outler insists that it is important for all to reappropriate "our *common Christian* history," and he himself has greatly helped to render *our* history as Methodists accessible to others, so that the possessive pronoun may acquire an inclusive rather than an exclusive sense.[40]

Individual Methodists have in fact made prominent contributions to the modern ecumenical movement from the early days of John R. Mott, the roving American, and Sir Henry Lunn, the British travel agent. In Faith and Order, there have been Ivan Lee Holt, Clarence Tucker Craig, the unforgettable Robert Newton Flew, Albert Outler himself (so important in the Montreal agreement on Scripture and Tradition), J. Robert Nelson, and A. Raymond George. Philip Potter, the present general secretary of the WCC, is unmistakably Methodist.

Methodist churches have been members of the WCC from its inception. They have also engaged in various official bilateral dialogues in the different countries, notably with Roman Catholics and Lutherans, and it is with these that the World Methodist Council has engaged in conversations at the "world confessional" level. By this stage of the ecumenical movement, however, the crucial test must be that of Methodist participation in concrete transconfessional unions. First in Canada and then in Australia, the Methodists have joined with the Congregationalists and the majority of Presbyterians to form, respectively, the United Church of Canada (1925) and the Uniting Church in Australia (1977). In 1938 most of the French Methodists entered the Église Réformée de France. The more difficult, and perhaps therefore more exciting, unions have issued in the Church of South India, which in 1947 brought Methodists, Presbyterians, and Congregationalists together with Anglicans in an episcopally ordered church, and the Church of North India (1970), which included Baptists and Brethren, in addition to the others. The American Methodists remain outside the two Indian churches, and we gather that the reasons are more financial than theological. Apart from their forcible inclusion in the rather unsatisfactory unions contrived by the secular authorities in Japan (1940) and Zaire (1970), American Methodists have—in comparison with the British achievement in India and the rather thwarted promises in Sri Lanka and several African countries—a somewhat poor record of participation in unity schemes.[41] Financial reasons apart, we may wonder whether the contrasting perceptions indicated in our first section have not also played a part in the attitudes fostered among those who have received the gospel from American and British missions respectively. That makes all the more crucial the outcome of participation by The United Methodist Church, and indeed the three black Methodist Churches, in the U.S. Consultation on Church Union as it seeks to move, by way of some form of mutual recognition, toward a Church of Christ Uniting. In Britain, the Methodist Church was twice jilted at the altar by the Church of England—in 1969 and 1972. And more recently a somewhat looser covenant arrangement has been rejected by most Baptists, by the Roman Catholic Bishops' Conference, and at the last minute by a sufficient spoiling minority of the house of clergy in the Church of England synod. It seems unlikely that the Methodists, the United Reformed, and the Moravians will proceed into the episcopally ordered relationship that the covenant envisaged as a step toward fuller unity. In 1979, the Methodist Synod in Scotland turned down a union with the Church of Scotland despite the fact that the latter staunchly Calvinist body, while retaining its inveterate opposition to the very name of "superintendent" and rejecting the stationing implications of connectionalism, had been willing to accept a statement of faith that was all an Evangelical Arminian could desire. This experience with the difficulties of a tiny minority church in relation to the national Church of Scotland should give British Methodists as a whole some fellow feeling with the small Methodist churches in the midst of the *Volkskirchen* of Germany and Scandinavia. What two very small minority churches can do together is illustrated by the "integrazione" (1979) of the Methodists and the Waldensians in Italy, where the governing synod is united while the scattered local congregations retain their traditional name and flavor.

One final aspect of "our history" needs to be mentioned in the present connection. Wesley's stand on the universal offer of the gospel naturally led Methodism to play a leading role in the great missionary expansion of the nineteenth and early twentieth centuries. It is a fact of abiding ecclesiological significance that membership in the British Methodist Church has carried with it automatic membership in the Methodist Missionary Society: the mission is recognized to be part of the church's very being. Yet historically, as Outler once again notes, "the very success of denominational missions served to expose the anomaly of a divided Christianity trying to carry the Gospel message to every creature," and we recall that the modern ecumenical movement is conventionally dated from the Edinburgh Missionary Conference of 1910.[42] If "the mission is one," a divided Christianity is no more tolerable "at home" than it is "overseas": the being of the church and the credibility of its message are everywhere called into question by division.

IV. The Eponymous Hero in the Communion of the Saints

It may not be superfluous to admit and explain that Wesley's name has already been, and will again be, invoked in this essay with an intention that goes beyond the historical into the theological and even into the spiritual. For Albert Outler, John Wesley is both the "eponymous hero of [our] particular denomination" and an "ecumenical theologian."[43] For Colin Williams, it is by sympathetically and critically "analyzing the Methodist tradition at the point of its origin," namely *John Wesley's Theology*, that we shall be enabled to make an authentically Methodist contribution to the changed ecumenical situation of *today*.[44] As already mentioned, Francis Frost recognizes the theologically and spiritually decisive imprint of Wesley on the whole of Methodism, and the other Roman Catholic, John Todd, not only recognizes the continuing historical influence of an inimitably great man but ends up confessing: "As I have come to know Wesley I have believed him to be [in heaven] and have prayed to God through him—not publicly as the Church prays through those declared to be saints—but privately as I pray for and to those who have been close to me."[45] The Wesley brothers figure in the new Anglican calendars in both England and the United States and in the calendar of the new North American *Lutheran Book of Worship*. Should Methodists be less open to the Wesleyan presence, in person, words, and deeds?

A few catchwords removed from their context have sometimes been used to make out that Wesley was an ecclesiological laxist, particularly in matters with a doctrinal import. But in his sermon "Catholic Spirit," he gives a full credal, experiential, and practical content to "Is thine heart right, as my heart is with thy heart?" before he will say "Give me thine hand."[46] In the third part of the sermon, Wesley expressly denies any charges of "speculative latitudinarian-ism ("A catholic spirit . . . is not indifferent to *all* opinions. . . . A man of a truly catholic spirit . . . is as fixed as the sun in his judgment concerning the main branches of Christian doctrine") or of "practical latitudinarism" whether in worship ("The man of a truly catholic spirit . . . is clearly convinced that [his] manner of worshipping God is both scriptural and rational") or in ecclesical allegiance ("A man of a truly catholic spirit is fixed in his congregation as well as his principles"). In other words, while "a difference in opinions or modes of worship may prevent an entire external union," the "union in affection," which it need not prevent, is limited to those who are recognizably Christian, "brother[s] in Christ," "joint heir[s] of his glory." Again, when in *The Character of a Methodist* it is stated that "we think and let think," this magnanimity is limited to "opinions which do not strike at the root of Christianity."[47] And when Wesley writes in the *Letter to a Roman Catholic* that "if we cannot as yet think alike in all things, at least we may love alike," he has already expressed the faith of "a true Protestant" through an amplified version of the Nicene Creed that is set in a context of worship and Christian practice.[48] An unfortunate phrase in *A Plain Account of the People Called Methodists*—that "orthodoxy, or right opinions, is at best a slender part of religion, if it can be allowed to be any part at all"—is best understood along the lines of Saint James' refusal of saving efficacy to the devil's impeccable monotheism.[49]

Nor may Wesley's exegetical point in his sermon "On Schism"—that Paul's usage of the word *schisma* in I Corinthians refers to divisions within a religious community which continues outwardly united—be used fairly to father on him the view that renders Christian disunity as we know it relatively innocuous by talk of the church as being in a state of internal schism.[50] Internal disunion was already bad enough in Wesley's eyes, but we have heard earlier his even fiercer description—in the latter part of that same sermon—of the nature and consequence of visible separation, and *that* is what the ecumenical problem is about. Wesley's position on Christian disunity and the unity of the church is in fact rather complex. Taken as a whole, it is not directly applicable to our situation two hundred years later—with Methodism having become "an autonomous Christian confession," the modern ecumenical movement having grown and developed the way it has and the possibilities for institutional relationships with the Roman Catholic Church having opened up in a manner quite unforeseeable in the eighteenth and indeed the nineteenth and early twentieth centuries; but there are elements in Wesley's historically conditioned position that may help us toward a characteristically Methodist perspective on the present form of some apparently perennial issues.

To the Roman Catholic bishop Challoner, Wesley defined "the Catholic Church" as "the whole body of men, endued with faith working by love, dispersed over the whole earth, in Europe, Asia, Africa, and America. And this Church is 'ever one' [the quotations are from Challoner]; in all ages and nations it is the one body of Christ. It is 'ever holy'; for no unholy man can possibly be a member of it. It is 'ever orthodox'; so is every holy man, in all things necessary to salvation; 'secured against error,' in things essential, 'by the perpetual presence of Christ and ever directed by the Spirit of Truth,' in the truth which is after godliness."[51] To the Baptist minister Gilbert Boyce, Wesley wrote: "I do not think either the Church of England, or the people called Methodists, or any other particular society under heaven to be the *True Church of Christ*. For that Church is but one, and contains all the true believers on earth. But I conceive every Society of true believers to be a branch of the one true Church of Christ."[52] How far this insistence on "true believers" and on holiness is removed from invisibilism or from Donatism will appear in a moment. Meanwhile we note, on the one hand, the practical generosity which flows from this attitude. The Anglican Wesley refuses to damn Quakers.[53] The words of the sermon, "Catholic Spirit," concerning congregational loyalty—matched by Wesley's practical advice to all his hearers and followers not to separate from the ecclesial body in which they found themselves—imply an unwillingness on the part of the mature Wesley to unchurch the Dissenting bodies.[54] Wesley also followed the hitherto traditional Anglican recognition of continental Protestant churches, even though they lacked the preferred form of episcopal government.[55] At times he appears to hold that Roman Catholics could be Christians only in spite of their Church.[56] Thus he says to Boyce: "If I were in the Church of Rome, I would conform to all her doctrines and practices as far as they were not contrary to plain Scripture."[57] But that limitation would surely have presented difficulties for one who, say, shared the view of the Anglican Articles on Roman eucharistic doctrines and practices. Wesley, in fact, points to much "error," "superstition," and even "idolatry" in the Roman Catholic Church.[58] But his attitude even on doctrinally more significant matters appears to have been in line with his remarks on the miracles at the grave of a certain French *abbé*: "The 'times of ignorance' God does 'wink at' still; and bless the faith notwithstanding the superstition."[59] Wesley aims not only at popular but also at official credulity when he calls Roman Catholics "volunteers in faith," "believing more than God has revealed." Yet, he says, "it cannot be denied that they believe all which God has revealed as necessary to salvation. In this we rejoice on their behalf." And "we are glad that none of those new articles, which they added at the Council of Trent to the 'faith once delivered to the saints' does so materially contradict any of the ancient articles, as to render them of no effect."[60] What, we may wonder, would Wesley have said of the subsequent Marian dogmas and, more fundamentally, that metadogma of 1870 which qualifies all the others, namely papal infallibility?

If Wesley's position on "true believers" and on "holiness" allows in some directions a certain ecclesiological generosity, it also permits him to be more restrictive on other scores. In his *Letter to a Roman Catholic*, he denies the name of "true Protestant" to "all common swearers, Sabbath-breakers, drunkards, all whoremongers, liars, cheats, extortioners—in a word, all that live in open sin. These are no Protestants; they are not Christians at all. Give them their own name: they are open heathens. They are the curse of the nation, the bane of society, the shame of mankind, the scum of the earth." Wesley was no Donatist in the technical sense, for he maintained the Roman and Anglican position that the unworthiness of the minister does not hinder the grace of the sacrament.[61] But he certainly held that holiness belonged to the essence of Christianity and was indeed the realization of the human vocation: "That course of life tends most to the glory of God wherein we can most promote holiness in ourselves and others."[62] Holiness is thus the key to all Wesley's ecclesiology, theoretical and practical. But the broad terms of admission to the Methodist societies ("a desire to flee from the wrath to come, to be saved from their sins")—coupled with fruits evidencing the desire of salvation as a condition for continuing in membership—show that the holiness is one of aspiration before it is one of achievement.[63] Methodism cannot fairly be accused of being a perfectionist sect, as long as its members consider perfection as a goal to be pressed on toward (Philippians 3). Nor can Wesley properly be charged with invisibilism, when we note his insistence— over against Moravian quietism—on the use of the instituted means of grace even by seekers, let alone by those who have already received the new birth. Wesley's teaching and practice of the Lord's Supper are firmly sacramentalist. Nor would an anti-institutionalist have devoted such attention as Wesey did to questions of church order.

The historical context and chief practical problem of Wesley's preaching of a New Testament holiness Christianity were of course provided by the large number of purely nominal Christians in the Church of England. The qualitative tension of growth in holiness that marks all original and authentic Christianity had been turned into a daunting quantitative discrepancy between the vast number of the baptized and the much smaller "congregation of English believers."[64] The gap between the "multitudinous" and the "gathered" conceptions of the church is one of the problems bequeathed by what Wesley called "that evil hour, when Constantine the Great called himself a Christian."[65]

The relics of Constantinianism remain a major though rarely named issue in contemporary ecumenism. They affect in yet another way the question of a national church. In his sermon "Of the Church," Wesley finds some New Testament justification for the use of "church" to refer to the Christian congregations dispersed throughout a civil province or country. But Constantinianism meant legal establishment— what Wesley calls "a mere political institution";[66] and even the Reformation retained *cuius regio eius religio*. Already by the time of his 1749 sermon "Catholic Spirit," Wesley was confessing the abatement of his earlier zeal for the view that "the place of our birth fixes the church to which we ought to belong; that one, for instance, who is born in England ought to be a member of that which is styled the Church of England

and, consequently, to worship God in the particular manner which is prescribed by that church." He realized that on those principles "there could have been no reformation from popery." Wesley, in fact, respected the laws of the Church of England only to the point where conscience or evangelistic need obliged him to vary. If he loved its liturgy and preferred its episcopal constitution, it was on account of their consonance with Scripture rather than for their Englishness. The test remained the primitive church, and it is interesting that from first to last, Wesley considered America a place where those pristine conditions might be approximated, away from the constraints of England. A line leads from his attempt to restore supposedly apostolic rites and disciplines in Georgia in the 1730s to the closing statement in his letter to "Our Brethren in America" of September 10, 1784: "As our American brethren are now totally disentangled both from the state and from the English hierarchy, we dare not entangle them again either with the one or the other. They are now at full liberty simply to follow the Scriptures and the primitive church. And we judge it best that they should stand fast in that liberty wherewith God has so strangely made them free."[67]

This section may be closed, and the next prepared, by briefly noting the specific views of Wesley on some questions of faith and order. Wesley held the creedal truths concerning the Trinity, the Incarnation, and the Atonement, and he viewed Arians, semi-Arians, Socinians, and Deists as having departed from the Christian faith.[68] Their heart was not right with his heart, and he did not offer them his hand as brothers and sisters in Christ. For collaboration in preaching to non-believers Wesley demanded agreement—as, for instance, his "Letter to Various Clergymen" reveals—on the articles of "original sin, justification by faith, and holiness of heart and life."[69] Granted this unity in evangelistic witness, Wesley was willing to allow that differences over predestination or perfection—which "are important in the nurture of Christians," as Colin Williams says, "rather than in the missionary proclamation of the gospel"—should not be church-dividing, though they would be apparent in the distinction between his own societies and, say, Whitefield's.[70]

In its more official sense also, the ordering of the church was strictly subservient to the conversion of sinners and their edification in that holiness without which no one shall see the Lord: "What is the end of all ecclesiastical order? Is it not to bring souls from the power of Satan to God; and to build them up in his fear and love? Order, then, is so far valuable, as it answers these ends; and if it answers them not, it is nothing worth."[71]

With that, we are structurally at the midpoint in this essay. The second half will be shorter, however. The diachronic lines drawn in the first half still allow a vector of choices on various issues in our present ecumenical situation. I will in each case simply indicate my own preferences within the authentically Methodist range. Section V—on Faith and Order—links up with section IV on Wesley. Section VI—on choice of partners—corresponds back to section III on our institutional history. Section VII—on Methodism's ecumenical contribution—matches section II on the parts and the whole. The opening section on schism and pluralism finds its pendant in the concluding section on reconciled diversity and costly unity.

V. Faith and Order

The most important ecumenical document before the churches at the moment is the Lima text *Baptism, Eucharist and Ministry* (1982), a fruit of fifty-five years' work in Faith and Order. Under the mandate given by the WCC's Fifth Assembly at Nairobi in 1975 and renewed by its Central Committee at Dresden in 1981, the Faith and Order Commission "now respectfully invites all churches to prepare an official response to this text at the highest appropriate level of authority, whether it be a council, synod, conference, assembly or other body." Having worked closely for the past several years on the final stages of its production, I am persuaded that this document can be received from a Methodist standpoint as stating "the faith of the Church through the ages." The ecumenical question then becomes that of "the consequences your church can draw from this text for its relations and dialogues with other churches, particularly with those churches which also recognize the text as an expression of the apostolic faith."

The treatment of infant and believers' baptism perfectly reflects the persistent tension in Wesley—which he himself never clearly thematized theologically—between a baptismal regeneration in infants and the necessity of a subsequent spiritual rebirth.[72] The statement on the eucharist might well have served as the text for the Wesleys' *Hymns on the Lord's Supper*, and Dean Brevint himself would have been pleased with it; it is actually the fruit of the recent biblical, patristic, and liturgical renewal. The knottiest problems in ministry are those concerning the priesthood and the episcopal succession. While the relation of ministerial priesthood to the general priesthood is directly addressed only in section 17, the whole document presents a description of the ordained ministry within the whole church, which is fully in line with the emergent consensus expressed by three such different voices as the following. First, the British Methodist *Statement on Ordination* of 1974:

As a perpetual reminder of this calling [of the whole people of God to be the body of Christ] and as a means of being obedient to it, the Church sets apart men and women, specially called, in ordination. In their office the calling of the whole Church is focused and represented, and it is their responsibility as representative persons to lead the people to share with them in that calling. In this sense they are the sign of the presence and ministry of Christ in the Church, and through the Church to the world.

Second, the seventh chapter of the text of the Consultation on Church Union in the United States, *In Quest of a Church of Christ Uniting* (1980): "Their ordination marks them as persons who represent to the Church its own identity and mission in Jesus Christ."

Third, David N. Power, a leading Roman Catholic theologian on orders and ministry:

The needs of the church and of its mission are what determine ministry. . . . The office-holder, through the service of supervision and presidency, represents back to the church that which in the faith of the ordination ceremony it has expressed about itself. . . . Because [the eucharistic president] is empowered to represent the church in this vital action, to represent to it its own very ground of being, we say that he is empowered to represent Christ. . . . The role of the ordained minister is to represent in the midst of this community its work for the kingdom, its eschatological nature, and its relationship to Christ. . . . The validity of ministry, to use the word loosely, is not assessed on the ground of it ecclesiastical provenance, but on the ground of its benefit to the church.[73]

Wesley had no difficulty in defining the ministerial office in priestly terms.[74] He also believed the bishop and the threefold order to be scriptural and apostolic, though not exclusively prescribed for all times,[75] and he valued continuity in ministry highly, while denying the provability of an uninterrupted episcopal succession.[76] This is consonant with the Faith and Order text on ministry—which suggests that all should now adopt the existing episcopal succession as a *sign* ("though not a guarantee") of continuity in that apostolic tradition whose *substance* may be recognized beyond the episcopal churches, which themselves need to "regain their lost unity." Granted Wesley's views on the historical variability of church order and its subservience to evangelical needs, Methodists may without disloyalty now accept an historic episcopate for the sake of a unity whose absence is a countertestimony to the gospel.[77]

The work of Faith and Order on *Baptism, Eucharist, and Ministry*, together with a more limited study, *How does the church teach authoritatively today?*, will be taken up into the next big project, entitled "Towards the Common Expression of the Apostolic Faith Today."[78] I know of no more ecumenically acceptable description of the interdependence of authoritative functions than that provided by the thoroughly Wesleyan statement on doctrine and doctrinal standards included in the 1972 *Discipline* of The United Methodist Church: it speaks of "a 'marrow' of Christian truth that can be identified and that must be conserved. This living core . . . stands revealed in Scripture, illumined by tradition, vivified in personal experience, and confirmed by reason."[79] And the Lima decision to take the Nicene Creed as the determinative foundation for the project on "the common expression of the apostolic faith today" follows exactly the procedures of Wesley's own confession in his "Letter to a Roman Catholic."[80]

VI. Choice of Partners

I have concentrated on WCC Faith and Order work because—whatever other denominations may believe concerning their own achievements in bilateral conversations— those multilateral WCC statements, in whose elaboration Methodists and indeed Roman Catholics have strongly participated, are doctrinally much further advanced than anything yet produced by Methodist bilateral dialogues wih the Roman Catholics or, more recently, the Lutherans. At least since Vatican II, considerable tensions of procedure and emphasis have run through the ecumenical movement: multilateral versus bilateral, local versus worldwide, organic versus federal. People tend to opt consistently for either the first or the second term in the series of pairs, so that the multilateral, the local, and the organic line up against the bilateral, the worldwide, and the federal. At the Lima meeting of Faith and Order in January 1982, Father Jean Tillard suggested that the local unions among non-Catholics should see themselves as a rather loose "communion de groupes," which did not prejudice the particular denominational constituents in their respective worldwide confessional relations, notably with the Roman Catholic Church. Granted that any entry into communion with Rome would be a great step for another confession or denomination to take, might we not look for a concomitant stride by Rome which would in fact reverse Tillard's emphasis? Could not Rome—in bold application of its own principle of subsidiarity—permit Catholic Bishops' conferences to enter into local unions with other churches in ways that did not impair their own relationship with the Roman see but rather invited the other local participants to join them in it?[81] The most significant version for Methodists of the general tension concerning "choice of partners" is put in the very title of Gerald Moede's article in the *Journal of Ecumenical Studies:* "Methodist Participation in Church Union Negotiations and

United Churches: Possible Implications for Methodist-Roman Catholic Dialogue."[82]

In ecumenical relations, much depends on the partners we choose or get chosen by. If the partners are Lutheran, we deal with a denomination which—in the Lutheran World Federation—has a strongly developed world confessional structure, where the dominant model for ecumenical unity is one of "reconciled diversity" among the continuing confessions. If the Roman Catholics are the partners, we are dealing with a church that is organically united throughout the world, and the model nearest to hand for integrating other traditions is a kind of uniatism in the Roman obedience—though that existing model itself includes the problem of geographically overlapping jurisdictions among the various rites.

Whatever the complexities of interpreting *place* when the New Delhi definition speaks of "all in each place," unity must first or last find a *local* embodiment.[83] It is locally that the scandal of disunity is most obvious, and it is locally that the day-to-day need arises for united worship, mission, and decision-making. That is doubtless why the World Methodist Conference in 1951 declared that it could only rejoice to see Methodism giving up its denominational existence in order to find new life in the wider community of the United Church of Canada and the Church of South India.[84] And that is what British Methodists have realized from the earliest days of modern ecumenism. It explains their positive response to the Archbishop of Canterbury's sermon in 1946; and had the Anglican-Methodist scheme succeeded in 1969 or 1972, it would have created in two stages an organic union with the possibility of an interesting modification of the Constantinian pattern, so that the new church's national responsibilities would have been fulfilled in its mission to the peoples of Britain (which is not an un-Wesleyan thought). Later on, the British Methodists joined with several other bodies to explore an invitation from the United Reformed Church. With the adverse decision of the Church of England's Synod in July 1982, the heart has gone out of the ensuing covenant proposals, for full ecumenism in England cannot get on without Anglican participation. These disappointments are serious, not only nationally but also in their international repercussions. Of the Anglican refusal of union with the Methodists, the Roman Catholic writer Francis Frost has observed that "this unhappy event has contributed to a tangible lowering of the influence of British non-Roman Catholic churches in the ecumenical movement as a whole."[85] The effect of the 1982 collapse of the English covenanting proposals on the Consultation on Church Union in the United States remains to be seen. Unity in England, where several of the now universal confessions took their origin in whole or in part, could still have a powerful effect for good elsewhere in the world.

That unions at the national level need not cut churches off from the wider world is shown by the newly developing relationships of united churches among themselves within the context of the WCC. Internationalism will also be furthered by the world confessional bodies, as long as they exist, and by whatever universal structures emerge from a process in which the special position of the Bishop of Rome is recognized more and more widely. That is why it may now be the moment for British Methodists—without giving up their concern for unity at the national level, and without turning their backs on the historically close Moravians or the United Reformed Church with which they now have hundreds of joint local congregations in one shape or another, or indeed on those Anglican friends who have desired unity with us—for British Methodists (I say) to abandon the reticence of the last generation toward the World Methodist Council and find in it an organ of international ecclesial fellowship and a valuable instrument in carrying on negotiations with the Roman Catholic Church in particular, but also with the Lutherans and with any others who are willing. In his last letter to America, written to Ezekiel Cooper on February 1, 1791, John Wesley summoned American Methodists to "see that you never give place to one thought of separating from your brethren in Europe. Lose no opportunity of declaring to all men that the Methodists are one people in all the world." Perhaps that same summons, *mutatis mutandis*, will now be heard by the British brothers and sisters. Their commitment to the WCC need in no wise be impaired.

VII. Methodism's Ecumenical Contribution

It has become rather unfashionable to envision the denominations bringing their separate treasures into the service of the coming great church. Perhaps we have all become aware that our partners do not always see our gifts as we ourselves see them but sometimes even look upon them as an embarrassing and unwanted offering. Certainly we need to be aware of the temptation to compare our ideal self-image with the unpolished actuality of others' conditions. With all due tentativeness we must, however, state the values we would like others to share for the sake of the gospel. Let me briefly risk it for Methodism. Two points will suffice.

First, I consider that Methodism holds what Wesley called the "proportion of the faith."[86] I find it typically expressed in the liturgical corpus of the Wesleyan hymns. What I mean is the connected, coherent, and balanced configuration of the great doctrinal truths of Christianity held with a real assent as the content of a living relationship with the God confessed. At the level of theology, it is remarkable how often writers refer to what Howard Snyder calls "the Wesleyan synthesis." Colin Williams sees Wesley's theology as enabling the combination of traditional Catholic, classical Protestant, and Free Church Protestant concerns. Albert Outler manages to see Wesley's "evangelical catholicism" as vitally fusing such eclectic elements as "Marcarius the Egyptian" and Jonathan Edwards—a "conjunctive theology" indeed.[87] The spiritual integrity of the Wesleyan synthesis—important both for its own substance and as an example of method—is evident even to some observers outside of Methodism, particularly Roman Catholics. Maximin Piette's brave thesis in the 1920s—that Wesley represented a Catholic "reaction" to the Protestant extremes of Luther and Calvin[88]—was followed by John Todd's recognition in the 1950s of "Wesley's genius to combine two commonly separated Christian truths, the truth of the divine call to every man to surrender himself, totally, to God, and the truth of the Church established for the purpose of enabling each man to respond in the fullest possible way to the call."[89] Recently there has been the most perceptive and generous article, already several times referred to, of Francis Frost in the encyclopedia *Catholicisme:* Methodism there appears as a unified spiritual heritage with a precious witness to bear in the reconciliation of divided Christianity.

The second value is the drive for holiness which characterized Wesley's manhood, ministry, and mission, and which has never entirely disappeared from Methodism, however serious our mistakes and failings. It is a comprehensive thrust, embracing the person, the church, and the world—linking the present age with the age to come. At the moment it is finding expression in the often transconfessional search for patterns of spirituality, in Methodist participation in the liturgical movement for an ecumenical renewal of worship, and in those widely desired connections between sanctification and liberation to which the Oxford Institute gave special attention in 1977.[90]

There is a third Methodist contribution to ecumenism which I will reserve for the concluding section.

VIII. *Reconciled Diversity and Costly Unity*

Hints have already been dropped concerning the differences between "reconciled diversity" and "organic union" as models of church unity. But signs of a rapprochement are not lacking. One mediating category may perhaps be found in the idea of "conciliarity" developed in Faith and Order from the Salamanca consultation in 1973. That notion was not intended to present an alternative to "local churches which are themselves truly united." "Conciliar fellowship" was meant to designate the structure of "sustained and sustaining relationships" to be maintained among such churches, which would allow the calling of councils whenever needed to make decisions affecting all. But some supporters of "reconciled diversity" happily appear to have found the notion of conciliarity to allay some of their fears about organic unity. In a positive move from his side, Harding Meyer—the leading Lutheran proponent of reconciled diversity—has allowed that reconciled diversity may in some circumstances appropriately extend to organic union.[91]

At the time of the English unity scheme between Anglicans and Methodists, Reginald Kissack argued strongly for federalism as a left-wing alternative to the catholic model of organic union.[92] Kissack appeared to think federalism desirable in itself, but with an advocate's skill he allowed that it would not exclude a more organic pattern in the longer run. Such a concession was needed if Kissack was to dodge the full force of John Kent's trenchant critique: "Christ is more than the President of a Federal Republic of Christian Associations; He is the Head of the Body which is His Church."[93] We might put the point sacramentally by saying that something more than federalism is required to bring to an end the situation in which it is possible, and sometimes even necessary, to ask whether baptism and confirmation initiate a person into a denomination or into the Christian church, whether the eucharistic celebration is that of a particular communion or of the Body of Christ, whether ordination admits a person to official ministry in a conventicle or in the church of God.

At one point Kissack contemplated the possibility that "scriptural holiness can keep alight and be spread abroad by a company of Christians if they make themselves an Order inside a Church, but not if they make themselves a self-sufficient Church. . . . Does holiness become significant again in the new ecumenical context, in the sense that nostalgia for its traditional function should encourage Methodism to unmake itself as a Church, but to remake itself as an Order inside a new Church in England?"[94] About the same period C. J. Bertrand was suggesting that the reintegration of Methodism into the Anglican communion would make of Methodism the unique historical phenomenon of a "province in time" rather than a province in space.[95] To accept temporal limitations, the Christian might say, is to be ready to die in the hope of resurrection to a more glorious life.

To universalize the scene, let us listen one more time to Albert Outler. He visualizes for the future "a united Christian community really united in *communicatio in sacris* (in membership, ministry, and sacraments) in which the distinctive witness of divers denominations, functioning as 'orders,' 'societies,' or 'movements' under their own self-appointed heads, will be conserved within a wider catholic perimeter, organized constitutionally on some collegial and conciliar pattern."[96] That that vision entails more than reconciled diversity is made clear by Outler's ensuing sentences:

Who should know better than we [Methodists] that denominations may be justified in their existence for this "time being" or that, but not forever? We were commissioned by the Spirit of God "for the time being" to carry out an extraordinary mission of witness and service, for just so long as our life apart is effective in the economy of God's providence. We are, or ought to be, prepared to risk our life as a separate church and to face death as a denomination in the sure and lively hope of our resurrection in the true community of the whole people of God. . . . The price of true catholicity may very well be the death and resurrection of the churches that we know—in the faith that God has greater things in store for his people than we can remember or even imagine.[97]

It is because Dr. Outler is so firmly committed to the ecclesiological provisionality of Methodism that I am willing to reappropriate the words with which he closed his lecture at the Oxford Institute in 1962, in order to close my essay some twenty years later: "Every denomination in a divided and broken Christendom is an *ecclesiola in via*, but Methodists have a peculiar heritage that might make the transitive character of our ecclesiastical existence not only tolerable but positively proleptic."[98]

Notes

1. On the practical tensions, despite the ideal correspondence, between truth and unity, see Colin W. Williams, *John Wesley's Theology Today* (Nashville: Abingdon Press, 1960), pp. 207ff.
2. Dietrich Bonhoeffer, *No Rusty Swords: Letters, Lectures and Notes 1928-1936* (New York: Harper & Row, 1965), pp. 86-118.
3. Entry in John Wesley's *Journal* for Mar. 25, 1743.
4. *Journal*, Feb. 19, 1761.
5. In his Sermon CVII, "On God's Vineyard" (1787-89), Wesley refers to "the body of people commonly called Methodists" as "that Society . . . which began at Oxford in the year 1729, and remains united at this day."
6. The "Rules of the United Societies" (1743)—from which come the quotation in the text and the next following it—define a society as "a company of men having the form and seeking the power of godliness, united in order to pray together, to receive the word of exhortation, and to watch

over one another in love, that they may help each other to work out their salvation."

7. See Albert C. Outler, "Do Methodists Have a Doctrine of the Church?" in *The Doctrine of the Church*, ed. D. Kirkpatrick (Nashville: Abingdon Press, 1964), pp. 11-28, in particular p. 18.

8. To the very end, "I live and die a member of the Church of England" ("Farther Thoughts on Separation from the Church," written Dec. 11, 1789 and published in the *Arminian Magazine*, Apr. 1790).

9. See C. Williams, pp. 230-31.

10. See Frank Baker, *John Wesley and the Church of England* (London: Epworth Press, 1970), p. 311: "Dr. Coke puts me in mind of a German proverb, which I may apply to himself and to myself. 'He skips like a flea; I creep like a louse.' He would tear all from top to bottom. I will not tear, but unstitch."

11. For Wesley's own death as the most precise date of Methodism's separation from the Church of England, see Reginald Kissack, *Church or No Church? The Development of the Concept of Church in British Methodism* (London: Epworth Press, 1964), p. 71.

12. John M. Turner, "From Society to Church," in *London Quarterly and Holborn Review*, 188 (1963), pp. 110-15.

13. At the Conference of 1766, Wesley declared that Methodist preaching services were intended to *supplement* the public prayer of the church and its celebration of the Lord's Supper (see Williams, p. 213). Note also Wesley's Sermon CIV, "On Attending the Church Service" (1788).

14. On Methodism's "self-confidence," see Kissack, pp. 68-95.

15. The Methodist reaction against the Oxford Movement and later Anglo-Catholicism may sometimes have been overemphasized by historians, but the anti-Puseyism of the 1840s was real enough; see John Kent, *The Age of Disunity* (London: Epworth Press, 1966), pp. 56, 138. Nor should one ignore Methodism's difficulties with a resurgent (Calvinist) Evangelicalism in the Church of England.

16. C. J. Bertrand, "Le méthodisme, 'province' méconnue de la communion anglicane?" in *Aspects de l'Anglicanisme: Colloque de Strasbourg 14-16 juin 1972* (Paris: Presses Universitaires de France, 1974), pp. 103-22.

17. For hints that some Methodists, including Wesley himself, toyed with the idea that Wesley and perhaps others might be made "itinerant bishops," see F. Hunter, *John Wesley and the Coming Comprehensive Church* (London: Epworth Press, 1968), chapters 7 and 8; see also Baker, pp. 279-80.

18. See Bertrand's own remarks, pp. 119ff.

19. Admittedly, Stevens had a peculiar view of the apostolic age and of the "coming great Church," ignoring all the problems of "denominationalism": "Members of any denomination, or of none, can enter the spiritual Church which [Wesley] organized, provided they possess the necessary moral qualifications. 'One condition,' he continues, 'and one only, is required—a real desire to save their souls. Where this is, it is enough; they desire no more. They lay stress upon nothing else. They ask only, Is thy heart herein as my heart? If it be, give me thy hand.' Such was Wesley's 'United Society,' such the Church of Methodism; and as such, is it not a reproduction of the Church of the Apostolic age, and a type of 'the Church of the future' "? (Abel Stevens, *History of Methodism*, II, 1861, p. 353.

20. Workman's essay, under the title "The Place of Methodism in the Life and Thought of the Christian Church," first appeared in W. J. Townsend, H. B. Workman, and G. Eayrs, eds., *A New History of Methodism*, I (London:

Hodder, 1909), pp. 1-73. A revised edition, under the new title, was published separately in 1921. He wrote: "Unfortunately the dogmatism of certain theologians renders it necessary for us to claim that Methodism has a place in the development of the kingdom of God, and, so far as we can judge from existing phenomena, forms part of His divine plan. . . . No larger reunion is possible which either implicitly or explicitly ignores the *fact* of a [Methodist] Church which is today the largest Protestant Church in the world, with the possible exception of the Lutherans." Outdated triumphalism? Or a still necessary reminder?

21. The British union of 1932 brought together Wesleyan, Primitive, and United Methodists (the latter dating from a union of 1907). See Kent, pp. 1-43.

22. To be fair, the Bradford statement immediately continues: "It is their duty to make common cause in the search for the perfect expression of that unity and holiness which in Christ are already theirs."

23. Howard A. Snyder, *The Radical Wesley and Patterns for Church Renewal* (Downers Grove: Inter Varsity Press, 1980), p. 151.

24. Wesley would certainly not have allowed a "spiritualizing" distinction between a "visible" and an "invisible" church as a way of evading the concrete problems of disunity. In his confrontation with Calvinism, Wesley could admit a distinction between "the outward, visible church" and "the invisible church, which consists of holy believers" (*Predestination Calmly Considered*, 1752, sec. 71). But his more characteristic usage (as in *An Earnest Appeal to Men of Reason and Religion*, 1743, secs. 76-78) took the visibility and invisibility of the church as referring respectively to its *assembled* and *scattered* existence. This needs to be borne in mind even in the "holy believers" definition he gives to Bishop Challoner: "Such is the Catholic Church . . . the whole body of men, endued with faith working by love, dispersed over the whole earth, in Europe, Asia, Africa, and America." For Wesley, even the "spiritual" church remains visible by word and sacraments, and his views on the gravity of "separation" reveal how evangelically intolerable for him was all disunity which could not fail to have an institutional manifestation. For further elaboration, see secs. III and IV.

25. Colin W. Williams and Albert C. Outler appear to have popularized the "ecclesiola in Ecclesia" account of Methodism. They personally are to be absolved of all denominational complacency in its use.

26. C. Williams, p. 216.

27. R. N. Flew, "Methodism and the Catholic Tradition," in *Northern Catholicism*, N. P. Williams and C. Harris, eds., (London: SPCK, 1933), in particular pp. 515-31.

28. Albert C. Outler, *John Wesley* (New York: Oxford University Press, 1964), p. 306. That Wesley tended to look on his traveling preachers as such an order is apparent from his address to the 1769 Conference (see C. Williams, pp. 214-15). It is a broadening of the idea to let it include all Methodists, but from the viewpoint of social organization, Michael Hill does in fact argue that early Methodism had "a status close to that of a religious order in the Church of England." See "Methodism as a Religious Order: A Question of Categories," in *A Sociological Yearbook of Religion in Britain*, VI, Michael Hill, ed., (London: SCM Press, 1973), pp. 91-99.

29. As in note 7.

30. John M. Todd, *John Wesley and the Catholic Church* (London: Hodder and Stoughton, 1958), in particular p. 12. This sounds like a "vestigia ecclesiae" understanding of non-Roman Christianity. While that view

probably remains dominant even in Vatican II, A. Dulles has shown that the conciliar documents open up other approaches too: "The Church, the Churches, and the Catholic Church," in *Theological Studies* 33, 1972, pp. 199-234.

31. Francis Frost, "Méthodisme," in G. Jacquemet, ed., *Catholicisme, hier, aujourd'hui, demain* (Paris: Letouzey et Ané, 1948ff.), vol. IX, cols. 48-71.

32. This phrase or a similar one occurs in several places, for example, the Minutes of the 1763 Conference.

33. Letter of Mar. 20, 1739 to James Hervey.

34. Kissack, in particular pp. 89-95, 142-46.

35. E. G. Rupp, "The Future of the Methodist Tradition," in *London Quarterly and Holborn Review*, 184, 1959, pp. 264-74.

36. Sermon LXXV, "On Schism" (1786).

37. *A Farther Appeal to Men of Reason and Religion* (1744-45), III. 4. 6. The Catholic John M. Todd comments: "What seems so admirable about this passage is its serenity, from a man who certainly did believe that the Catholic Church was grossly in the wrong in his own time on fundamental points of doctrine" (*John Wesley and the Catholic Church*, pp. 180-81). In other places, Wesley allows that the Reformers were "thurst out" (see, e.g., Sermon CIV, "On Attending the Church Service").

38. Outler, *That the World May Believe: A Study of Christian Unity and What It Means for Methodists* (New York: Board of Missions of the Methodist Church, 1966), in particular p. 64.

39. Outler, *The Christian Tradition and the Unity We Seek* (New York: Oxford University Press, 1957). The distinctly theological motivation of ecumenism must be maintained in face of such a sociologically reductionist account of the reunion of British Methodism as R. Currie, *Methodism Divided: A Study in the Sociology of Ecumenicalism* (London: Faber & Faber, 1968).

40. "The discovery of our total Christian past is the means of fuller initiation into the whole Christian family" (Outler, as in note 39, p. 41).

41. Belgium and Pakistan are voluntary, though small, exceptions.

42. Outler, *The Christian Tradition and the Unity We Seek*, p. 22.

43. Outler, *John Wesley*, pp. vii-xii.

44. C. Williams, pp. 5-10.

45. Todd, pp. 182-83, 192.

46. Sermon XXXIV, "Catholic Spirit" (1749-50); over lesser matters, Wesley is prepared to "talk of them, if need be, at a more convenient season." See also the letter of July 3, 1756 to James Clark.

47. See Outler, *John Wesley*, p. 92. On "opinions" as distinguished from "essentials," see C. Williams, pp. 13-22; and J. Newton, "The Ecumenical Wesley," in *The Ecumenical Review*, 24, 1972, pp. 160-75.

48. Letter of July 18, 1749 (text in Outler, *John Wesley*, pp. 492-99).

49. See Outler, *John Wesley*, p. 92; see also letter of July 3, 1756 to James Clark.

50. Sermon LXXV, "On Schism" (1786).

51. *Journal*, Feb. 19, 1761.

52. Letter of May 22, 1750 to Gilbert Boyce.

53. Letter to Boyce.

54. Under Non-Juror influence, the earlier Wesley favored the (re)baptism of Germans and Dissenters who had not received "episcopal" baptism. As late as Oct. 21, 1738, an entry in Charles Wesley's *Journal* shows John to have taken up a stricter position than the Bishop of London on this point. See Hunter, chapters 2 and 5.

55. On the "foreign reformed churches," see the Minutes of the 1747 Conference (Williams, p. 221).

56. To Bishop Challoner he countered: "*Whatever may be the case of some particular souls*, it must be said, if your own marks be true, the Roman Catholics in general, are not 'the people of God' " (letter of Feb. 19, 1761). Yet Sermon LXXIV, "Of the Church" (1786), sec. 19, appears to consider the Church of Rome as "a part of the catholic Church"; see also above, at note 3.

57. Letter of May 22, 1750 to Gilbert Boyce.

58. See Sermon CIV, "On Attending the Church Service" (1788).

59. *Journal*, Jan. 11, 1750.

60. Sermon CVI, "On Faith" (1788).

61. Todd shows that Wesley mistook the Roman Catholic doctrine of "intention" for one of "worthiness," but that Wesley then defended the *true* Roman (anti-Donatist) doctrine against his own misunderstanding of it (pp. 149, 175-76)!

62. The date is early and the context is autobiographical, but what Wesley thus wrote in a letter to his father on Dec. 10, 1734, concerning the incumbency of Epworth, he undoubtedly held to throughout his ministry as universally applicable.

63. See Outler, *John Wesley*, pp. 177-80 for the rules of the United Societies.

64. For "the congregation of English believers," see the Minutes of the 1744 Conference (Williams, p. 208); see also *An Earnest Appeal to Men of Reason and Religion* (1743), sec. 76.

65. See Sermon CXV, "The Ministerial Office" (1789). For further references to Constantine in Wesley, see Snyder, pp. 80-82, 95-96.

66. Minutes of the 1747 Conference (Williams, p. 222).

67. On this, see Hunter, chapter 2.

68. See, for example, letter of July 3, 1756 to James Clark.

69. Letter of Apr. 19, 1764 to "various clergymen."

70. Williams, pp. 154-55; see also pp. 16-20.

71. Letter of June 25, 1746 to "John Smith."

72. See Robert E. Cushman, "Baptism and the Family of God," in D. Kirkpatrick, ed., *The Doctrine of the Church* (Nashville: Abingdon Press, 1964), pp. 79-102; B. G. Holland, *Baptism in Early Methodism* (London: Epworth Press, 1970). Wesley might have done well to take with permanent theological seriousness the advice of Tomo-chacki, the American Indian in Georgia: "We would not be made Christians as the Spaniards make Christians: we would be taught before we are baptized" (Todd, p. 67).

73. Composite quotation from David N. Power, "The basis for official ministry in the Church," in *The Jurist*, 41, 1981, 314-42, and *Gifts that Differ* (New York: Pueblo, 1980).

74. Sermon CXV, "The Ministerial Office" (1789).

75. See the Minutes of the 1747 Conference (Williams, p. 222).

76. "The uninterrupted succession I know to be a fable, which no man ever did or can prove" (letter of Aug. 19, 1785 to Charles Wesley).

77. On "accidental variations" in church government, see the Minutes of the 1747 Conference (Williams, p. 222).

78. Faith and Order Paper No. 91, reprinted from *The Ecumenical Review*, 31, 1979, pp. 77-93.

79. For the ecumenical dimensions of authority, see the work of the British Methodist Rupert E. Davies, *Religious Authority in an Age of Doubt* (London: Epworth Press, 1968).

80. See Commission on Faith and Order Lima, 1982, *Towards Visible Unity*, I (Faith and Order Paper No. 112, 1982), 89-100; II (No. 113), pp. 28-46.

81. A. D. Falconer, "Contemporary Attitudes to the Papacy," in *The Furrow*, 27, 1976, pp. 3-19.

82. Gerald E. Moede, in *Journal of Ecumenical Studies* 12, 1975, pp. 367-88.

83. For the New Delhi definition, see, for example, L. Vischer, ed., *A Documentary History of the Faith and Order Movement 1927-1963* (St. Louis: Bethany Press, 1963), pp. 144ff. On the complexities of "place," see the WCC publication *In Each Place: Towards a Fellowship of Local Churches Truly United* (Geneva: WCC, 1977).

84. See Frost, col. 70.

85. Frost, col. 70.

86. In the Preface to his *Notes on the Old Testament*, for example, Wesley writes of "the analogy of faith, the connexion and harmony there is between those grand fundamental doctrines, original sin, justification by faith, the new birth, inward and outward holiness" (*Works*, XIV, p. 253).

87. Outler, *John Wesley*, pp. 3-33; see also his *Theology in the Wesleyan Spirit* (Nashville: Discipleship Resources, 1975); and "The Place of Wesley in the Christian Tradition," in K. E. Rowe, ed., *The Place of Wesley in the Christian Tradition* (Metuchen: Scarecrow Press, 1976), pp. 11-38.

88. Maximin Piette, *La réaction wesléyenne dans l'évolution protestante* (1925); English trans.: *John Wesley in the Evolution of Protestantism* (London: Sheed and Ward, 1937; reprint 1979).

89. Todd, p. 183.

90. Theodore Runyon, ed., *Sanctification and Liberation* (Nashville: Abingdon Press, 1981).

91. H. Meyer, " 'Einheit in versöhnter Verschiedenheit'—'konziliare Gemeinschaft'—'organische Union': Gemeinsamkeit und Differenz gegenwärtig diskutierter Einheitskonzeptionen," in *Oekumenische Rundschau*, 27, 1978, pp. 377-400.

92. Kissack, especially pp. 113f., 131-34, 148-59.

93. Kent, pp. 193-206.

94. Kissack, p. 130.

95. Bertrand, p. 121.

96. Outler, *That the World May Believe*, p. 54.

97. Outler, pp. 74-75.

98. Outler, "Do Methodists Have a Doctrine of the Church?" p. 28.

Ecclesiology and Sacraments in an Ecumenical Context

Working Group Paper

Introduction

To give focus to our theme "Ecclesiology and Sacraments in an Ecumenical Context," we studied and discussed the convergence statements on Baptism, Eucharist, and Ministry finalized at Lima in January 1982, after more than fifty years of work by the Faith and Order Commission of the World Council of Churches. This procedure commended itself, inasmuch as these are the most broadly based agreements on these topics in the history of the modern ecumenical movement (including Roman Catholic and Orthodox participation), and the churches of world Methodism will be asked to respond to the entire statement by December 1985 from our Wesleyan and Methodist perspective.

The statements proved to be a fruitful point of initiation for our careful study of Methodist ecclesiology and sacramental theology. Although we ourselves, as members of the same world family, did not agree at all points, we found that we were in substantial agreement with many elements of the text. Since these are vital parts of our own ecclesiology, we will share with the Institute the major points of our agreement. We will also list issues that we think require research and further development by Methodist theological scholarship.

I. *Baptism*
   A. Points of agreement with the *Baptism, Eucharist, and Ministry* (*BEM*) text from the point of view of Methodist theology:

(1) Baptism is both God's gift and our human response to that gift. Its objective grounding is in the total ministry of Jesus Christ. Baptism is one of the dominical sacraments.

(2) God bestows on all baptized persons the anointing and the promise of the Holy Spirit, and implants in their hearts the first fruit of this inheritance as children of God.

(3) The Holy Spirit nurtures the life of faith in the baptized person.

(4) Both infant and believers' baptism embody God's initiative in Christ and express a response of faith made within the believing community.

(5) Those baptized are pardoned, cleansed, and sanctified by Christ, and are given as part of their baptismal experience a new ethical orientation under the guidance of the Holy Spirit.

B. Issues for further research, reflection, and articulation:

(1) What is the relationship between God's prevenient grace, flowing out of the work of Christ, and the process of initiation? How do we understand the universality of grace?

(2) What is the relation between baptism as an event and initiation as a process? That is, what is the relation between God's gift of grace in baptism and God's continuing gift of grace in the process of initiation, a process which includes and requires a person's faith commitment?

(3) In what way does our one baptism, and our acceptance of each other's baptism, constitute a call to the churches to overcome their separateness?

II. *Eucharist*

In regard to eucharist, our study centered on Christ's presence and his sacrifice, and derivatively, frequency of celebration and the treatment of the elements.

A. Points of agreement with the *BEM* text from the point of view of Methodist theology:

(1) Emerging agreement on *anamnesis* was noted and appreciated; the supper is the living and effective sign of Christ's sacrifice. Christ's sacrifice is unique, accomplished once and for all on the cross. The sign character can be seen in different ways. It is the same Jesus who died who is present in the eucharist to give us benefits now.

(2) Word and sacrament belong together.

(3) We note that the eucharistic hymns of the Wesleys reflect a doctrine of Christ's presence in the elements. Accordingly we concur with the statement on eucharist that the presence of Christ does not depend on our faith, but that faith is vital to discern Christ's body and blood. It is by the Holy Spirit that the bread and wine become the sacramental signs of Christ's body and blood. Jesus Christ is present in a special way to the Christian community and the individual Christian in the celebration of the eucharist.

B. Issues for further research, reflection, and articulation:

(1) John Wesley and early Methodists received the sacrament frequently, and the *BEM* document suggests that eucharist be the normal Sunday service. Should eucharist be celebrated at least every Sunday in Methodist churches?

(2) The treatment of unused elements reflects the theological understanding of eucharist. More work needs to be done on this question among Methodists.

(3) The *mystery* always present in the eucharist is recognized in the *BEM* document. We appreciate the inclusion of this dimension. Because Methodism incorporates elements of both Eastern and Western thought, it may serve as a model of legitimate diversity in unity concerning the eucharist.

III. *Ministry*
   A. Points of agreement with the *BEM* document:
      (1) Ministry is grounded in Christology, with a trinitarian basis.
      (2) The question of ministry begins with the whole people of God.
      (3) Ordained ministry is representative of the normative ministry of Jesus Christ and also of the ministry of the whole church.
      (4) Tradition comprises the continuity of the faith and life of the church; episcopal succession is one element within this tradition.
      (5) Ordained ministry includes calling by God, prayer for the Spirit, discernment of gifts, and authenticating by the church. Ordination is not merely a functional differentiation; it is a sacramental act for Methodists.
      (6) The ordained minister is involved in a ministry of word and sacrament, in a community of discipline and accountability.
      (7) When representative ministry is open to women, it is blessed by them. We commend this to the whole church.
   B. Issues for further research, reflection, and articulation:
      (1) What is the relation between ordination and education?
      (2) Serious attention needs to be given to theological concepts of the three-fold ministry by Methodists. In particular we note the need for attention to historical, theological, and ecumenical concerns with the *diaconate*. The group notes its concern with proposed unilateral and unecumenical action toward the creation of a "lay diaconate" among United Methodists.
      (3) Are there elements in our tradition that move us to accept the "sign of episcopal succession" as the *BEM* document suggests?
      (4) The focus of ordained ministry may be in the local eucharistic community, but its relation to

the whole church (international fellowship) needs attention as well.

IV. *Ecclesiology*

In this section we will mention several issues of systematic importance to consideration of the doctrine of the church in Methodism.

A. *Membership*

The *BEM* document says that baptism unites the one baptized with Christ and with his people, and this directly raises questions about membership of the church. Christ died for all, and God seeks by prevenient grace to work in every human heart. "When an infant is baptized, his personal response will be offered at a later moment in life." Baptized infants are received in an important sense as members of the church, but in some churches it is not until a later time in their lives that they are received as members in some other sense. This difficulty, which concerns many churches, also is made more acute in Methodism because of our societary origins.

In Methodist usage, the membership of infants is described in various ways such as "real but incomplete," or "preparatory membership," and the later membership as "membership of society," "full membership," or "membership of the church as an organization." The relation of the two is not always clear. Although the term "confirmation" was not originally used in Methodism at all, it is often used now to refer to this later completion of baptism in church membership. This uncertainty about the status of baptized children also affects the question of whether they should receive Holy Communion.

B. *The Denomination and the Church Universal*

The discussion of liturgical acts raises the question whether baptism, confirmation, or ordination are related to the universal church or to the denomination. It might perhaps be said that they are performed for the universal church (whether or not they are recognized by other denominations, as they should be), but they are also performed within a particular denomination that has the immediate responsibility of discipline, pastoral care, and support.

Geoffrey Wainwright, in his paper, suggests that the New Testament and the mission to spread scriptural holiness alike require the structural unity of the church. Denominations, according to this view, must be regarded as provisional. He considers the possibility that the particular spiritual tradition now represented by a denominational family might be kept alive by something like a religious order within the universal church. The universal church should consist of locally united churches (however locality is defined), bound together in conciliar fellowship where decisions are made together in matters which concern all.

The religious orders within such a universal church would need some organization, but much less than the present denominations have. These religious orders would be in some tension with the structures of the church, but here tension would be kept within bounds. Are some of our traditions mere preferences, which need to be judged by the great Tradition of the universal church?

There are serious questions, however, whether Methodism's mission might be impaired by entering into structural unions; whether local unions whittle down the strength of the denominational family; whether it would be better to await the results of the bilaterals; whether there is not danger in the idea of a "super-church" (despite the fact that no one favors the term), and in the creation of national churches which lack adequate international links. The question also arises whether the full unity of the church does not beong to the "last things." Should we begin within the Methodist family, for instance, through closer relations, or even union, among the historic black Methodist Episcopal churches and United Methodism?

Another question concerns the continuing role of the World Methodist Council. Should it be transmuted into a pan-Methodist church or in some other way maintain a strong international denominational emphasis seeking closer relationship with other world bodies through multilaterals. Or should it, without any strengthening of its organization, be engaged in the development of a Methodist order in the *Una Sancta?*

C. *Authority*

The question arises where the teaching authority of the church resides. Is there a role for the Bishop of Rome as a unifying factor within the church? The present claims for the magisterium in the Church of Rome are not acceptable to many Christians, yet the nature of teaching authority needs fuller investigation, as does the relation of primacy to conciliarity.

In all of these questions, issues, and concerns, the group recognizes that there are serious historical, societal, and cultural realities at work in the life of the church which complicate application of theological principles. Moreover, for Methodism, theological principles are not easily invested with authority for ordering the life of the church.

D. *Theological Traditions within Methodism*

Our group is aware through its study and discussion that world Methodism contains elements of what might be called "low" and "high" understandings of ecclesiology and the sacraments. We think that continuing serious study, reflection, and articulation of the intentions of the diverse theological strands of Methodism will prove fruitful. Without such attention, these differences will be problematic. Methodism is both evangelical and catholic; John Wesley himself always held these dimensions together. Insistence on the unity of these dimensions is a hallmark of Methodism in the universal church.

Conclusion

We, as a group, are mindful of the fact that all we have discussed is in service to the total worldwide mission of the church. The sacraments are gifts of God through which God's grace is given unto us all. The structures of the church are intended to enable and enhance our love for one another and all persons. The urgent needs of the world and its peoples are uppermost in our minds as we seek to understand the way Methodism can be free to be about God's work of deliverance, mission, and unity. Personal and social holiness are gifts of God; they also involve determined human engagement.

Finally, to the Oxford Institute of Methodist Theological Studies, the group suggests that the *BEM* document, aiming as it does to provide the churches with a reconciling statement of what we can say together, challenges us to rethink our own Wesleyan and Methodist positions. What are the elements more or less unique to us that we want to commend to this emerging consensus? What, on the other hand, are idiosyncracies that have crept into our thinking, which we might relinquish with no great loss?

Having thus commented on these *BEM* texts, we wish as an Institute to recommend to churches in the Methodist family a serious study of and response to these documents, to the end that we may make a contribution to the growing agreement, identifying and rectifying any eccentricities among us that take us beyond acceptable diversity within the church catholic.

Evangelism and Wesley's Catholicity of Grace

S. Wesley Ariarajah

It has become difficult to speak on evangelism, not because it is a new or abstruse subject, but because so much has been said and written about it from such a vast range of perspectives. It has been defined and redefined, recycled and restated so many times, that I hesitate at the very thought of adding yet another view.

An attempt to reconceive evangelism at the present time is nonetheless important, for at least three reasons. First, there is a sense in which our understanding of evangelism is what really reveals our theological convictions. Evangelism emanates from an understanding of God, of the human person, of Christ, and of what God has done in Christ. Our understanding of evangelism is but the tip of the iceberg; underneath lies a whole theological worldview.

Second, at least in some Christian traditions, evangelism is the basic rationale for the existence of the church. In these traditions, evangelism is not a concept to be discussed, but a mandate to be fulfilled—the primary and permanent task of the church without which it has no right to exist.

Third (and perhaps we should take note of this more carefully than we have done so far), understanding what evangelism is and how to go about it may well become one of the most divisive issues of the church in our time. There is already a growing polarization that cuts across all traditional lines of division. Labels have appeared; trenches are being built; and from time to time one can hear the sound of artillery exchanges. As confessional differences become less and less pronounced, the new division based on the understanding of the nature of evangelism comes to the fore.

Elements in Evangelism

The irony is that, in a sense, it is unwise and counter-productive to try to agree on a common understanding of evangelism. For in reality, evangelism is not a concept nor even a program, but a response of a person who comes to a particular knowledge and experience of God in Jesus Christ. A person's understanding of evangelism and commitment to it, therefore, will depend to a large extent on that knowledge and experience and the nature of the obedience demanded in a given situation.

This is not to deny that, on the basis of scripture and the corporate experience of the church, we can draw out some elements involved in the evangelistic task, nor that it is useful to arrive at some definitions. Nevertheless, evangelism is often much more complex than we wish to admit, rendering discussion of the task difficult and frequently confusing.

To begin with, evangelism has to do with sharing the good news of Jesus Christ. But there are so many aspects to the life and ministry of Christ, and so many ways of perceiving his life, death, and resurrection, even within scripture, that there is the abiding problem of discerning the content of the gospel. To some of us, this presents no problem; we consider the message to be clear in the scriptures. But as more and more people begin to reread the scriptures from various historical perspectives, there is much less agreement on what it is that makes the good news "good."

The second difficulty with regard to evangelism is that the good news has been, and always will be, mediated through persons whose own experience of the gospel invariably affects their understanding and presentation of the message. Even within the scripture, the presentation of the gospel by John, Paul, Peter, and the writer of the Letter to the Hebrews, for example, have all been conditioned by the specific experiences from which they themselves responded to the message of Christ.

In the third place, evangelism is effective only insofar as the gospel is heard and received. Just as the one who presents the gospel mediates it out of his or her own experience, the hearers of the gospel can hear it only from the specific context in which they live. One of the exciting things about the second half of this century is that we are witnessing a great proliferation of ways in which the gospel of Jesus Christ is heard, understood, and received in different parts of the world. Increasingly, peoples of Latin America, Africa, and Asia are hearing the gospel in new ways, and in so doing they are also challenging what traditionally has been accepted as evangelism.

Finally, and most importantly, in all evangelism we believe that the Holy Spirit is acting to fulfill God's intention in each specific situation. Ultimately there is only one mission—God's mission, and one evangelist—God. Evangelism happens, therefore, not when the evangelist's intentions are fulfilled, nor when persons cross from one commitment to another, but when *God's* intention is fulfilled in a given life or situation. What ultimately matters in evanglism is whether more of life and life-situations have come under the rule of God. The temptation in evangelism is to forget that what we are about is God's mission, and for the evangelist to set goals and priorities as though God does not act. Such goals can become so absolutized that they can contradict God's own purpose, for the intention of God and the intention of the evangelist do not always coincide.

To summarize, any reconception of evangelism should include: (1) an understanding of the content of the gospel; (2) a recognition that the gospel is mediated and experienced in a variety of ways; (3) a deeper appreciation of the ways in which different situations and cultures affect the hearing of the gospel; and (4) a recognition that ultimately it is God's own purpose that should be fulfilled—all of which make the task of evangelism complex and our understanding of it difficult.

Wesley's Context

The purpose of this rather lengthy introduction is to set a context within which we might consider Wesley's own understanding and practice of evangelism. His perception of the gospel was very much influenced by the continuing debate within Reformation theology, his Puritan heritage, his study of the seventeenth-century Anglican divines, and by the new awakening in personal piety.[1] But his evangelical experience was very much a part of his own spiritual pilgrimage, which began under the wing of his mother, Susanna. His upbringing, his intense study of the scriptures, the search for personal holiness, the experience of assurance commonly said to have been received at Aldersgate Street, and his quest for perfection, were all part of the pilgrimage. Some have tried to build a model for evangelism out of Wesley's experience at Aldersgate Street, and there is no doubt that this was a significant turning point in his spiritual life.[2] But he himself refused to make it the norm. Further, while Wesley insisted that religious truth has to be "experienced," he refused to make experience the sole authority, and insisted primarily on the guidance of the scripture and on the corporate authority of the church.[3]

At the same time, the evangelical message he proclaimed was very much directed to a particular historical and spiritual condition of British life in the eighteenth century.[4] He believed that God had raised the people called Methodists to "spread scriptural holiness throughout the land." This he did with all the vigor he could muster. Moreover, one of the healthy features of the Methodist tradition is that it has been a growing tradition. While the marks of Wesley's own teaching can still be seen in Methodism as a whole, the Methodist churches have grown in their own ways in different parts of the world, and have always maintained ecumenical relations with other churches.

Reconceiving evangelism today, therefore, should not be an attempt to go back to the Methodist tradition in order simply to reaffirm it. Rather it should be an attempt to look into the tradition to see what resources there are to guide us today. It is in this spirit that we can turn to the life and teachings of Wesley and early Methodism.

Catholicity of Grace

One of the crucial issues in evangelism is our theological evaluation of the world, and especially of the peoples of other faiths and convictions. Evangelism is urgent, it is sometimes claimed, because millions are perishing without the gospel. In this view, the gospel has to be preached to save the world from damnation, with a sharp distinction between the "saved" and the "unsaved." The urgency of evangelism, from the perspective of potential believers, lies in the fact that if they do not hear, repent, and believe in the gospel, they will be "lost," perhaps eternally. The urgency for evangelists is that they are under a mandate to preach the gospel, and in some sense or other become responsible for the destiny of the potential hearers.

This view tends to produce a savior complex in the evangelist, with all of its attendant problems. Those who seriously hold this position, but who for one reason or another are unable to engage in active evangelism, must carry in their hearts a big burden of guilt. The real problem, however, is theological, concerning God's nature and relationship to the created world. If we believe that God's relationship of love and grace to humanity has always been the same, then the significance of the gospel event must be seen in that context and not outside it.

Wesley faced this problem. Even though he subscribed to the view that the human being is a sinner, and that it is God's grace alone that can redeem, Wesley found it difficult to subscribe to the theory of total depravity as did some of the Reformers. On the contrary, he held that God's law is written in the heart of every human being. Human conscience helps the person to know what is right, even if it is not possible to fulfill the law as God requires.[5] Similarly, Wesley valued the human faculty of reason, asserting that there is a measure of freedom which makes it possible for someone to accept or reject God's offer of salvation.

Wesley was able to hold such views because of the catholicity of his doctrine of grace. He talked of grace in at least three aspects: prevenient (or preventing) grace, justifying grace, and sanctifying grace. With the doctrine of prevenient grace, he was able to modify the extreme position that the "natural" human condition "belongs to the devil." He claimed that God's grace is already present and active in the natural person, moving and inviting towards saving grace, and commonly identified as conscience:

Can it be denied that something of this is found in every man born into the world? And does it not appear as soon as understanding opens, as soon as reason begins to dawn? Does not everyone then begin to know that there is a difference between good and evil, however imperfect the various circumstances of this sense of good and evil may be?[6]

But he rejected the idea that conscience is natural. It is rather "the supernatural gift of God above all his natural endowments."

No; it is not nature, but the son of God, that is "the true light, which enlighteneth every man that cometh into the world." So that we may say to every human creature, "He," not nature, "hath showed thee, O man, what is good." And it is his spirit who giveth thee an inward check, who causeth thee to feel uneasy, when thou walkest in any instance contrary to the light which he hath given thee.[7]

The significance of this doctrine was twofold. It declared God's grace to be available to all human beings—"free in all, and free for all"—and what others considered natural Wesley insisted was the work of God's grace in each person.[8] More significant, however, was the Christological and pneumatological dimension which Wesley gave to the doctrine on the basis of the Johannine prologue. Grace in its prevenience (its relation to nature as such) presupposes the Triune God of the Christian faith. It is prevenient in the sense of "before faith" and not "before Christ." For Wesley, there was no "before Christ." He believed that through faith we move in freedom from prevenient grace to justifying and sanctifying grace. His doctrine of original sin was severe: that total depravity was the result of the fall. But God was already at work with redeeming grace! With his doctrine of prevenient grace, Colin Williams says, Wesley "broke the chain of logical necessity by which Calvin's doctrine of predestination seems to flow from the doctrine of original sin."[9]

Nor did Wesley hesitate to draw some of the implications of this view for the universality of God's grace. He believed that Christ works even in those who do not hear the gospel in this life. Such persons are judged, he held, according to their response to the universal grace by which Christ works within them in a hidden way.[10] Wesley saw no contradiction between this view and his belief in justification by faith. Those who have not had the opportunity of hearing the gospel, yet have responded to prevenient grace, are, like the patriarchs, justified by faith in anticipation of the full revelation of Christ.

Wesley's thoughts were of course conditioned by the limits of his own knowledge and the theological boundaries recognized within his inherited theology. But his concept of grace and the concern that is expressed in it are of much relevance to our own understanding of evangelism in a culturally and religiously plural world. Our evangelistic task is set, not in a world that is lost and deprived of God, but in one in which God is very much active, and where, moved by God's grace, people already experience the love of God in good measure through Christ and the Holy Spirit. The evangelistic task is not to deny this universal grace, but to help persons move from "grace to grace." The theological task lies in trying to understand the nature of the relationship between this universal grace of God available to all and the salvation offered to humanity in the life, death, and resurrection of Jesus Christ.

Some would argue that such a generous doctrine of grace will undercut the urgency in evangelism. Wesley's own life remains the answer to this objection, for the same Wesley who held this doctrine of universal grace was also the greatest evangelist of his time.

The Whole Gospel for the Whole Person in the Whole Community

One of the important contributions that the Methodist tradition can make today, holds Mortimer Arias of Bolivia, is the "holistic or integral approach" to evangelism. The Evangelical Methodist Church in Bolivia puts it this way:

True evangelism is holistic; the whole gospel for the whole man and the whole of mankind. Evangelism addresses the person in the totality of his being: individual and social, physical and spiritual, historical and eternal. We reject, therefore, all dichotomies, ancient and modern, which reduce the gospel to one dimension, or fragment man who was created in the image and likeness of God. We do not accept the idea that evangelism means only "saving souls" and seeking exclusively "a change in the eternal status of the individual." These concepts are biblically insufficient. We reject also the reduction of the gospel to a program for service or social development or a mere instrument of socio-political programs.[11]

The problem that we face today is not so much that our evangelism reduces people to "souls with ears" or "stomachs with souls." The real problem lies in the fact that those who believe in saving souls have not, despite serious attempts, been able to expand their concept of evangelism beyond personal assurance, moral reformation, and a general concern for the poor and marginalized in society. The fundamental problem of sin as a structural reality in the social, economic, and political order somehow remains out of place. On the other hand, those who strive to act on the gospel imperatives to work for the kingdom within society, and who choose to stand in solidarity with the poor and the oppressed in order to resist the powers of structural sin, have not been able to integrate into their conception of evangelism the individual's need of forgiveness and the demand of the gospel for a radical change in the inner life of the person. Though they always claim, rightly, that there is an evangelical dimension to their work, they have not always succeeded in changing evangelical dimensions into evangelical intentions. Somehow the frontier between faith and nonfaith remains undefined.[12] Labels such as "fundamentalists," "radicals," "evangelicals," and "ecumenicals" have made the situation no better. Much ink and energy have been spent in mutual accusation and defense. Any reconceiving of evangelism has to take this situation seriously. There are now some attempts to initiate dialogue between these two perspectives on evangelism, but not always with much success. For many reasons it proves difficult to close the theological gap. The question, therefore, is—can we transcend it?

Obviously, early Methodism did not face the question in this specific form, but Methodist faith and practice can at least point us in some direction. Wesley saw the individual as a whole person, whose total life should be brought under the grace of God. He therefore emphasized sanctification alongside justification—the true mark of religion being discipleship as expressed in a life of holiness.[13] And since he could not conceive of a Christian life apart from social living, he extended the concept of personal holiness to social holiness, emphasizing social service and political responsibility, with strong attitudes on social evils.[14] His eschatological vision was one in which the whole creation would be transformed, when God would establish the fullness of the kingdom, the foretaste of which was already present in historical reality. Thus, even though Wesley saw his own life as a pilgrimage towards personal holiness, in his vision of redemption, the personal, the social, and the universal were held together.[15]

Perhaps most significant in Wesley's understanding of evangelism is that, contrary to what is often assumed, he never saw its purpose merely in terms of conversion. He began with the premise that God's grace was already in operation, and looked for the fulfilment of God's new creation, when all would be "perfected into one." His brother Charles captured the spirit of this evangelism in his familiar hymn:

> Finish, then, thy new creation;
> Pure and spotless let us be.
> Let us see thy great salvation
> Perfectly restored in thee:
> Changed from glory into glory,
> Till in heaven we take our place,
> Till we cast our crowns before thee,
> Lost in wonder, love, and praise.

The "wonder, love, and praise" are not that the individual has reached heaven, but that God has finished the new creation—that all have been perfectly restored in God.

Widening the Vision

While the Methodist traditions can, as we have observed, help us avoid some of the pitfalls of contemporary evangelism, we should not forget that Wesley was a man of his time, and that in our own time Methodism and Christianity in general face new challenges and possibilities. There is a sense in which we have entered into a new era in our relationships with other religious traditions. The witness of other faiths and our dialogue with them have thrown new light on our own perception of witness and service. This, for example, was not an immediate issue for Wesley.

The social, economic, and political problems we face today have changed vastly in character and magnitude. Emphasis has moved from social service to questions of international economic order; millions starve and thousands actually die of hunger, even though enough food is produced to feed all mouths. The world is facing not only the horrors of war, but the real possibility of a nuclear catastrophe that can wipe out life from the surface of the earth. Social organization and international and interpersonal relations have become so complex that personal decisions and life-styles seem to have little or no impact on society. Similarly, individuals are unable to escape the impact and influence of social structures on their own lives.

In the midst of all these, there is the search for meaning, peace, and spirituality, but in the images and language of a new age. In our attempt to reconceive evangelism today, we should not only draw insights from our past, but also bring the complexity of our contemporary world into it, so that tradition, in its attempt to speak a meaningful word, may remain a "living tradition."

The question we face is this: Are we, in our attempt to understand the task of evangelism today, able—in the spirit of John Wesley—to look upon the *world* as our parish? If we do, our task will not be easy, but will certainly be worthwhile.

Notes

1. Albert C. Outler, ed., *John Wesley* (New York: Oxford University Press, 1964), pp. 7ff.

2. A. Skevington Wood, for example, in *The Burning Heart: John Wesley, Evangelist* (Devon: Paternoster Press, 1967), attempts to make a strong case that John Wesley was actually converted at Aldersgate Street. See especially pp. 66-69.

3. "The scriptures are the touchstone whereby Christians examine all real or supposed revelation. . . . For though the Spirit is our principal leader, yet He is not our rule at all; the scriptures are the rule whereby He leads us into all 'truth' " (*Letters* 2:17), quoted in Colin Williams, *John Wesley's Theology Today* (Nashville: Abingdon Press, 1960), p. 35.

4. Rupert E. Davies, *Methodism* (London: Epworth Press, 1976). A good discussion on the intellectual, spiritual, and social setting is found on pp. 21-37.

5. *The Works of John Wesley*, 14 vols. (London: Wesleyan Conference Office, 1872; reprint, Grand Rapids: Baker House, 1979), 6:512.

6. Wesley, *Works* 7:187. Cf. Wesley's sermon, "The Scripture Way of Salvation," in *John Wesley*, ed. Outler, pp. 271-82. "If Wesleyan theology had to be judged by a single essay, this one would do as well as any and better than most" (ed.'s introduction, p. 271).

7. *Works*, 7:188.

8. *Works*, 7:373-74.

9. Williams, *Wesley's Theology*, p. 46.

10. *Works*, 7:188. Cf. 6:206.

11. Mortimer Arias, "That the World May Believe," in *Mission Trends No. 3: Third World Theologies*, ed. Gerald H. Anderson and Thomas J. Stransky (New York: Paulist Press, 1976), p. 91.

12. Arias, p. 92.

13. Cf. Wesley's sermon, "Christian Perfection," in *John Wesley*, ed. Outler, pp. 252-71.

14. Williams, *Wesley's Theology*, pp. 196 ff.

15. *Works*, 6:295-96, 430-31.

Evangelism in the Wesleyan Traditions

Working Group Paper

"The Gospel is the Good News of the Kingdom of God. It is God's offer of life through repentance and faith in Jesus Christ as risen Savior and Lord, participation in His Body the Church, and His call to become partners in the work of His Kingdom of love, peace, and justice in the world."

"Evangelism is the proclamation of the Kingdom of God. It means presenting the love of God in Jesus Christ through the power of the Holy Spirit so that persons repent, place their trust in the resurrected Christ, worship Him as Lord in the fellowship of His Body, and invest their lives in the work of His Kingdom."

With these definitions, the evangelism group of the Institute summed up days of research and discussion. The major areas of investigation and the main conclusions reached are as follows.

1. Wesleyan Evangelism

The message of the evangelism of John and Charles Wesley was the historic faith of the Christian church. The Wesleys were orthodox believers, remaining always in the main-stream of Christian truth and tradition.

In "offering Christ" John Wesley developed a clear understanding of the way the Holy Spirit works in "the Order of Salvation." Beginning with prevenient grace, the Spirit leads people through convincing, converting, and sanctifying grace. At the heart of this process are conversion and assurance, brought about through justification by faith. After conversion comes the call to seek holiness, including social holiness.

2. Wesleyan Evangelism Today

Is Wesleyan evangelism valid in the vastly different modern world? Yes, for underneath the changes and the complexity of life today are vital constant factors. Human nature is the same: shameful, splendid, sinful, saintly, needing salvation. The Christian gospel, rooted in the historic birth, life, death and resurrection of Jesus Christ, abides. The gospel needs to be reinterpreted, but Jesus is the name for today.

3. The Context of Evangelism

The Evangelism Group, representative of the six continents, examined the context for evangelism today. Reports were discussed from churches in the First, Second, and Third Worlds. A time of opportunity has opened for the proclamation of the Christian faith, as young people grope after the transcendent, and adults are discovering that the secret of life is not in the means but in the ends of living. Many are seeking afresh a faith to live by.

4. The Message of Evangelism

The message of the gospel in every age and in each place and culture is a first concern of evangelism. What is the message now?

Conversion Christianity is the message of the church and the need of the world. The message must be contextualized in each society and undertaken in concrete historical situations, taking note of religious and cultural diversity. The message must be at once personal and social; especially it must represent good news for the poor. In a nuclear age it is essential to present Christ as the Prince of Peace.

5. The Methods of Evangelism

The maintenance church is called again to be a missionary church, reaching, as did John Wesley, for those beyond its boundaries, inviting them to a living faith. The effective church is the indigenous, contextualized church. Under the challenge of Latin American members of the group, it was recognized that ways must be found to undertake evangelism among the poor with sensitivity. Jesus proclaimed good news to the poor, who understand and relate to the gospel in a unique way.

With surprising frequency, the house group, or the "little church," emerged in worldwide reports. As Methodism seeks to use this method of evangelizing, John Wesley has much to say through his system of bands and class meetings. The gospel is to be expressed today in deed as well as word, in acts of mercy to the victims of suffering and oppression and in social action in relation to the power structures of society and the corporate sins of humanity. The little church facilitates this.

Finally, as the spiritual sons and daughters of John Wesley, we cannot overlook preaching and preaching for conversion. Evangelical preaching inside and outside churches is one great need of today.

6. *A World Vision*

World Methodism, established in ninety countries, is powerfully placed to see afresh the world vision of John Wesley and can reach the world through its world evangelism program. By the intellectual and scholarly search for the meaning of evangelism and by the doing of it, we may yet experience this in our time.

Some Areas of Concern

1. How are social, political, and economic realities related to the kingdom of God? What does personal evangelism mean in this context? What help can we get from Wesley on this question?
2. What is the relationship between the gospel and the experiences of the poor? What does it mean to speak of the gospel *of* the poor and *for* the poor? How do we avoid platitudes in this regard?
3. What does evangelism mean in situations where people live, as in Africa, in socially integrated communities with common bonds and loyalties? What is the nature of the gospel to be preached in such situations?
4. In societies where traditional churches are declining in numbers, which forms of church community and outreach

can help to foster new growth? Is the Wesleyan model of bands, classes, and societies relevant in this context?

5. How can we ensure that evangelism is an act of sharing in love? Since women form the majority of the membership of the church, can their experience tell us anything about male-dominated concepts in evangelism—e.g., the common use of military language, such as "campaign" or "crusade"?

Some Issues for Further Reflection, Study, and Dialogue

1. What can we learn about the meaning and practice of evangelism from churches which really are churches of the poor?

2. How do the themes of poverty and oppression and the actual life of the poor relate to the *content* of the gospel?

3. How do militarism, the arms race, and in particular the growing awareness of the worldwide nuclear threat, impact our evangelistic message and practice? What does the gospel promise of universal *shalom* have to say to humankind's hunger for peace today?

4. How are the social, economic, and political dimensions of God's kingdom to be correlated with our evangelistic witness? Can we learn anything from Wesley in this regard?

5. Can we come to a fuller understanding of the psychological and sociological meaning of awakening, conversion, and sanctification by attending to secular interest in and study of spiritual experience?

6. What can we learn from Africa and other communal cultures about the nature of evangelism and the meaning of the gospel as a call to and an offer of socially integrated community?

7. The concept of prevenient grace and its implications for evangelism and social witness need further investigation.

8. Given the historical dimensions and concrete historical expressions of sin, how is the historical meaning of love, justice, peace, and salvation to be understood in context?

9. What is the theological significance of evangelism as part of the *praxis* out of which theological reflection arises? Is

theological reflection not inherently deficient and incomplete if it is not grounded in the practice of evangelism?

10. The need for evangelism *within* the church needs further attention. How can we proclaim the gospel to professed Christians so that the radical demands of the kingdom of God may be heard and heeded?

11. The relationship of dialogue and evangelism, and the place of dialogue as part of evangelism need further clarification. Are dialogue and evangelism complementary or contradictory? In particular, as Wesleyans, what is our stance towards other living traditions of the Christian faith in the practice of evangelism?

12. What does it mean to speak of the eucharist as a "converting ordinance"? What is the place of liturgy and worship in evangelism?

13. Organizational structures of the church as vehicles for (or obstacles to) evangelism need careful study. What structural forms or changes tend best to further the church's evangelistic witness?

14. The relevance of Wesleyan *ecclesiolae* has been affirmed by our group. Such structures seem particularly suited to ministry among the poor. Why do they seem to die out, however, as churches become more affluent? Is this an inherent social dynamic, or is it due to other factors?

15. The significance of the priesthood of all believers and the gifts of the Spirit for evangelism need further emphasis. Have we adequately appreciated the evangelistic significance of the priesthood and our gifted laity in general, and women and the poor in particular?

16. Our group affirms the urgency of the evangelistic task and the need to offer life in Christ to all. To this end we commend and call for such research and study as may help to further this work. Given the theme of this Institute, we therefore express concern about the inadequacy or unavailability of theological publications—especially in Africa—and the need for a Spanish edition of Wesley's works. (Drafted by Alan Walker.)

A Praxis Approach to Evangelism: Reflections on the Realities of Contemporary Evangelical Outreach

David Lowes Watson

It was an important and welcome decision to have a working group on evangelism at the Seventh Oxford Institute, and for two reasons. If theology is to avoid the abstraction of critical reflection for its own sake, the theologian is well advised, not only to practice Christian living, but to take the gospel as a message into the rough and tumble of ordinary human existence. Proclaiming the truth on which one reflects is a searching exercise. It is at once the test and the purpose of a Christian's engagement with theology as a discipline of the faith, and it is precisely this dimension of Christian *praxis* which the evangelist brings to theological discourse. By the same token, it is salutary for the evangelist to be exposed to the critical enquiry of the theologian. The theme of this Institute, with its emphasis on theological traditioning in the quest for God's future, was particularly pertinent to such an exposure. Without a faithful appropriation of the Christ event and the scriptural witness of the church across the centuries, evangelists are all too susceptible to the pressures of contextual exigencies, allowing their own priorities to subsume God's gracious initiatives.

Far from being separate functions of the church's ministry and mission to the world, therefore, evangelism and theological reflection are quite interdependent. They are of course distinct, since evangelism is the pointed and relevant presentation of the gospel in its essentials. Theological reflection is out of place in the immediacy of such a communication, just as critical commentary by a musicologist is anomalous during the playing of a piece of music. Criticism and reflective response are necessary for authentic interpretation, but they should not interrupt the immediacy of a happening. At the same time, evangelism is always the tip of a theological iceberg, to use Wesley Ariarajah's vivid metaphor.[1] A wide range of ecclesiology, soteriology, eschatology, and pneumatology will inevitably extend deep below the surface of the communicated message, rendering theology *de facto* a substantial component of evangelistic outreach, and dialogue between the evangelist and the theologian of paramount importance.

The lack of such dialogue in the church invariably leads to a weighty missional error: engagement in theological controversy to the neglect and even the exclusion of authentic evangelistic outreach. This is not to deny the place of dispute in theological enquiry, something quite pivotal to the critical reflection it affords. But if it is not tempered by the realities of defining the gospel as a communicable message—the task which more than any other Christian activity provides the church with its distinctive identity in the world—then theology, lacking a proper accountability, becomes ecclesially introspective and intellectually self-indulgent. This in turn, with a harsh irony, permits the practice of an evangelism which, insensitive to the *missio Dei*, is theologically brittle rather than tensile. Strategy and method are substituted for the faithful traditioning of the *evangel*, and theologies which ought to be seriously questioned are adopted as little more than motivational techniques. The result is that whenever evangelism does become the subject of serious theological reflection, issues are all too often prejudged and attitudes entrenched.

The working group on evangelism sought to avoid this error by adopting praxis as the theological method of its deliberations. Because this required the discussions to be grounded in the realities of historical context, the subject matter could not be evangelism as a concept, nor yet as an ideal. It had to be *the evangelism that is currently being practiced in the church*. This perforce locked the group into an agenda which was not only comprehensive but polemical, and it was hardly surprising that the working papers evoked a number

155

of candid and forthright disagreements. Yet the discussions took place in an atmosphere of trust and collegiality, and always with a sure sense of evangelistic priorities in appropriate tension with the criteria of theological reflection.

This was due in no small part to the overall focus of the Institute on the Methodist theological traditions, which time and again took us back to Wesley himself—perhaps *the* exemplar for thoughtful and accountable evangelism. Even a cursory study of his ministry reveals that, while the touchstone of the Methodist contribution to the eighteenth-century revival was Wesley's driving concern to take the gospel the length and breadth of the land, this was never to the detriment of his concern for right doctrine. On the contrary, he honed his theological positions in the exigencies of the revival: in preaching the evangel to audiences which were hostile as often as they were receptive; in the plotting of a tortuous course though minefields of clerical opposition; and in the pastoral anguish of very mixed fortunes with his assistants and society leadership. Most remarkable about this doctrinal pilgrimage is that he did not markedly change his stance on what he regarded as the essentials of the faith. The passing years tempered his language and gave added depth to his perspective, but the gospel which he preached remained essentially the same—the offer of salvation through the merits of Christ's atonement and a summons to the obligations of a changed life-style in the power and grace of the Holy Spirit as a necessary consequence of accepting God's forgiveness and reconciliation.[2]

To insist on the necessity of obedient discipleship as an integral part of the evangel was the distinctive dimension of Wesley's evangelistic outreach and the principal reason for the efficacy of early Methodism as a spiritually reforming movement. The polity of societies, classes, and bands was the embodiment of this message no less than the expression of its founder's organizing genius, and could not have been forged as a disciplined structure had he and his preachers not proclaimed Christ in law as well as gospel:

It is our part thus to preach Christ, by preaching all things whatsoever He hath revealed. We may indeed, without blame, yea, and with a peculiar blessing from God, declare the love of our Lord Jesus Christ . . . but still we should not preach Christ according to His word, if we were wholly to confine ourselves to this; we are not ourselves clear before God, unless we proclaim Him in all His offices . . . not only as our great High Priest . . . but likewise as the Prophet of the Lord . . . who, by His Word and His Spirit, is with us always, 'guiding us into all truth'; yea, and as remaining a King for ever; as giving laws to all whom He has bought with His blood . . . until He hath utterly cast out all sin, and brought in everlasting righteousness.[3]

The implications of this are profound, for evangelism and theological reflection alike. As he took the gospel "into the highways and byways," Wesley found that the theological question with which Protestantism had wrestled since the Reformation—the question of faith and works—was altogether moot in the practical realities of discipleship.[4] The truth of the matter is that the great majority of Christians, whose chief occupation in life is not theological reflection, find faith and works quite indistinguishable. They perforce must live out their faith or lose it, and their instinctive understanding of this was the underlying strength of the weekly class meetings which, far from being intensive group experiences per se, were times of mutual accountability for faithful discipleship—the "sinews" of the societies.[5]

Yet Wesley remains largely unheard in this regard, and the issue continues to occasion divisions in the Western Protestant church, which Christians elsewhere in the world find difficult to understand and are increasingly unwilling to accept. The problem is the conceptual distinction between the inward faith of commitment to Christ and the outward works of discipleship. Because each is viewed as having its own integrity, albeit contingent upon the other, missional outreach becomes a two-fold activity: the proclamation of an evangel that offers salvation through faith in Christ and the working out of that salvation through social and personal obligations to the global community. Every attempt is made to stress that faith must result in costly discipleship, and that authentic discipleship must be rooted in grace. But as long as the one is viewed as the occasion or corollary of the other, there is a tendency for the distinction to become a polarization, and even a dichotomy. Personal faith and accountable discipleship are stretched to the limits of their semantic connotations, and dedicated Christians are importuned by the perceived need to make one or the other an evangelistic priority.

The pressing issue for evangelism is not the bridging of this dichotomy when it occurs, but the prior question of whether the conceptual distinction from which it proceeds is appropriate. Clearly the proclamation of the gospel is not all that the church does as it engages in God's mission to the world. Good works are as much a part of that mission as the announcement of God's salvation—indeed, as is everything else that the church is sent into the world to be and to do as a sign of Christ's new age. But to define evangelism as the proclamation of God's grace in Christ, and the works of discipleship as the corollary of that proclamation, albeit a necessary corollary, is to draw a false and unscriptural distinction. The call to an accountable discipleship of good works is as much a part of the evangel as the offer of forgiveness and reconciliation through faith in Christ, and acceptance of the atoning work of Christ is as necessary for true discipleship as the works of obedience for which grace empowers.[6]

The first priority of the evangelist, therefore, is to get the gospel message clear in its essentials in order to proclaim it in its fullness. Failure to do this in the contemporary church merely results in attempts to correct defective evangelism with more intensive discipleship—a perpetuation of the false dichotomy between word and deed. If, on the other hand, the properly scriptural distinction is made between evangelism and the task to which it calls, the gospel and Christian discipleship both retain their proper integrity: evangelism as the announcement of God's salvation in Christ *and* the call to an accountable discipleship in the world; discipleship as joyful obedience to the continuing gracious initiatives of the Holy Spirit *and* an acceptance of God's saving righteousness in Christ.

This was well argued in Plutarco Bonilla's working paper for the group, "The Content of the Evangelistic Message." Bonilla suggested that the Latin American Protestant evangelical churches, including those of Methodism, have been more concerned about winning people away from Roman Catholicism than converting them to the gospel of Jesus Christ. Their preaching of the gospel has thus centered on personal salvation, drawing on the Pauline epistles for a doctrine of the death and resurrection of Jesus in isolation from his life and teaching. Social concern has been confined to areas such as education and health, with little weight given to the scope of the kingdom announced by Jesus. When Paul is viewed in the light of the gospels, however, there is no dichotomy between the personal and social dimensions of the gospel. Faith in Christ means obedience to the One who is ultimately to reign over history, and discipleship consists of the exercise of love, justice, and peace which brings us into the reality of that new age. Just as sin is not an abstraction, but a concrete reality in history, so must the gospel be proclaimed as historical hope.[7]

Once it is perceived that the gospel proclaimed in its fullness calls to a discipleship that actively anticipates the true scope of God's new age, many of the theological concepts which govern the evangelistic outreach of the church emerge in a very different light. A good example of this was the discussion stimulated by Robert G. Tuttle's working paper on prevenient grace. Wesley emphasized prevenient grace, Tuttle argued, "so as to portray God as the principal character in the drama of rescue, while preserving the freedom of human response." It was the universal efficacy of grace that made valid the evangelistic ministry of early Methodism. And since people today, no less than in Wesley's time, are being drawn by the Spirit of God at work throughout the world, those of us in the church should evangelize not only with energy, but with expectancy.[8]

This proves to have significant social as well as individual implications. If the promise of the *evangel* is the new age of Jesus Christ—the fullness of *shalom*—then the Holy Spirit is at work, not only in personal lives, but in human communities, societies, nations, and international systems, drawing by prevenient grace to that *novum* which is promised for the world as well as for each human being. The evangelist must look for God's grace in the entire panorama of human history, discerning those evidences of God's love, power, and justice in historical moments that a sinful world cannot recognize. And once discerned, these workings of prevenient grace must be interpreted, announced, and affirmed. For they are not random manifestations of God's gracious activity. They are nothing less than the breaking in of Christ's new age, the signs of that which *is* to come, on earth as in heaven.

An equally stimulating session was initiated by Ronald Crandall's paper on the centrality of Christian experience in the Methodist tradition. Advocating a restoration of this emphasis to contemporary evangelism, Crandall argued that the "inward witness" of Wesley was the distinctive core of the evangelical tradition. Whatever its manifestations throughout the history of the church, the essential evangelistic message has always been the offer of a salvation which can be experienced—a knowledge of God in the power of the Holy Spirit, at once liberating, transforming, and empowering. The present pluralism of religious expressions notwithstanding, evangelists should continue to affirm this experience as the center of Christian faith, and the source of authentic discipleship.

The ensuing discussion made clear the extent to which the Christian tradition must now be viewed in a global context of interreligious dialogue.[9] While it was agreed that Christian experience is a necessary component of the evangelistic message, serious questions emerged about its holding a central emphasis in what is proclaimed. This was not to deny the significance of religious experience. On the contrary, the issue for evangelism proved to be the very commonality of such experience throughout the human family. Studies in comparative religion, as well as in adjunct disciplines such as social psychology and anthropology, have fostered a new openness among Christians to the spiritual reality behind all world religions, constituting a whole new area of evangelistic research.[10]

This presents the contemporary church with a task very similar to that of the early church as it sought to establish the particularity of its spiritual gifts in the midst of first-century religions. Then and now, the criteria for true Christian experience are two-fold: the fruits of God's righteousness in the life of the believer and the honoring of Christ as the end of true faith. Christian experience must evince faithfulness to the imperatives of Jesus' own life and work, and the gospel which offers the assurance of salvation in Christ must also issue a clear call to discipleship. Put differently, Christian experience as the inward witness of God's saving righteousness is authentic only to the extent that it is grounded in the historical reality of the prophet from Nazareth. The invitation to be a disciple of the risen Christ is a call to work for the new age to which the ministry of the Jewish carpenter has already given definitive shape.

This is not to imply that contextual reality displaces experience at the center of the evangel, for involvement in human history lacks the authenticity of Christian discipleship if it is divorced from the experiential power of the Holy Spirit. It is rather to affirm that the central core of the gospel is a dialectic: of inward assurance and outward commitment, of spiritual experience and worldly involvement, of self-awareness and historical vision. Grace and accountability alike must be proclaimed in their personal, social, and cosmic dimensions. It is a dialectic which Wesley came to understand at an early stage of his evangelistic ministry, and which he maintained by giving his message only one center—Jesus Christ: "In strictness, therefore, neither our faith nor works justify us; that is, deserve the remission of our sins. But God himself justifies us, of his own mercy, through the merits of his Son only . . . therefore in that respect we renounce, as it were, again, faith, works, and all other virtues."[11]

To make Christ "the flaming center" of the evangelistic message provides at once a freedom from contextual limitations, and freedom for authentic Christian experience.[12] This emerged with some cogency from three contextual studies presented to the group. The first, by Zablon Nthamburi, stressed the need in the African context for a gospel which speaks to the strong community consciousness of the continent. A message that propagates the individualism of Western Christianity, Nthamburi explained, renders the gospel incongruous to African

Christians. Indeed, the more the Christian faith is traditioned in the African context, the more it becomes clear that Western individualism is both cause and effect of an undue reliance on the printed word for the propagation of the gospel. In Africa, where there is a vital sense of human community, the oral tradition plays a much more significant role and to great evangelistic effect. Not only does Jesus Christ occupy center stage quite effortlessly when the story is told by word of mouth, but neglected dimensions of the tradition emerge with new force and clarity. The saints of the church, for example, assume their proper place in the faith of a people whose sense of ancestry is foundational to their culture.

The most important praxis question of Nthamburi's paper, however, was missional moratorium—an issue which the group found to be very much alive.[13] There was a strong feeling on the part of African participants that the mission and the health of their church had been threatened by too much receiving, and that only a self-propagating, self-governing, self-reliant church could become incarnate in its own culture. Emerging leadership and initiative had to come from the indigenous church and could not depend on a limitless supply of missionaries from other countries—not all of whom were willing to step aside when there was a clear opportunity to do so.[14] Non-Western members of the group were at pains to stress that this was not a rejection of Western cooperation in the task of reaching people with the gospel. But they insisted that the whole concept of "unreached peoples" required careful attitudinal examination.

It was at this point that the dialectic of contemporary world evangelism, so clearly articulated in plenary session by Wesley Ariarajah and Alan Walker, came most pointedly to the fore in the group's deliberations.[15] On the one hand, as Ariarajah eloquently demonstrated, the Christian must expect to meet the risen Lord already at work in the mission field. This is to do no more than affirm prevenient grace as the theological undergirding of evangelism, accepting that the human contribution to the task is not so much initiative as facilitation, for which the requisite gifts are sensitivity and empathy as well as enthusiasm. There will always be a degree of mutuality in the proclamation of the gospel, the evangelist receiving new dimensions of Christian insight from those with whom the gospel is shared quite simply because Christ is already in their midst. Evangelism cannot therefore be a church-centered activity—only Christ-centered. For the Christian is called "outside the gate" to engage in the *missio Dei*.[16]

On the other hand, as Alan Walker convincingly argued, if the gospel is indeed the good news of Jesus Christ, then evangelists are needed urgently, whatever contextual adjustments might be required to render their work effective. The missionary work of Paul is a constant reminder that the gospel carries its own authority, provided the messenger is sent in the power of the Holy Spirit. The proclamation by the early church of God's salvation in Christ was by definition a cross-cultural if not supra-cultural message, and the point of the Apostolic Conference between Paul and the Jerusalem leaders was not so much the issue of Jewish legal observances, but the fact that Paul, in taking the gospel to the gentiles, had found it received by faith *before* its implications were contextualized.[17] The evangelist who, like Paul, travels to foreign parts, must observe the particulars of contextualization. But in the final analysis, he or she will be heard, not through the technics of cultural communication, but as one whose message has the authority of divine revelation and eternal truth.

The commitment of the group to a praxis method of theological reflection brought this issue to a very particular imperative. The challenge of missional moratorium emerged, not as a suspension of evangelistic activity by Western churches—which must surely be censured as altogether contrary to the impulse of Christian tradition—but as a question of basic Christian collegiality. Of course there must be a deference to indigenous workers, where indeed they are at work. But the real test for evangelists throughout the world is whether they are willing, as a global task force, *to respect each other's work for what it is.*

The history of Christianity over the past three hundred years lays the onus for developing such a collegiality squarely on the evangelists of Western countries. As they evangelize at home, they must be willing to receive help from colleagues in the other parts of the world with the same graciousness they wish to be accorded when they go abroad. Alan Walker's words are prophetic: the Western world is now the most difficult mission field of all. Yet Western churches continue to view their mission through traditionalisms which blind them to the neopaganisms of their contexts, whether it be North American folk religion or European secularism. As the Holy Spirit moves throughout the world church, imparting new vision, power, and hope, Western Christians must learn to welcome the collegiality of their global sisters and brothers, who can assure them of the reality of God's coming new age and strengthen their resolve to witness to their faith. North American churches, for example, must increasingly receive missionaries from Latin America, whose biblical message will perhaps be disturbing, challenging their ecclesiocentricity and their culture-bound theology.[18] Christians in Europe must invite African and Indian colleagues, not merely to minister to immigrant peoples or gratuitously to confirm well-diagnosed racisms, but to preach in their churches and cathedrals, giving new expression to the tradition which for centuries was the lifeblood of their culture.

A pointed reminder of this need for renewal in Western Christianity was brought to the group by the second contextual case study, in which Kenneth Thompson compared John Wesley's mission in Ireland with the traditioning of the gospel by Irish Methodism. His conclusions were sobering. While Wesley ministered in Ireland as a strategist for church renewal, Irish Methodists over the years have allowed theological and political considerations to distort their witness into a narrow denominationalism. A very special type of evangelism is now required, which, avoiding triumphalism and defeatism alike, will liberate people from their tribal and political idolatries.

Thompson suggested that the answer lies in a secularization of the gospel, thereby providing a ferment of creative action that can lead to renewal and reform. The enculturation of the church in Ireland, as in much of the Western world, has led to an unacceptable measure of religious and ideological confusion. The essentials of the apostolic tradition have been subverted by racial fraction and cultural conflict, with the result that pastoral obligations have been consumed by the more immediate demands of ministering to people whose faith owes more to three hundred years of history than the living word of the gospel.[19] In such a context, nothing less will suffice than a radical quest for the gospel regardless of, or even in spite of, the church.

It is important in the light of this discussion to clarify a semantic confusion which, in the absence of serious dialogue between evangelists and theologians, causes much mischief. Secularization is not *secularism*, the rejection of traditional religious values altogether, but rather a critical examination in the light of the gospel of those values which the church has assimilated from its surrounding culture.[20] Just as an evangelist to another culture must be sensitive to the need for indigenous expressions of the gospel, so an evangelist in a Christianized culture must be sensitive to the need for a faithful expression of the gospel, especially if this requires a reorientation of ecclesial attitudes and structures. In short, the evangelist must be constantly discerning and defining the gospel for the church as well as the world—a task well modelled by Wesley.

The third case study by Norman Thomas returned the discussion to the African context. Drawing on Max Weber's concept of "elective affinity,"[21] Thomas examined Wesley's synthesis of personal piety and social witness in relation to the values of African culture as found in Zimbabwe. Citing political leaders such as Canaan Banana, Kenneth Kaunda, and Abel Muzorewa, he showed how any dualism between the spiritual and the physical was foreign to African culture which, like Hebrew thought, emphasized the unity of human personality and existence. In the words of Canaan Banana:

The need of facing this issue in dualistic terms is typically western. . . . If western theologians are unable to see that the spiritual message of the Gospel is contained in the historical temporal realities by which Jesus was surrounded, that is their problem, not ours. The poor of the world know very well what Jesus is saying. That is why they find in him the plenitude they are looking for. They will never accept any longer the disincarnate "spirituality" of western Christianity, "scornfully superior to all earthly realities."[22]

It was the embodiment of this unity in the early Methodist class meeting, Thomas suggested, which provided the affinity for its ready adoption in Zimbabwe, both in its original form, and through the women's societies known as *Manyanos* in South Africa, and *Ruwadzanos* or *Rukwadzanos* in Zimbabwe—"the fellowship." These groups now cut through traditional tribal patterns, and provide sociability, status, security, and approval, especially for migrant peoples. Their rules of practical piety, the role of their leaders, and their impact on society as a whole, are highly evocative of the eighteenth-century model. During the liberation struggles in Zimbabwe, for example, they formed an important link for churches wherever worship services had been banned or suspended due to the conflict, adopting as their symbol of unity the ritual of foot washing.

There were two responses to the paper which served to focus the work of the group in the closing days of the Institute. The first was to note the role of women in these African *ecclesiolae*. Evangelism, with very few exceptions, has been projected in the contemporary church as a predominantly male-oriented ministry, with strategies and concepts couched for the most part in language of initiative and even aggression. This was questioned by the two women in the group and brought to the fore in a short but pointed presentation by Lois Miller. If indeed the Spirit of God is the power of the evangel, should there not be a passive as well as an active mode of evangelism? Should there not be a more rigorous evaluation of evangelistic outreach, in which the gracious initiatives of the Holy Spirit are sought rather than assumed? Without discounting the urgency of taking the gospel to the world, should there not be a waiting for God as well as a seeking of lost souls? The caring, receiving, and mothering of the *Ruwadzanos* seemed to have as powerful an evangelistic outreach as any other model considered by the group, and it could well be that the next major contribution to the field of evangelism will be from women, providing not only a nurturing complement to the cutting edge of the message, but a complementary form of outreach and ingathering with its own evangelistic integrity.

The second response was a growing awareness of the significance for evangelism of the whole phenomenon of the *ecclesiolae,* rightly given a major emphasis in Alan Walker's plenary report. They were the subject of three working papers, each of which drew distinctive inferences from the early Wesleyan model of class meetings. The first, by George Hunter, was an innovative and detailed survey of early Methodist polity, correlated with contemporary strategies of church growth. Wesley's methods and models of evangelism, suggested Hunter, were selected on the basis of pragmatic discoveries, which were tested and verified according to three principles: (1) The choice of method is primarily pragmatic, but is guided by the Christian ethic; (2) If a method ought to work, but doesn't, reject it—even if you like it; (3) If a method is effective, use it to the maximum— even if you don't like it. Accordingly, Wesley adopted two principal strategies: an intentional and even disproportionate move towards receptive areas and peoples, and the multiplication of "cells" as a means of recruiting people through "ports of entry."

In discussion of the paper, it was questioned whether pragmatism, albeit ethically guided, is an appropriate principle for evangelistic outreach. Things can succeed for the wrong reason, and even though the *ecclesiolae* are once again to be found in the church worldwide, the fact of the matter is that they died out in American and British Methodism during the nineteenth century, when the denomination in its various branches experienced its most substantial growth. Yet Hunter's question was wholly apposite to the method of the group's deliberations: What *in practice* is being done in evangelism today, and how should we reflect on it? His argument was convincing—that Wesley acted as he reflected, and so must we. Most assuredly this is preferable to constant deliberation about what ought to be done in evangelism, with implementation a wholly optional exercise. More than once the metaphor was used of the ship at sea. Course corrections are possible if the vessel is under way. If it is becalmed, the matter of direction is always subject to hypothesis.

Stein Skjorshammer presented a working model of the class meeting in the United Methodist Church of Norway, a project funded directly by their Board of Global Ministries and implemented by First UMC, Bergen. The purpose is directly evangelistic, since only 14 percent of the Norwegian people consider themselves intentionally Christian and a mere 8 percent attend church. The plan has been to find leaders who after training will recruit from local neighborhoods for membership in house churches, and to date, more than forty persons have joined such groupings. The challenge of the work is proving a stimulation for further outreach, though the problems that emerge for church renewal in a neopagan society point chasteningly to the importance of always keeping the church in the larger view of God's eschatological horizon.

Howard Snyder brought some final reflections on *ecclesiolae* structures by drawing attention to their social function, both for their members and for society at large.[23] Their evangelistic dynamic, he suggested, was five-fold: the stabilizing of new converts; instruction and discipline; the imparting of a sense of mission; their openness and accessibility to the poor; and their vitality over a long period of time. In society at large, they provided the poor with an identity and a training in leadership for social change, affirming personal dignity, and often providing the education necessary to play such a role. If the contemporary church will look to the poor today, it will find that this is where God is still at work. It is not that the *ecclesiolae* provide the possibility of new structures for the church as *ecclesia*. They offer rather a whole new way of understanding its life and work in the world. And the touchstone for this is the faith of the poor. They are the ones who receive the gospel most readily, who respond most faithfully in committed discipleship, and to whom above all others belongs the new age.[24] Among them, therefore, is to be found the surest sign of that which is to come—the little church.

The authoritative word on this came from two members of the group whose direct participation was impeded by differences of language, but who, in the closing sessions, bore witness to *ecclesiolae* in their own countries. Rosangela Soares de Oliveira from Brazil shared her experience of the *comunidades de base*, and Harry Windisch from the German Democratic Republic described the development of house churches in areas where there are no church buildings or established parishes. The pattern was similar to the other forms of *ecclesiolae* studied by the group, but in these two instances the witness was poignant and powerful: a grass-roots working of the Holy Spirit with the presence and the promise of the new age. In this outworking of the evangel, the Methodist theological tradition was found to be alive and well—a sign that the church in our day is being called to discipleship, perhaps as never before, with the commission to announce the coming on earth as in heaven of that for which the followers of Messiah Jesus have prayed ever since he taught them the words.

Notes

1. See above, p. 138. The assignments for the evangelism group, as with all of the working groups at the Institute, were three-fold: a plenary thematic statement, presented by the co-convenor of the group; a plenary report, based on the deliberations of the group; and a series of working papers, which provided the subject matter for group discussions. The plenary statement by S. Wesley Ariarajah and the plenary report drafted and delivered by Alan Walker comprise the two preceding papers. Working papers were presented as follows: Plutarco Bonilla A., "The Content of the Gospel as found in Wesley's Sermons, viewed from a Latin American Perspective"; Robert G. Tuttle, Jr., "Prevenient Grace: The Divine Initiative in the Drama of Rescue"; David Lowes Watson, "Christ Our Righteousness: Grace and Accountability in Wesley's Message"; Ronald King Crandall, "The Centrality of Christian Experience in the Methodist Heritage"; Zablon John Nthamburi, "Crisis in Mission: Contextualization and Enculturation of the Gospel"; Norman E. Thomas, "Personal Piety and Social Witness: A Case Study in Zimbabwe"; Kenneth H. Thompson, "Wesley's Mission in Ireland"; George G. Hunter III, "Wesley's Strategies for Christian Expansion"; Stein Skjorshammer, "The Wesleyan Class System in Parish Development Today"; Howard A. Snyder, "The Evangelistic Relevance of *Ecclesiola* Structures in Early Methodism and Moravianism"; and Alan Walker, "Wesleyan Evangelism Today."

2. See, for example, "The Principles of a Methodist" (1740), in *The Works of John Wesley*, 14 vols. (London: Wesleyan-Methodist Book-Room, 1872; reprint, Grand Rapids: Baker Book House, 1979), 8:359-74. This short polemical essay has all of the essential components of Wesley's mature work of the 1760s and 1770s.

3. John Wesley, *The Standard Sermons*, ed. Edward H. Sugden, 2 vols. (London: Epworth Press, 1921), 2:76-7. Cf. *Minutes of the Methodist Conferences, from The First Held in London by the Late Reverend John Wesley, A.M., in the Year 1744.* Volume 1 (London: Conference Office, 1812), p. 20.

4. *Minutes*, p. 10; Wesley, *Works*, 8:300.

5. *The Letters of the Reverend John Wesley, A.M.*, ed. John Telford. Standard ed., 8 vols. (London: Epworth Press, 1931), 4:194.

6. There is no better exposition of the scriptural texts in this regard than the third chapter, "The Evangel," in Michael Green, *Evangelism in the Early Church* (Grand Rapids: William B. Eerdmans, 1970), pp. 48-77.

7. Bonilla emphasized this point with regard to Wesley in particular: "It is necessary to make a re-elaboration of Wesley's thinking about sanctification and its historical implications. But this re-elaboration should take as its starting-point not mainly Wesley's sermons and theological writings, but his pastoral and caring ministry, his actions as an actual missionary to the poor and disinherited of his times. This is to say that we should read Wesley 'backwards' from his praxis."

8. Tuttle's paper was notable for some striking metaphors: "People want faith. They want to belong to something that is important, even costly! Believe it or not, they want to become disciples. God's prevenient grace is at work everywhere and in everyone. Let's get our shirts off and start flagging down traffic because the bridges are out all over the world."

9. A theme well explored in Gerald H. Anderson and Thomas F. Stransky, ed., *Christ's Lordship and Religious Pluralism* (Maryknoll, N.Y.: Orbis Books, 1981). Cf. Richard W. Rousseau, ed., *Interreligious Dialogue* (Scranton, Pa.: Ridge Row Press, 1981).

10. See, for example, Gerald H. Anderson and Thomas F. Stransky, ed., *Mission Trends No. 5: Faith Meets Faith* (Grand Rapids: William B. Eerdmans; New York: Paulist Press, 1981).

11. Wesley, *Works*, 8:362.

12. So K. E. Skydsgaard, "The Flaming Center, or The Core of Tradition," in *Our Common History as Christians: Essays in Honor of Albert C. Outler*, ed. John Deschner, Leroy T. Howe, and Klaus Penzel (New York: Oxford University Press, 1975), pp. 3-22. Cf. Carl E. Braaten, *The Flaming Center: A Theology of the Christian Mission* (Philadelphia: Fortress Press, 1977).

13. For an informative account and stimulating discussion of the "moratorium" proposal, see P. A. Kalilombe, "Self-Reliance of the African Church: A Catholic Perspective," in *African Theology En Route*, ed. Kofi Appiah-Kubi and Sergio Torres (Maryknoll, N.Y.: Orbis Books, 1979), pp. 36-58.

14. The graduate research of one of the group members, Leslie Shyllon of Sierra Leone, has revealed a number of instances where indigent African churches have not been permitted to fulfil their potential for precisely this reason.

15. In addition to providing a rich dialectic for discussion, it can be noted that the two papers afford the necessary tension of praxis—the reflection of Ariarajah's thoughtful argument and the direct evangelism of Walker's statement. The one explores several facets of the theme in depth; the other takes a wealth of data and hones it into a forthright challenge.

16. So Orlando E. Costas, *Christ Outside the Gate: Mission Beyond Christendom* (Maryknoll, N.Y.: Orbis Books, 1982).

17. Acts 15:1-35; Galatians 2:1-21.

18. Costas, *Outside the Gate,* pp. 174ff.

19. Thompson gave a simple example to illustrate his point: "Recently a group of Protestant churchmen, convinced that what Northern Ireland needs is spiritual revival, have been pressing the American evangelist, Dr. Billy Graham, to conduct a campaign in the province. Dr. Graham, who has become more ecumenical in recent years, has stated that one of his conditions for coming would be that both Catholic and Protestant churches should work together in preparation. It has been found impossible to agree to this, either out of conviction or for fear of the kind of backlash from the reactionary sections of the churches noted above; so there the matter rests."

20. A good discussion of these semantic and conceptual factors remains the fourth volume of the Geneva Documents, *Man in Community,* ed. Egbert de Vries (New York: Association Press, 1966). See especially pp. 293-382.

21. Whereby ideas, including religious ideas, enter into the processes of social action and change by gaining affinity with the interests of certain social groups. See *From Max Weber: Essays in Sociology,* trans. H. H. Gerth and C. Wright Mills (New York: Oxford University Press, 1946), pp. 62-63.

22. *Your Kingdom Come: Mission Perspectives.* Report on the World Conference on Mission and Evangelism, Melbourne, Australia, May 12-25, 1980 (Geneva: World Council of Churches, 1980), pp. 109-10.

23. Snyder's argument is given full treatment in his book, *The Radical Wesley and Patterns for Church Renewal* (Downers Grove, Ill.: InterVarsity Press, 1980), which received many appreciative comments during the Institute.

24. See Elsa Tamez, *Bible of the Oppressed* (Maryknoll, N.Y.: Orbis Books, 1982), p. 74.

6

John Wesley's Development in Faith

James W. Fowler

To address the issue of spirituality and faith development in the Wesleyan tradition means to begin with the life and pilgrimage in faith of John Wesley. For no other major reformer or founder has so endeavored to make of his life an open book. None other that I know has so extensively made public what Gandhi (whom Wesley in some significant ways resembles) would have called "his experiments with truth." Indeed, Wesley's preaching, teaching, and spiritual direction arose out of his own struggles for and within faith. The distinctive emphasis and contours of the Methodist approach to faith and growth in grace have their origins directly in Wesley's own fiducial and vocational walk with God. My contribution, therefore, consists in a brief review and analysis of Wesley's pilgrimage of faith. Aided by the research and theory in faith development, which I and my associates have pursued over the last ten years, I shall try to identify some of the decisive turnings and transformations in Wesley's pilgrimage.[1]

I

In our research on faith development we are learning to pay special attention to earliest infancy, a time for the formation of what we call *Primal* faith. It is in this time—and, indeed perhaps before, *in utero*—that the neonate forms its first pre-images of the character of life in this world. Birth brings both the trauma and the release of entry into our first physical and social environment. Pre-potentiated for recruiting care and tenderness, at birth we begin our first formative experiences of mutuality and intimacy with those powerful adults who welcome and care for us. Rapid cognitive and physical developments in the first year of life require our dealing with a succession of differentiations and separations. We learn that objects and persons are separate from us; we awaken to deep anxieties and fears of abandonment and loss. Faith has its origins in the trust evoked and confirmed by *their* faithfulness in caring for us. A first sense of self is awakened under the benign gaze and in response to the encouraging voices, of those who give us primary care. The material of which we will construct our first representations of God is taken from our experiences of maternal and paternal presence and care. Primal faith involves some mixture of deepgoing trust and hope, with inevitable distrust and tendencies toward the rudimentary ego's defensive centering of the world in itself.

John Wesley was conceived in the midst of a time of reconciliation between his strong-willed parents. Children of dissenting families, both Samuel and Susanna Wesley had early made principled decisions to reunite with the Church of England. In 1701 they had quarreled over Susanna's refusal to pray for the King (William of Orange), whom she considered to be a pretender. Samuel Wesley, who had reason to be in London to attend Convocation, left home in anger and did not return to his own house until after March 8 of the following year (1702) after King William died. When Samuel returned he intended to stay only long enough to pack more of his things. Some of his parishioners set fire to the rectory while he was there, however, and the resulting crisis led to a tenuous reconciliation between the parents. Nine months later, June 17, 1703, John Wesley was born. John's birth position—fourteen years younger than his only living brother, and youngest brother to seven sisters, plus his coming after the death of an infant brother, Benjamin—gave him a very significant, special place in the family system. (Charles Wesley would not be born until 1707.)[2]

Much has been written about the remarkable Wesley household. By one year of age, Susanna wrote that the children "were taught to fear the rod and to cry softly, by which means they escaped abundance of correction which they might otherwise have had. . . ."[3] For Susanna, obedience was the fundamental foundation and goal of child development:

In order to form the minds of the children, the first thing to be done is to conquer their will, and bring them to an obedient temper. To inform the understanding is a work of time; and must with children proceed by slow degrees, as they are able to bear it: but the subjecting the will is a thing which must be done at once, and the sooner the better; for by neglecting timely correction, they will contract a stubbornness and obstinacy which are hardly ever conquered. When a child is corrected it must be conquered. . . . I insist upon conquering the will of children betimes, because this is the only strong and rational foundation of a religious education.[4]

We can be certain that John Wesley, who throughout his life would be centrally concerned with doing the will of God, responded compliantly to Susanna's firm efforts to instantiate obedience and self-control. Modern sensibilities may reject the suppression of spontaneity and willfulness implied in Susanna's approach. But we should note that her firmness, clarity, and even-handed consistency in dealing with her children did create for them a sense of order and meaning in what could have been a chaotic household. (When John was two, Samuel was imprisoned for some four months because of inability to pay his debts.)

In addition to conquering their wills, Susanna Wesley early taught her children to pray. Her own seriousness about this and daily family devotionals at dinner provided for tangible and powerful actualization of the reality of God.

In early childhood—roughly ages two to seven—children enter upon a way of being in faith that we call the *Intuitive-Projective* stage. Language is now available, stimulating and evoking imagination. Lacking cognitive operations that allow us to grasp cause and effect relations or to reverse and test our perceptions and conclusions, we find our dreams and fantasies to be as real as everyday experiences. Religiously we respond to story and ritual; we are terrified of images of the supernatural and of evil. We experience ourselves as separate from others, but we do not differentiate their experience or points of view from our own. Dreams and illusions of our omnipotence struggle with terrors of helplessness and weakness. While we dream of being big and powerful, we have nightmare anxieties about the possible deaths of those we love and depend upon. Conscience is taking form and we internalize the judgments and expectations of parental figures far more harshly than they intend. We can form powerful and long-lasting images of God and God's expectations—harsh or benign—during this stage.

Taught by his mother and older siblings, John Wesley received many gifts to his imagination for the awakening of conscience and faith. Robert Moore in his book *John Wesley and Authority* contrasts Wesley's experiences with those of Susanna and Samuel during this period. Susanna's orderly, methodical, and rational approach to childraising bore fruit in John Wesley's approach to authority as an adult. Her by-laws, that a child would not be beaten if he confessed his transgression and promised to amend, were stern but just. Samuel, on the other hand, was mercurial, unpredictable, unorganized. His explosive temper and impetuous judgment, Moore suggests, evoked in the Wesley children elements of both *mysterium tremendum* and *mysterium fascinans*. Samuel was reported to have said that young John was so committed to arguing his position that he "would not attend to the most pressing necessities of nature unless he could give a reason for it."[5] This remark discloses something of Samuel's character, even as it suggests a measure of oedipal impatience with this youngster who began to claim so special a place in his mother's and sisters' attentions.

In John's fifth year a much reported event must have made a particularly powerful impression on this precociously serious lad. The Epworth rectory again caught fire. So rapid was the fire's spread that father, mother (who was ill), and children had to scramble out doors and windows to safety. When the panicked family assembled in the garden, five-year-old John was not present. When his futile attempts to enter the holocaust failed, Samuel Wesley knelt down and commended to God the soul of his little son. Meanwhile John, who had been awakened by the flames and the noise, appeared in a window. By way of a human ladder he was pulled from his second-story room even as the flaming thatched roof crashed down onto the house. Susanna Wesley saw John's rescue as evidence of providential intervention. She referred to him—as he often would refer to himself in the future—as a "brand plucked from the burning." Susanna resolved to be "more particularly careful of the soul of this child, which God had so mercifully provided for."[6]

Between ages six and eight we find a significant transition occurring in the way a child composes and maintains meaning. The emergent new stage we call *Mythic-Literal* faith. For most of us, operations of thought and reasoning begin to take form at this time, which allow us to "stop the world." We begin to form stable categories of thought by which to understand cause and effect relations. We can reverse the operations of our reasoning, testing its adequacy. Thought is no longer so dominated by feeling and perception. More consistently we differentiate our own experiences, wishes, and interests from those of others. The world becomes a more predictable and lawful place. We sort out the real from the make-believe, and we impute to God (now understood more anthropomorphically) the same commitment to fairness and reciprocal justice that seems so "natural" to us. In this stage our meanings are grasped and conserved in stories: stories we hear, stories we tell. Not yet theologians or philosophers who form abstract concepts about our stories, as school-aged children, our meanings inhere in the narratives we hear and tell. In this stage—in fairly literal and one-dimensional understandings—we are drawn to the stories of our people: to know and thrill to their stories is to belong.

We know that after the rectory fire the Wesley children were dispersed to the homes of friends and parishioners. Following the several months it took to rebuild the rectory, Susanna reassembled the family, noting that their stays with strange families and their servants had set back much of the careful work she had invested in the formation of her brood. School, which met for six hours a day, was re-commenced under Susanna's demanding leadership. When the children reached six they were taught the alphabet in one day. Soon after that they were put to reading from Genesis. Not only did they *hear* the stories of their people: they were able to read and reread them for themselves. In addition, Susanna set aside one hour a week to spend, usually in the time after dinner, with each child alone. During this time of what Wesley would eventually call "close conversation," this remarkable mother took time to enter each of her children's worlds—and to give them access to hers. Until he was well past thirty John would write her asking her judgment about a doctrinal issue or a matter of ecclesial policy. And with sympathetic care she would respond, showing balance and judgment, orthodox passion, and impressive logical lucidity. Susanna took special pride in teaching her daughters to read and think before teaching them to sew. Hetty, and perhaps some of the other girls—as well as the boys—learned some Greek and Hebrew from their father, as well as receiving exposure to classical and Christian poesy.

From the richness and orderly care of this schoolhouse for faith John Wesley went, at age ten-and-a-half, to London to the Charterhouse school for boys. There, in an institution that combined a retirement home for men with a preparatory school for boys—both under religious auspices—Wesley augmented his considerable skills in language and received a first-rate preparation for Oxford. Dr. John King, headmaster to the school during most of Wesley's seven years there, always carried with him a copy of Thomas à Kempis's *The Imitation of Christ*. This may help account for the later significance of this book in Wesley's young adulthood. The schoolmaster, Dr. Thomas Walker, had the reputation of a man with an excellent knowledge of the ancient languages. He had a high regard for Wesley, and it is said that Wesley "acquired great facility in the composition of Latin verse, while he learned Hebrew with unusual rapidity."[7]

The Charterhouse period is not very fully documented in the biographical studies of John Wesley. It spans the time in Wesley's youth when we have learned to expect another period of transition and regrounding in the life of faith. Between the ages of eleven and thirteen, typically, new modes of thought and reflection emerge, which both make possible and require a reorganization of beliefs, emotions, and awareness of self. Neither adolescence nor childhood were thought of in the eighteenth century as the distinctive developmental periods we hold them to be in the twentieth. Except for those gifted and privileged youth who went on to "public" school and university, those we call teenagers in the eighteenth century entered into jobs or apprenticeships in their teen years, and before many years would be married and starting families. For those in Wesley's position, however, the rigorous leisure of studies gave space and provocation for the kind of revolution in mental operations we see occurring in adolescents today. Such a revolution begins with learning to think about our thinking. It involves the capacity to reflect upon the previous era's stories, to compare, contrast, and sift out meanings. It means the ability to formulate propositional statements, employ abstract ideas, to grasp and communicate the thrust or truth of a narrative or situation.

In interpersonal relations this emerging stage brings new capacities for self-awareness. Previously we could differentiate our perspectives from those of others, making cooperation and bargaining possible. But in this new era we form the ability to do a new and fateful kind of construction: we now begin to construct the perspectives which trusted others have toward ourselves. We begin to see ourselves as others see us. And more, we begin to know and allow for the fact that they see us seeing them. Writing about this period in his own adolescent development Augustine said, "And I became a problem to myself." Erik Erikson has captured the struggle of young persons in integrating the images of self they get from others with their own feelings of self with the phrase, "identity crisis."

Identity crisis, for a youth reared like John Wesley, would also be a crisis of religious belief and practice. Such evidence as we have suggests that Wesley experienced considerable continuity in his religious belief and practice at Charterhouse with what he learned at home.

Writing immediately after Aldersgate, Wesley said of this period at Charterhouse:

The next six or seven years were spent at school; where, outward restraints being removed, I was much more negligent than before, even of outward duties, and almost continually guilty of outward sins, which I knew to be such, though they were not scandalous in the eyes of the world. However, I still read the Scriptures, and said my prayers, morning and evening. And what I now hoped to be saved by was 1. Not being so bad as other people. 2. Having still a kindness for religion. And, 3. Reading the Bible, going to church, and saying my prayers.[8]

Although he accuses himself of leniency, the image of a fifteen-year-old boy praying twice a day, reading the Scriptures, and attending communion at every opportunity, suggests that Susanna had little to worry about regarding this special boy.

The quote from Wesley's *Journal* suggests that during the latter part of his Charterhouse period he made a transition to what we call the *Synthetic-Conventional* stage of faith. *Synthetic* here means a drawing together of the images of self into a first sense of identity. It means drawing together in a tacit, but real integration, the beliefs, values, and attitudes that support a sense of identity. *Conventional* in this stage means that the youth's integration of self-images and beliefs into a first synthesis involves drawing upon ideological contents available in the contexts of interpersonal relationships that have most importance for us.

At age seventeen John Wesley carried his Synthetic-Conventional identity and faith to Oxford where he became a member of Christ Church college.

II

Charterhouse school had been for Wesley a home away from home. Now with this entry into Oxford he, in a sense, leaves home—at least physically and intellectually. Leaving home emotionally and spiritually, for a boy like Wesley, would be a much more protracted, difficult, and dangerous journey.

During his five years at Christ Church, Wesley widened his world of experience and knowledge. He read in history and literature, philosophy and religion. In addition he allowed himself time to read and attend plays, to converse in pubs, and to participate modestly in tennis and rowing. Walking in the fields around Oxford was a favorite activity. Evidently he preserved both the forms and the feelings of his religious life, but not with the intensity which his graduation and decision to enter holy orders would soon bring. Reviewing his life under the impact of Aldersgate, Wesley wrote of this period:

When I was about twenty-two, my father pressed me to enter into holy orders. At the same time, the providence of God directing me to Kempis's "Christian Pattern," I began to see, that true religion was seated in the heart, and that God's law extended to all our thoughts as well as words and actions. I was, however, very angry at Kempis, for being too strict; though I read him only in Dean Stanhope's translation. [Wesley would eventually make his own translation for his preachers.] Yet I had frequently much sensible comfort in reading him, such as I was an utter stranger to before: And meeting likewise with a religious friend, which I never had till now, I began to alter the whole form of my conversation, and to set in earnest upon a new life. I set apart an hour or two a day for religious retirement. I communicated every week. I watched against all sin, whether in word or deed. I began to aim at, and pray for, inward holiness. So that now, "doing so much, and living so good a life," I doubted not but I was a good Christian.[9]

The "religious friend" Wesley refers to in this passage is likely Sally Kirkham, a sister of a college friend of Wesley's. His correspondence with "Varanese"—his nickname for her—indicates that in his relations with her sentiments of piety were intermixed powerfully with affections of another kind. As she was already engaged to another, and as Wesley was moving toward a post as Tutor in Lincoln College, which required that he remain unmarried, the issue of deeper romantic intimacy was, for the time, avoided. She played a crucial role in his early adulthood, nonetheless, apparently introducing him not only to Kempis, but to Jeremy Taylor's books on *The Rule and Exercises of Holy Living* and *The Rule and Exercises of Holy Dying*. The circle of friends around the Kirkham family included a young, vivacious widow, a bit Wesley's senior, named Mrs. Pendarves. With her, also, Wesley maintained a relationship and correspondence in which lively seriousness about religious life provided a medium for the sharing of lightly veiled romantic emotions.

With the deepened and focused attention to religious life that emerged in Wesley in 1725 (age twenty-two), many writers have urged that we see this period as the time of Wesley's conversion. Faith development theory offers a somewhat different and necessarily more complex perspective on this young adult time of transition.

Leaving home, in all of the senses I mentioned earlier, can precipitate for us the beginnings of one of the most consequential transitions in the course of faith development—the transition from a Synthetic-Conventional stage to the way of knowing and committing we call *Individuative-Reflective* faith. (A significant number of adults do not make this transition. For others it comes later—in their thirties, forties, or fifties. Even when it occurs in the twenties, as I shall argue that it did for Wesley, it is at best a protracted and difficult passage.)

Essentially what happens in the transition to the Individuative-Reflective stage is a double movement. In one of these movements our previous tacitly held worldview of the Synthetic-Conventional era comes to be an object for our reflection and decision. Our tacit beliefs, values, and assumptions must now be made explicit; as such they will require our making choices and entering upon a new quality of self-aware commitment. In the other movement of this transition we come to terms with issues of authority in our lives. We begin to form and trust what I call an "executive ego." This means a capacity for self-responsibility, a responsible freedom to commit our lives—in faith, in work or career (vocation), and in intimacy and love.

The intensification of religious involvement and commitment we see emerging in Wesley in 1725 seems to me to hallmark the beginnings of his transition into the way of knowing and committing that is the Individuative-Reflective stage. During this year he engages in his first theological dispute (over the stringency of Kempis's ideal of the imitation of Christ). He begins to correspond with his parents, as well as his peers, about issues of Christian doctrine and Christian praxis. Though admittedly at the urging of his father, he is moving toward ordination and the tangible shaping of a vocation. And he is beginning his struggles with risking himself in intimacy—in the intimacy of "close conversations" about spiritual matters, and in the (more difficult for him) intimacy of the closeness of bodies in love.

In view of what we know is coming in the next fourteen years of Wesley's life, and in view of that dramatic year, 1738, which assumes such pivotal significance in both Wesley's life and the Methodist movement, I must ask you to probe more deeply with me into some peculiar features of Wesley's transition toward Individuative-Reflective faith. In this probing I will magnify a bit some of the features of Wesley's personality through lenses provided by psychoanalytic ego psychology. Though I will reach conclusions somewhat at variance with his own, I must acknowledge my indebtedness to the penetrating work of Robert L. Moore in *John Wesley and Authority*.

Moore refers to an insight of V. H. H. Green in his *The Young Mr. Wesley*. Green, he says, "has noted that the dominance of Susanna led to an intense dependency upon her in all of the Wesley children, and that though "in some respects the brothers were less tied, more especially Samuel as the eldest . . . even in *their* (the brothers') development the powerful, loving, counselling and warning figure of Susanna Wesley was never far away."[10] With documentation Moore supplies, and on the basis of patterns we will see in Wesley's life from ages twenty-two to thirty-five, I think we are in a position to grasp some of the unique dynamics of Wesley's growth. These features, in turn, will make their distinctive contribution to later Wesleyan spirituality.

Specifically, I think we have to entertain the likelihood that Wesley brought to his transition into young adulthood a personality dominantly organized along patterns shaped by his superego. This means, oversimply put, that in his experiences of early nurture—the expectations, standards, and ideals of his parents assumed an overbalancing power in the shaping of Jacky Wesley's motivations and desires. His own will, wishes, and purposes could scarcely be formed or acknowledged by himself, let alone others. Consciously, he claimed the parental aspirations for him as his own, including the powerful religious dimensions and groundings of those ideals. My assumption, based on clinical data, is that

Wesley's deeper feelings of infantile anger, raw selfishness, lust, or murderous intent, were so powerfully repressed by his precocious conscious that they rarely showed themselves in his attitude or behavior. John Wesley was, and became a *very* good boy.

Through Charterhouse school and his undergraduate years at Oxford the organization of his growing personality along superego lines would account for a certain seriousness of purpose, a feeling of special responsibility and occasionally of special privilege. Apart from a vague sense of not fully being "one of the boys" (or as Wesley put it, "Not being so bad as other people"), it is unlikely that Wesley ever felt or experienced much inner or outer conflict.

Entering young adulthood, however, with his feeling the twin issues of making considerable choices about his beliefs and values, and his risking the self in vocational and romantic commitment, the superego domination of his personality felt threatened with a painful split. Intellectually, Wesley's able mind and penetrating curiosity served him well in the transition toward an Individuative-Reflective style of faith. His difficulty would come in regard to the emergence of an executive ego.

In a personality organized or directed out of the superego, there is a sense in which we are not our own persons. Our goals and values serve as the internalized aspirations and standards of parent or parent-like persons. Our initiatives and purposes are likely to be the results of the expectations and hopes of respected authorities. In a religious person, sharply attuned to doing the will of God, the superego-organized personality experiences great difficulty when God seems to sanction two mutually exclusive options equally. The ego in such persons had little leeway in early childhood to develop its own autonomy and initiative. The ego early identified with the parental program, avoiding most rebellion, and put its energies and drives in the service of their visions and aspirations.

Wesley's life from age twenty-two to his return from Georgia at age thirty-five presents us with a study in the early adulthood of a strongly religious, superego-dominated personality. On the one hand, there is much about Wesley's strenuous efforts to be a worthy Christian in those years that is admirable and heroic. On the other, there is a great deal that is filled with pathos, pain, and even low comedy. Wesley, returning from Georgia, characterized his time in the new world as "beating the air." There is a sense in which this phrase seems apt for describing the overt fruits of most of his ministry and labor in his young adulthood. Most of the images of Wesley as fastidious, priggish, naive, and rigid come from this period. Psychologically, Wesley was doing his utmost to give himself to God, when in fact he had never taken possession of himself. Little wonder that there was not inner freedom to give himself to another in love or marriage.

The personality pattern I have been describing means that as Wesley increasingly confronted situations requiring adult choices and commitments, he would intensify his efforts to be a "right" person. Increased self-watchfulness and scrupulosity and ever-renewed commitment to images of perfection would be required to deal with the ambiguities he encountered. Likely, he experienced oscillations between times of inflation, when he felt that his being congrued with his ideals, and times of abject deflation, when he felt that the gap between what he was and what he ought to be, was a yawning canyon. For most such persons there is a largely unconscious but pervasive feeling of unsoundness or lack of integrity—a vague sense that their lives have a sham quality or that they operate behind a facade. Erik Erikson, writing of this pattern, says, "It is as though the culture forces a man to over-advertise himself. While all along he knows that his mother really never believed it." It is not surprising that Wesley, confronted in Savannah by a Spangenberg, should feel such dis-ease at the Moravian's probing questions as to whether Wesley knew Christ as *his* savior and Lord.

We can surmise, further, that the superego-dominated young adult is likely to be carrying a considerable fund of unconscious anger. Much of this will be turned upon the self in times of self-criticism and depression, and in the maintenance of continual scrupulosity. Some of the anger may be directed at "safe" objects, displacing it from those most responsible for the contents of the superego. Wesley's anger at Kempis in 1725 may have something of this character. His hostile break with William Law, about the time of the Adlersgate release, seems to me to have that quality of overdetermination about it, which suggests that it was fueled by anger Wesley felt toward others. My supposition is that Law symbolized Susanna and Samuel for John, and that the unconscious transferring of his wrath to Law was internally permissible in ways that overt anger toward the parents was not. In one incident in 1726 John confronted Samuel Wesley over his brutal and utterly insensitive treatment of Wesley's sister, Hetty. He confronted his father, however, only from the safety of the pulpit, and was later surprised that his father responded to his attack and reproof in kind. Upon feeling the force of his father's objection Wesley crumbled, doing penance by transcribing his father's voluminous manuscript on Job for the rest of the summer.

Certainly a critical step toward release from the domination of his superego and the emergence of his own executive ego came when John declined to accept the living at Epworth and Wroot. Over a period of two years, from 1733-35 Wesley resisted his father's pressures. In doing so he also withstood the argument that by replacing his father he could assure the continuity of a home for his mother and sisters.

Resistance to parental wishes in the Epworth matter, however, may have played a significant role in Wesley's decision to go to Georgia. There are reasons to suppose that Wesley felt considerable guilt over turning his father down (or, more properly, over having avoided a final decision for so long that by the time he accepted it, the post had already gone to another). At a deeper level, he likely felt both guilt and grief that in not returning to Epworth he tacitly passed judgment on the quality of his father's career-long ministry there. From his own writings it is also evident that the Georgia mission promised relief from Wesley's deep ambivalence regarding relations with women. His long correspondence with Mrs. Pendarves had just ended with his feeling futile and rejected. It appears that in his images of Georgia, he saw it as a land without women of his own race.

A kind of final breakdown—or breakthrough—from the dominating superego came with Wesley's failure and disgrace in Georgia. To be crude about it, we could say that in the Georgia experience Wesley developed a "superego leak." The self-deception (or better, lack of self-knowledge) from which Wesley to this point had unknowingly suffered, was punctured in the events surrounding his abortive romance and failed mission to the Indians. The strategy of self-perfection and disciplined self-relinquishment to the will of God had proven disastrous. Pardoxically, it is on the return ship to England as Wesley begins to face his disillusioning situation, that his ego begins to have some room to take responsibility for his life. It is further paradoxical that only with the breakdown of his scrupulous, overaccusing, and controlling superego, could Wesley really see himself as a finite-sinner, in deep need of the grace of God. Georgia, for all its pain, was John Wesley's point of entry into a sense of real identification with the human race. It was to become a gateway to grace.

III

The profound experiential appropriation of the doctrine of justification by grace through faith freed Wesley to complete his protracted transition to the Individuative-Reflective stage of faith. The reality of justification by grace through faith gave him the leeway to begin exercising an executive ego. Not having to ground himself by his holiness began to give him the abandonment to *be* a self. A felt knowledge of the love that God had for him, John Wesley empowered him to love himself. The experience of being grounded in the love of God in Christ released him from the self-coercive love of neighbor under the domination of duty. He began to know in his gut that we love because God first loves us.

The transformation, however, was not sudden—the mere twinkling of an eye. From February to June of 1738, Böhler worked with the Wesley brothers, patiently, resourcefully, inspiredly, meeting them with scripture, doctrine, and affection-arousing prayer. One of the most moving moments in this spring of growth and struggle is reported in the journal of Peter Böhler for May 4, 1738. Böhler had brought three Moravians who related to Wesley how the onset of saving faith for them had been sudden. Wesley had been objecting to this possibility. I quote now from the summary of Böhler's journal entry by Martin Schmidt:

At first "Wesley and the others who were with him" were "as though struck dumb at these narratives." Nevertheless he still held out. He said that four examples—obviously including Böhler's own account with the others—were not sufficient to convince him as yet. Straightway Böhler offered to bring eight more in London. After a short time Wesley stood up and proposed that they should sing Christian Frederick Richter's hymn, *My Soul before Thee prostrate lies.* It was one of the hymns he had translated in Georgia. During the singing he repeatedly wiped his eyes. Then he took Böhler into his bedroom with him alone and said he was now convinced of what he had said about faith and that he would not raise any further points. He saw indeed that he did not possess this faith, which he had to recognize as the genuine kind. "But how could he now help himself and how should he attain to such faith?" He said that he was a man who had not sinned so grossly as other people. Böhler answered, just like Zinzendorf and Luther, that he had sinned enough in not believing in the Saviour. He ought not to go away from the door of the Saviour until he had helped him. Wesley then asked Böhler to pray with him. . . . Wesley assured [Böhler] that if he gained a true and complete relationship with the Saviour he would then preach only about faith.[11]

In the weeks and months after Aldersgate Wesley *did* preach only about faith. Some of the same anger he heaped upon Law he dumped on Anglican congregations to whom he proclaimed the message of grace. In the completion of his transition to the Individuative-Reflective stage Wesley exhibited a pattern typical for its early phases. He tended to see things in terms of sharp dichotomies. The espousal of grace meant the total rejection of anything that smacked of an effort to secure one's salvation by works. Wesley's brittle testimony, with its delivery fueled by outrage at the growing recognition of the extent of his previous self-deception, alienated Wesley from virtually every congregation he addressed. With impressive continuity Wesley's journal for these months records "was advised not to preach here again."

After his trip to Germany in the summer of 1738, however, Wesley's involvement with the Moravians in the Fetter Lane Society provided the kind of community in which he could "work out his salvation." No longer obsessively concerned with gaining his own salvation, Wesley—and the members of this society—could concern themselves with mission and the sharing of the gospel, as well as with holiness and purity of life. In the fall of 1739, Wesley's call from Whitefield to assist in field preaching around Bristol provided concrete opportunity to be in mission. In accepting that challenge—and being instantly confirmed in the response the crowds made to his preaching—Wesey began to shape the contours of his genuine vocation.

Before speaking briefly about the last major transition a developmentalist sees in Wesley's pilgrimage in faith, there are a few loose ends that need to be tied off: (1) While I have made a good deal of the negative aspects of Wesley's dominant superego, looked at over the span of his life it also had some critical positive consequences. Wesley's superego, we may say, was the "custodian" of his vocation. Through marriage or through a complacent settling into a living as a priest or bishop, Wesley might have cut the nerve of "his pressing on toward the mark of the high calling of Christ." Each time those possibilities arose, the scrupulosity and hidden wisdom of his "specialness" and special calling inhibited Wesley's response. In fact, we may say that in a way different than Wesley understood the matter at the time, his life and will *were* put at the disposal of God's will—not by his own choice, but by that of Susanna and Samuel. Moreover, Wesley's dominant superego gave him a long period for finding—and being found by—his calling. Erik Erikson calls this long period of time which creative people claim for the finding and shaping of their adult vocations a "moratorium." Wesley's superego gave him—or divine providence through it gave him—a rich and substantial time of preparation. (2) Pathology is not the point here. In nothing I have proposed do I intend to see Wesley as William James's "sick soul," or as an obsessive-compulsive neurotic. A developmental approach allows us to see how features of personality and behavior, which could be characterized in those ways from other perspectives, are part of the integrity of a life of faith and vocation in progress, and are in important respects, *indispensable to it*. (3) The Aldersgate appropriation of grace as the basis of his life did not entirely overthrow Wesley's superego. It did not end his careful self-scrutiny, his strenuous efforts to always "improve the time"; nor did it mark the end of all his difficulties regarding intimacy with women. Anna Freud in *The Ego and the Mechanisms of Defense* makes a vital distinction between defenses of the *ego*, which all of us need, and defenses of the *superego*, which perpetuate the kind of personality structuring we saw in the younger Wesley. Aldersgate, I would say, was the key event in a process by which Wesley was released from an excessive reliance on the superego and its defenses for the ordering of his life and faith. The marked changes in the responses of persons to his preaching and pastoral care, and the quality of calm confidence and courage that characterized his bearing in the 1740s and beyond, provide powerful testimony to his fundamental transformation.

IV

In some persons at or near midlife we see a transition to a stage beyond the Individuative-Reflective. We call this mid-life stage *Conjunctive* faith. The term comes from Carl Jung, who identified a number of polarities in our personalities that have to be acknowledged and integrated at midlife: polarities such as masculine and feminine, young and old, active and passive, creative and destructive, righteous self and shadow self, conscious and unconscious. The integration of these polarities at midlife involves a kind of balancing, a knowledge of the self that holds together our aspirations for excellence, moral and otherwise, with a chastened awareness of our capacities for evil, distortion, and self-deception.

Theologically, Conjunctive faith values multiple names and metaphors for God; it knows that we properly stutter when we address the Almighty. It affirms the quality of absoluteness that comes to expression in the event of Jesus Christ. But it knows the danger of idolizing the absolutes we formulate *about* Jesus Christ. Beyond tribal loyalties or denominational pride, Conjunctive faith is committed to justice, inclusiveness, and to the great church of those called of God.

The spirit of the theology, which Wesley evolved through his preaching in the years after Aldersgate, exhibits many of the qualities of Conjunctive faith. Certainly his theology of the grace of God held together—often under bitter attack and provocation—a number of great polarities: human bondage and human freedom (through his doctrine of prevenient grace); justification by grace through faith and the working out our salvation in fear and trembling; and grace as the power of salvation and law as the gift of God's grace. The qualities of Wesley's theology to which I want to call attention are the following: (1) Its integration of the Catholic and Protestant themes—sanctification and justification by grace through faith, respectively; (2) Its appreciation of the depths of our bondage in sin and its vision of the synergy of divine and human love in sanctification and the restoration of the *Imago Dei*; (3) Its evangelical fervor centered in the invitation to look to Christ and Christ alone for salvation, with its broad and irenic insistence on the universality of God's love. If there had been a theory of faith development (of the kind we work with) in the eighteenth century, certainly the theology of Wesley would have been a model for its version of Conjunctive faith.

Ultimately the question of using a stage theory developed in the twentieth century to examine theology and faith that flourished in the eighteenth becomes a tenuous and somewhat arbitrary effort. Perhaps the comparison does help somewhat, however, if it enables us to clarify ways in which Wesley's theology still strikes us as perennially solid and helpful, as well as clarifying some of the ways in which it has lost resonance in the intervening years.

From my standpoint the most difficult obstacles to a full embrace of Wesleyan spirituality today comes at two points:

(1) Despite all our emphasis upon the warm heart and experiential religion, Wesley's spirituality—his own and his movement's—retains a dominantly propositional, doctrinal mode of communication about faith. Very much an Enlightenment man, in this respect, Wesley's was and is a reasoned and reasoning faith. It was revolutionary for his own time, with its daring description of and address to the emotions. But it still partakes deeply of the Enlightenment's overtrust in words and reason. Wesley's mistrust of mysticism dictated that he stop short of an approach to prayer and scripture that could open up intercourse with the soul at the points of the will and the affections. The hymnody—and the poetry of Charles Wesley—were, of course, the saving medium in this

respect in Wesley's day. (2) Our century has witnessed two World Wars, Auschwitz and Buchenwald, Nagasaki and Hiroshima, Saigon and Beirut. We have been encultured into an intellectual world post-Feuerbach and Marx, post-Freud and Einstein. What we find so appealing in Wesley's "optimism of grace" and his witness to the transformation grace works toward wholeness in sanctification, makes us anxious at the same time. Desperately in need of visions of the calling and potential of our kind in relation to God, yet we have been burnt—burnt by our own and others' self-deceptions; burnt by rigid imperialisms of the soul, which ask us to direct our climb heavenward without helping us see the weight and drag of cellar voices within us. As our earlier discussion of Wesley's superego-dominated personality suggested, Wesley (and, of course, his era) had little inkling of the unconscious. Not until a century later, in Copenhagen, would any theologian begin to trace the ironic ways in which our movements toward perfection bring new oppressions and suppressions.

All of this is to say that we who stand and work in Wesley's magnificent wake have the contemporary task, as far as spirituality and faith development are concerned, of bringing a richer anthropology to our theologies of grace and transformation. We require not only a hermeneutics of holiness, to use Carl Michaelson's beautiful phrase, but also a hermeneutics of suspicion sufficient to help us avoid self-deception and the offering of shallow salvation. But we *do* need to offer the invitation to a walk with God that permanently and powerfully modifies what our culture takes to be normal human development. We are called to offer a spirituality of critical and constructive thrust, which shows men and women the way to a Spirit-empowered mingling of divine and human love, not for the perfecting of individual souls, but for the kingdom of God.

And as we work at this task, Wesley will be out there ahead of us. His teaching of perfection, his tireless, creative envisioning of justification, regeneration, and sanctification as a great ongoing drama of transformation in divine-human partnership, is still capable of informing and guiding our work. And Wesley himself, spending and being spent still among us, points to a horizon beyond Conjunctive faith which is truly *Universal*. Trying to describe the marks of the "genuine Christian," Wesley's characterization aptly expresses the shape of Universalizing faith, the last stage our research can identify:

Above all, remembering that God is love, [the Christian] is conformed to the same likeness. [The Christian] is full of love to [the] neighbor: of universal love, not confined to our sect or party, not restrained to those who agree with [us] in opinions, or in outward modes of worship, or to those who are allied . . . by blood, or recommended by nearness of place. . . . [T]his love resembles that of [the One] whose mercy is over all his works. It soars above all these scanty bounds, embracing neighbours and strangers, friends and enemies. . . . For the Christian loves every soul that God has made, every child of man, of whatever place or nation.[12]

Notes

1. See Jim Fowler and Sam Keen, *Life-Maps* (Waco, Texas: Word Books, 1978); James W. Fowler, with Robin Lovin et al., *Trajectories in Faith: Five Life Studies* (Nashville: Abingdon Press, 1980); and James W. Fowler, *Stages of Faith: The Psychology of Human Development and the Quest for Meaning* (San Francisco: Harper & Row, 1981); published in German by Suhrkamp Verlag, 1983.

2. For biographical background on Wesley, I rely primarily on Martin Schmidt, *John Wesley: A Theological Biography*, 3 vols., trans. Norman Goldhawk (Nashville: Abingdon Press, 1962, 1972, 1973); and Stanley Ayling, *John Wesley* (Cleveland, New York: William Collins, Publishers, 1979). Robert L. Moore's *John Wesley and Authority: A Psychological Perspective* (AAR Dissertation Series 29: Scholars' Press, 1979) marshals a considerable amount of biographical materials useful for my purposes here. Where I have drawn explicitly on the latter I indicate it in footnotes. Where I quote either Schmidt or Ayling, or where they may disagree, I also provide a footnote. In matters of biographical interpretation where the two former sources agree, I generally do not cite a specific footnote.

3. Moore, p. 42 (quoting from Wesley's *Journal*, 3:34 ff.).

4. Moore, p. 42.

5. Moore, pp. 44-45. (Quoting from G. Elsie Harrison, *Son to Susanna* (Nashville: Cokesbury Press, 1938), I:44.

6. Ayling, p. 20.

7. Schmidt, vol. I, p. 67.

8. *The Reverend Mr. John Wesley's Journal* from *The Works of John Wesley*, 3rd. ed. (Grand Rapids: Baker Book House, 1979), vol. I, p. 98, para. 2.

9. *Wesley's Journal*, p. 99.

10. Moore, p. 45, quoting V. H. H. Green, *The Young Mr. Wesley* (London: Edward Arnold, 1961), p. 54.

11. Schmidt, vol. I, pp. 240-41.

12. Wesley, *A Plain Account of Genuine Christianity*, sec. I., para. 5. Quoted in Albert Outler, ed., *John Wesley* (New York: Oxford University Press, 1964), p. 184.

Wesleyan Spirituality and Faith Development

Working Group Paper

Introduction

The working group on Wesleyan Spirituality and Faith Development represented a new focus of studies in the Oxford Institute of Methodist Theological Studies. Others are better able than we to trace why, in 1981-82, planners decided that the Institute could well afford to include a dialogue between John Wesley's theology and praxis of growth in grace, and some twentieth-century perspectives on faith and human development. As we pursued this dialogue we had a growing sense of its importance: importance as an approach to the study of Wesley's *theology in action*, and therefore crucial for our historical understanding of him and his movement; importance as a contribution to the contemporary and future efforts of the church to shape methods of sponsorship, which can discerningly midwife the work of the Holy Spirit in the transformation of lives towards holiness and happiness.

Elements of Wesleyan Spirituality

Spirituality concerns the Way, the Walk, and the Goal of Christian discipleship. It considers the direction of our course, the manner of our journey, its temper and discipline. It refers to our attitude to the world and to other people, and the end, the *summum bonum*, variously described as the vision of God, perfection, deification, entire sanctification, heaven, the kingdom of God.

Spirituality in English usage in the sixteenth and seventeenth centuries meant the "clergy," or sometimes "clerical property." The themes of *theologia spiritualis* would be described as "Holy Living and Holy Dying" or the "Practice of Piety," to name influential treatises, or simply "Godliness," or "Walking with God." The French wrote of "La Vie Spirituelle," though, at first perjoratively, to condemn the eccentricities of Madame Guyon or Molinos. Later the adjective became respectable. It presupposes that "there is a spirit in man," a faculty of human nature, which is able to transcend mortal responsibilities, utilitarian concerns, rational functions, and pursue ends beyond those of earthly existence—physical pleasure, getting and spending. This faculty controls and animates the whole.

In French, the word *spiritualite* means "liveliness." This also gives a clue. To put it colloquially, our spirituality is "what makes us tick." It is the whole variety of ideas, attitudes, intuitions that shape and inspire our living.

Thus understood there are two consequences:

(1) The term does not *ipso facto* define what is good. There are evil and erroneous spiritualities from which we need to be delivered. Hitler was a spiritual being: National Socialism a misbegotten spiritual movement.

(2) Our spirituality may not be what we think it is. We may pay lip service to certain forms and ideals, but our real, if unconscious, inspiration lies elsewhere. Our Christian progress may consist in being weaned away from false spiritualities and from self-deception as to the sources of our hidden life.

We, as Christians, believe that our beings may be animated by the Holy Spirit, the very life of God himself bestowed and released through Jesus Christ, his crucifixion and resurrection.

Christian spirituality needs for its elucidation and assessment the interplay of psychology, historical criticism, and theology.

When we turn to Wesley we may, through the use of all these disciplines, discern the following characteristics of his spirituality, stated in fairly nontechnical terms.

(1) His spirituality aims at a right relation to God and to persons. This is true throughout his whole life, though there were struggles to attain it, and some fluctuations afterwards.

(2) It was a synthesis of mystical and prophetic piety—to use the distinction of Friedrich Heiler. There was an ardent desire for God and for union with him, though this was never for an absorption into God which denied his own individuality or his need of other people. There was a strong sense of social reponsibility, of social joys, and of the need for men and women to be changed and society reformed. This coexisted in Wesley with opposition to revolution and a strong belief that good Christians conform to the existing order.

(3) The poor constituted a particular obligation, because Wesley was both a compassionate Christian, and one who lived by the Bible. He demonstrated a special quality of identification with the poor, and authentically manifested Jesus the Christ's concern for the dignity and redemption of the "little ones." While it may be anachronistic to speak of Wesley as "de-classing" himself, his identification with the poor is captured in this phrase.

(4) There is a requirement for human response to God's freely-given divine grace, and a call to human partnership and responsibility both in personal salvation and social transformation. The invitation of grace to "walk as Christ walked" leads to the imperative of "spreading scriptural holiness across the land."

(5) Wesley calls for a constant dependence on the means of grace. He adopted the classification of these into the "Instituted"—prayer; searching the scriptures (by reading, hearing, and meditation); the Lord's Supper—and the provisional, e.g., Christian conference (bands, classes, societies).

(6) Wesleyan spirituality envisions growth in grace and towards perfect love. There are stages in this growth, along with relapses and the possibility of being in more than one stage at once. The "dark night of the soul" was alien to Wesley as a theme in his theology, though not in his life. Wesley believed and taught that God intended progress and gave assurance to the believer by "the witness of our own

spirit" into which one could reason oneself by a syllogism, and "the witness of the Holy Spirit of adoption." Wesley believed perfection to be attainable in this life, though there are degrees of it, and there is always a tension between the "now" and the "not yet." In awareness of this the perfection may consist.

(7) Real holiness leads to true happiness, and both happiness and holiness found expression in Wesleyan hymnody. Wesley always insisted that the people called Methodists "sing with the spirit and with the understanding also," and the hymnody functioned as a major vehicle for the communication of Wesleyan theology. This is especially true of the eucharistic reality of Christ's presence in the Sacrament, the remembrance of Christ's sacrificial death for us, and the rejoicing that flows from both.

(8) Wesleyan spirituality is ecumenical. It is "pure Scriptural Christianity"; it follows the discipline and practice of the undivided church; and it avails itself of aids from every branch of Christendom and regards as its rightful partners all those who have sought holiness of life in the way of Christ.

An Approach to Wesleyan Spirituality and Faith Development

In documents circulated before the Institute we shaped a strategy that called for approaching Wesleyan spirituality from three directions:

(1) The study of Wesley's own life, with its distinctive pattern in the struggle for saving and sanctifying faith.

(2) A consideration of Wesley's various teachings and metaphors for illumining the drama of salvation and growth in grace.

(3) An examination of the concrete methods and contexts Wesley evolved for encouragement, education, and account-ability in the nurture of growth in grace. In addition, we determined to make an initial foray into twentieth-century psychosocial studies of faith development, with an eye to bringing these contemporary perspectives into a mutually constructive and critical encounter with Wesley's theology and praxis.

Prior to engaging in the study of these various topic areas, however, we realized that in the study of Wesleyan spirituality we had, in the group of twenty-three who had assembled in Oxford, a rich range of diverse (and similar) experiences of formation in the Wesleyan tradition. There-fore, for two of our early sessions we took the time for each participant to introduce her/himself and to share something of the ways the Wesleyan tradition had formed or marked our pathways into Christian faith. Some in the group remarked that at points the "testimony" approached the quality of a love feast. Certainly we, each one, felt enriched and informed by this sharing. The beginnings of understanding acquired in this time of introductions served us well as we soon came to points of difference and struggle over matters of great importance.

Our method of joint inquiry into the four major areas of our concern combined reports and presentations by members of our own group with several presentations from persons from other working groups in the Institute who have special expertise in some of our topics. A brief accounting will give a sense and sample of our ways of proceeding:

(1) *On Wesley's Praxis of the Nurture of Growth in Grace:* We were fortunate to have with us Tom Albin, of Cambridge University and a student of Gordon Rupp, whose computer studies of some five hundred members of early Methodist Societies (1740–1790) gave us fresh access to the character and religious experience of Wesley's early followers. Albin stressed the importance for understanding Wesley's doctrine of perfection, of studying those whom Wesley himself took to have been well on the way toward sanctification. He shared his finding that *lay* ministry, by means of band and class and written testimony, had been a catalytic factor in the rebirth of a majority of those he studied. Albin's dissertation will be extremely rich for this working group as well as for others. Paul Chilcote, a member of our group, is pursuing doctoral studies at Duke Divinity School with Frank Baker. Chilcote's topic of research is the role and influence of women in the Methodist movement in England from 1739-1830. He supplemented Albin's report at important points, and we expect that his work will be of critical importance for further

work on spirituality, as well as for Wesley studies and the group on Salvation and Justice.

Durwood Foster of our group presented a detailed review of David Michael Henderson's 1980 dissertation entitled *John Wesley's Instructional Groups*. A careful study of the Wesleyan bands, societies, and classes, Henderson's study correlates Wesley's theology of salvation and his principles and methods of nurture. This valuable resource was augmented by our hearing David Watson's rich account of the antecedents of Wesley's group approach and his illuminating understanding of the ways in which bands, classes, and societies actually worked. His dissertation, *The Origins and Significance of the Early Methodist Class Meetings* (Duke, 1978), is critical for our further work.

Our various examinations of the pattern of Wesley on nurture confirmed the following:

(a) Wesleyan spirituality assumes and gives tangible shape to the ecclesia—the congregation—as the fundamental context for conversion and growth in grace.

(b) Wesley's use of groups intentionally began with behavioral conversion. Like the catechumenate of the early church, the *classes* were evolved to help people, who intended to "live lives in Christ and flee the wrath to come" to begin the praxis of Christian living and mission. In the societies the crucial work of instruction was carried out through sermon and hymn as well as straightforward teaching. The bands served the function of forming the affections and aiding in the deep, convictional alignment of the will with the Divine will and truth as disclosed in Christ.

(c) Wesley's commitment to provide care for *each* member of the societies, to mark their growth in grace, and to sustain them with structures of accountability, points to the crucial dimensions of any faithful contemporary approach to spiritual nurture.

(2) *On Wesley's Theology of Salvation:* By way of review and clarification, three members of our group opened up our way into Wesley's teaching about what we in this Institute have called the *ordo salutis*. In quite distinct but complementary ways Gordon Wakefield and Rob Staples led us into Wesley's

teachings in this regard. We were impressed by the power of some of Wesley's images to arrest and hold us:

(a) His account of the three "states" indicating the primary orientation and grounding of our lives: "Natural Man," "Legal Man," "Evangelical Man." (Some of us noted similarities in these conceptions to Søren Kierkegaard's distinctions between the aesthetic, the ethical, and religious "stages of life's way.")

(b) Wesley's use of the developmental metaphor in his talk of "babes in Christ," "young men," and "fathers."

(c) We felt challenged by the richness of trying to combine the Wesleyan conception of stages and orientation of life with the developmental metaphor, while at the same time relating both these to the grand drama of the work of grace in the lives of those born of Christ: Conviction-Repentance; Justification-Rebirth; Sanctification-Perfection. Rex Matthews provided us with a comprehensive chart mapping the relations of these teachings in Wesley in an exceedingly rich way, drawing on the work of Harald Lindström and Colin Williams, as well as the original sources.

(3) *On Wesley's Life and Spiritual Growth:* Several windows into the life and growth in grace of John Wesley were shared in the course of our work together. These perspectives, each illuminative in important ways, reminded us that in Wesley we are dealing with an extremely complex figure. His century with its sensibilities and styles, its institutions and economics, its horizons of reason and experience, is in many ways alien to our own. Moreover, although Wesley's life may well be the best documented of any major reformer or founder, the self-presentation underlying much of that documentation has to be evaluated carefully as a source for biographical study. The various secondary studies of Wesley present problems of critical interpretation not entirely dissimilar to the synoptic problem in New Testament studies.

Chastened by these awarenesses, we nonetheless benefited from Robert Tuttle's sharing of his interpretation of Wesley's struggle for saving faith, which focuses especially on Wesley's immersion in the writings of certain Roman Catholic reformation mystics. Especially in the years 1725 to

1735, Tuttle argued, the essential lines of Wesley's spiritual stirrings and those of the Holy Club, were inspired in significant part by these Catholic mystics. Later, as Tuttle pointed out, Wesley would break with their teachings of "the dark night of the soul." And when he abridged ten of these mystical texts for the Christian Library, he rewrote the parts dealing with the dark night of the soul, substituting for them accounts of "Faith as the Evidence of Things Unseen." Wesley also replaced the mystics' goal of union with God with the sturdy theme of "perfection" as the goal of Christian life. Tuttle's thesis supplements important previous work in Orthodox, Anglican, Continental pietist, and Puritan sources for Wesley's teaching on the *ordo salutis*.

In his plenary address James Fowler employed the theory of faith development, for which he has been a principal researcher, as an interpretative framework for the study of Wesley's pilgrimage in faith. In this presentation he attempted simultaneously to introduce faith development theory and a fresh look at Wesley's life. For Fowler, Wesley's pattern of growth in faith was marked by an early domination of his personality organization by a powerful *superego* (which included the religious ideals and aspirations of his parents). The years 1725-1738, Fowler argued, marked the time when Wesley met the limits of his superego-dominated orientation to deal with the adult issues of conviction, authority, vocation, and intimacy—intimacy with God and other humans. Aldersgate—understood as a period beginning with failure and disgrace in Georgia and ending with his invitation to field preach in 1739—is to be seen as the time in which Wesley found his limits, helplessness, and needs, and became radically open to God's grace.

Following the discussion of issues raised by Fowler's paper, Mary Elizabeth Moore gave a précis of Robert L. Moore's *John Wesley and Authority* (1980). This psychoanalytic study offers penetrating light on certain dynamics of Wesley's personhood and faith. In it Wesley is portrayed as adopting a passive-aggressive approach to the exercise of authority. By attributing all initiative to God, Wesley was able to exercise rarely questioned authority over the early Methodist movement and its members. Our group felt that

Moore tends to overtrust psychological analysis and to give too little attention to the social and cultural contexts of Wesley. Despite Moore's effort to avoid reductionism, we judged that he failed to grant Wesley's theological grounding its own full measure of integrity.

Colin Archer of our group responded to Moore by asking us to acknowledge directly the pathological dimensions of Wesley's personality. He sees the "handicaps" of Wesley as a point of contact with a theology of the Cross, and an important link with vulnerabilities such as poverty and powerlessness in the contemporary dispossessed, which forms the basis of an essential interlocking with the liberation theologies.

Rex Matthews, in a carefully argued and documented study, helped us understand the ways in which reason and reasoning played central roles in Wesley's re-imaging of faith during the critical years between 1725 and 1738. Matthews' study of "Reason, Faith and Experience" in Wesley is a foretaste of his Harvard doctoral dissertation, now in progress. This study carefully demonstrates Wesley's consistent reliance upon the concepts of reason, which he derived from the eighteenth-century Oxford Aristotelian logical tradition, particularly Henry Aldrich's *Artis Logicae Compendium* (1691). Wesley, who taught logic at Lincoln College for six years, later translated, abridged, and published Aldrich's work as his own *Compendium of Logic* (1750). Matthews shows that Wesley's understanding of faith evolved from an initial approach to faith as rational assent to the propositions of doctrinal truths. In a second phase he understood faith as grounded in rational conviction of the credibility of the proposer of such truth. In a third phase, under the influence of the Moravians and the guidance of Peter Böhler, Wesley was brought to an understanding of faith as direct spiritual vision in Christ. This position may draw upon the thought of John Norris and Nicholas Malebranch, but it finds expression most directly in the language of Hebrews 11:1—Faith as "the assurance of things hoped for, the conviction of things not seen." Although Wesley never abandoned the language of faith as a rational assent, Matthews argues, it was his new understanding of faith as "divine evidence or conviction" which allowed him at Aldersgate to reappropriate the language of faith as "a sure trust and confidence" of salvation, found in the *Book of Common Prayer* and *Homilies* of the Church of England as truly his *own* language. After identifying the relationship between these three "languages of faith" in Wesley, Matthews' paper culminates in an account of how reason is regrounded for Wesley in the personal experience of rebirth brought about by God's gift of faith, and so is enabled to play its proper role in the guidance and governance of the spiritual life.

(4) *Faith Development Theory:* In addition to the plenary paper on Wesley's development of faith, James Fowler presented, in rather more detail, the background and leading assumptions of the research and theory of faith development. The presentation of his generic characterization of faith, with its sequence of structural stages brought to the surface a number of persistent issues for our group.

For some, both on Wesleyan and biblical theological grounds, Fowler's use of the term "faith" to describe the human capacity for commitment and shaping a meaningful world is incompatible with Christian understanding of faith as the gift of God's grace and as an overturning of any claims to human self-sufficiency. Some of these objected to a psychological approach which fails to grant the priority of scripture, revelation, and the work of the Spirit in any proper speaking of faith. Fowler answered that he sees the stage theory of faith as primarily a contribution to theological anthropology. He reminded the group, however, that the doctrine of prevenient grace in Wesley contends that the idea of human beings in the natural or fallen state is really a theoretical construct. Already, by virtue of God's universal prevenient grace, conscience is awakened and reason is able, however dimly, to discriminate right from wrong. Fowler observed that the stage theory in its present formulation (see Fowler, *Stages of Faith,* 1981) does not fully enough acknowledge its grounding in the conviction of God's sovereignty, nor does it explicitly develop its doctrine of prevenient grace.

From his own work on human development studies, Donald Joy pressed the group toward the effort to find linkages and overlays between stage theories of the kind Fowler has offered and Wesley's various ways of speaking of the conversion, which grace works by faith as depicted in the *ordo salutis*.

Major Learnings and Issues

It seems to us that one of the powerful points of common meeting between Wesley's teaching about the way of salvation and the emergent theory of faith development centers on the images that each offers of possibilities for the transformation of human life in the direction of wholeness. Each is concerned with the whole person—body, mind, and spirit. Each characterizes a sequence of ways in which the self is related to God, the neighbor, and the world. By virtue of the visions of excellence which each offers, they both have the effect of critiquing present modes of life with their centers of value and images of power. Each perspective takes seriously what is personal and unique in human lives, but each intends to view a person's becoming firmly in its social and corporate context.

Some important differences between these perspectives, however, have emerged in our discussions. Wesley's doctrine on the way of salvation begins clearly with the assumption of a human fall from a state of originally created perfection. Correlated with a radical understanding of human sinfulness in Wesley is an equally radical doctrine of divine grace and initiative. Thus the aptness of the characterization of Wesley's thought as holding together the twin emphases of "pessimism of nature" and "optimism of grace." The universally and freely available prevenient grace of God renders the "natural man" a fiction in Wesley's thought. Wesley's teaching about the way of salvation represents a sequence of events in the spiritual life through which reason is regrounded and the will and the affections are recentered. This dynamic process moves under the power of God's grace in the direction of perfecting a love *in* us that is increasingly like the love of God *for* us.

Faith development theory, at first examination, would seem to offer significant contrasts to Wesley's way of salvation. It offers no fully developed doctrine of sin. Nor does it fully give account of the pole of divine grace in the process which it depicts. It does begin, however, with the conviction of the sovereignty of God as creator, ruler, and redeemer. It is grounded in the belief that human beings are created for partnership with God—whether we know it and acknowledge it or not. The stages attempt to provide formal—that is to say, empty of specific content—descriptions of ways of being in faith. It is important to note, however, that each stage describes a way of situating the self in relation to the neighbor, and to that which has God-value and God-power for us. A transition from one faith stage to another, therefore, means a regrounding of self-understanding, of our orientation to God and neighbor, and of our patterns of action in the world. Each new stage brings a deidolization: a dethroning of the images of God or the ultimate held in the previous stage. With each new stage, a kind of decentering from self also occurs: This means an expanded capacity for taking the perspectives of others; it means a widened and deepened appreciation for the potential of all being in God's economy.

Wesley's way of salvation is more explicit about the transformation that God's grace works in our wills and affections. His doctrine preserves a useful fluidity regarding the phases of this transformation. Faith development theory gives greater attention to transformation in our modes of knowing and valuing, and attempts to specify differentiated stages in this process.

A fruitful area of overlap between the two perspectives may lie in the different ways in which each envisions a widening and regrounding of reason.

Wesley's way of salvation offers a powerful reminder that in God's grace persons described by any of the stages of faith development theory may need to undergo conviction, repentance, and conversion (or *metanoia*), and by virture of this become the recipients of God's graciously given salvation. And faith development theory enables us to understand that conversion, justification, and rebirth at different stages of faith may involve quite different conflicts and dynamics, therefore requiring different methods from those who would minister and give nurture to those in transition in faith.

In order to take this dialogue between Wesleyan spirituality and faith development theory further, future praxis and research will need to come to terms with the following issues:

(a) *The reconciliation of two kinds of perspectives on the self in community in relation to God:* One which starts from scripture and a theology centered in God's act in Christ, made contemporary with us through the work of the Holy Spirit in word, sacrament, and koinonia; the other which starts from empirical and phenomenological perspectives on human faith and fairly attempts to understand the human potentiation for, and vocation to, full humanity in partnership with God. Wesley's doctrine of prevenient grace, his understanding of reason before and after rebirth, and his own empirical and phenomenological interests in transforming experience, make him a far more helpful theological partner for faith development theory than most other reformation protestant theologies. Correspondingly, the "grace transforming nature" pattern common to Wesley and faith development theory together make them a strong informing perspective for the praxis of Christian nurture, spiritual direction, evangelism, preaching, and the care of souls.

(b) *The clarification of relationships and distinctions between faith stage change and conversion, rebirth and sanctification:* Repentance, rebirth, and justification literally may be approached as qualitatively different experiences by persons at different faith stages. Bonhoeffer's call for approaches to discipleship that take seriously a certain kind of "coming of age" should warn us against evangelism and education which take adolescent conversion and commitment as their dominant model—as important as that is.

(c) *The questioning and liberation from those forms of Wesleyan theology which view justification as the release from the neurotic guilt that results from an excessively harsh childhood conscience:* This has been and may continue for many to be the central dynamic in conviction and justification for many heirs of Wesley. But the *contents*, if not the structure itself, of the superego are changing in our time. Our doctrines of sin and salvation need to concern themselves equally with narcissism, complacence, anomie, and meaninglessness as besetting conditions of sin to which the call for conviction and repentance, justification and sanctification are addressed. A certain kind of narcotism and numbness in face of the grinding inequalities and brutal realities of our contemporary society may be the sins for which we most need forgiveness and rebirth.

(d) *The struggle, in praxis and theological-ethical reflection, to claim and explicate images of human excellence and full responsiveness to God and the neighbor, without boxing into new legalisms the specific contents or forms for the direction of God's work with us:* We need strong *Christian images of the human vocation* that are clear about our calling—our proper *entelechy*—but which preserve open-ended anticipation regarding the uniqueness of pattern and style resulting from the synergy of divine and human love worked in us by our ongoing response to God's grace.

(e) *Experimentation and praxis research on contemporary equivalents of early Methodism's bands, classes, and societies:* The interlocking structure of behavioral, instructional, and affectional-volitional formation and accountability in Wesley's model are indispensable for any spirituality that will sustain sanctifying faith and faithful mission.

(f) *Research and praxis investigation of Wesley's use of scripture—in personal prayer, in theological determinations, and in the contexts of the classes and bands:* A man of one book, a people of one book—In both belief and practice, in method and execution, we are sore in need of ways to enable persons to reenter what Karl Barth once called "the strange new world of the Bible," and to let it make in us the transforming linkages between the world it opens up and our own frenetic worlds.

(g) *The shaping of a spirituality faithful to God's calling in our time to be peacemakers and makers of justice:* Both Wesley's way of salvation and faith development theory envision our being citizens of the city of God, a global community of those born of God, who are restless, persistent, spending and being spent, in the human work of divine transformation toward inclusive justice and peace.

Some Specific Topics for Future Study

(1) "Wesley as *Homo Unius Libri:* How Wesley's Understanding and Use of the Bible Informs His Spirituality."

(2) "Wesley and the Dark Night of the Soul"—Was there in Wesley, and is there in the heritage of Methodist spirituality, a tendency to avoid the "shadow" within and without—a failure to plumb the depths of ambiguity and the demonic in us?

(3) "Wesley's Theology and Practice of Prayer."

(4) "The Seasons of Wesley's Life"—A study of relative emphases in theology and spirituality throughout Wesley's lifetime.

(5) "The Holy Spirit and Sacraments in Wesleyan Spirituality."

(6) "The Wesleyan *Ordo Salutis* and *Stages of Faith* Calmly Considered."

(7) "Wesley, Spirituality and the Poor"—Poverty and poverty of spirit; Wesley's spirituality as empowerment toward "declassing" and trans-class solidarity.

(8) "*The Psychology of the Methodist Revival* Revisited: The Convictional Experiences Engendered by Wesley's Evangelism"—A review needed of Sydney G. Dimond's *The Psychology of the Methodist Revival* (1926) and assessment in light of *Stages of Faith* and James Loder's approach in *The Transforming Moment* (Harper & Row, 1981).

(9) "Naturalism versus Justification and Sanctification"—Modern developmental theories and the Wesleyan way of salvation.

(10) "Wesley as Text: Hermeneutics of Holiness and Suspicion"—Deeper inquiry into Wesley's biography with judicious inquiry into the principles guiding his presentation of self in the journals. (The Wesley Wesley knew; the Wesley Wesley wanted us to know; the Wesley others knew [that Wesley didn't know]; the Wesley no one [but God] knows.)

(11) "Wesley and Universalizing Faith: The Extent and Limits of the Catholic Spirit"—Wesley's struggle to move beyond the clash of opinions of theological

dispute, his efforts to identify what is fundamental and essential in the gospel, bespeaks a theory of the relatedness (relativity) of religious approaches to truth. How does appropriation of this dimension of Wesley's work orient us in interfaith dialogue and the encounter with other spiritualities in our time?

(12) "Toward a Political Spirituality: Resources and Limits of Wesleyan Spirituality"—Are there resources in Wesley for a political spirituality, and what are the resources and limitations of Wesley's spirituality?

(13) "Methodist Spiritual Praxis in the Bands and Classes: the Dynamics and Possibilities of Group Spiritual Directions."

(14) "Wesley's Spirituality as Reflected in the Biographical Traditions: A Critical and Historical Survey."

(15) "Holiness and Happiness: Wesley's Vision of Fully Realized Humanity."

7

A Retrospect

Brian E. Beck

The seventh Institute broke new ground in being more of a working conference than its predecessors since 1958. Smaller specialist groups in which much of the work was done allowed deeper engagement with particular aspects of the subject. The seventh Institute also marked a further stage in the progressive narrowing down of the meaning of the words "Methodist Theological Studies" as traditionally included in the Institute's title, from "theological studies done by Methodists" to "studies of the Methodist contribution to theology." This was a welcome development, for there is little point in Methodists from all over the world gathering for study unless they consider some aspect of their specifically Methodist contribution. The Institute also succeeded in being more representative of that world constituency, including churches not officially counted in the Methodist "family" but which have inherited and value a Wesleyan tradition. It was not always clear, however, that the different voices were equally successful in making themselves adequately heard, and there is certainly scope for improving the representative character of the Institute, if the economic and other problems can be overcome.

The theme of the Institute, "The Future of the Methodist Theological Traditions," implies a question, and it is important to ask why we pose it. We cannot know what the future holds, and in predictive terms the question is unanswerable. But insofar as it lies in our hands to shape the future, we may properly ask how we may secure a place in it for our traditions, what form they might take, and whether we can now discern any undeveloped potential that we should exploit for future benefit. But in doing so, it is important to be clear about our motives.

Are we anxious about survival? It is natural to fear death, and institutions and social groups may fear it as much as individuals. Are we then seeking reassurance that what we believe in can survive in the next generation and so demonstrate the value of our belief even in our own? If so we might reflect that historically Christianity has taken many forms, which have proved to be impermanent because the social settings for which they were adopted have themselves not survived, but this does not entitle us to judge that they were without value in those settings. Even if it should prove to be the case that two centuries from now Methodism had had its day (not just as churches, as Professor Wainwright suggests, but as a family of traditions), why should we not now give thanks to God for the day he has given and be glad, like Charles Wesley, to "serve the present age?"

Is it a question of identity? In many parts of the world, Methodists form minority churches, surrounded by much larger communities of Lutherans, Roman Catholics, or Anglicans. The Methodist movement for world evangelism finds itself working alongside other evangelistic organizations. In such situations there is a natural urge to know who we are and why we are different. To say simply, on the analogy of the well-stocked supermarket, that variety of choice is good for the customer only trivializes the missionary enterprise. If we are doing no more than peddling the same goods under a different label, it is a poor witness to the Lord who offers to gather a fragmented and strife-torn world into one, and in John's gospel prays that his disciples may reflect the unity of Father and Son that the world may be better able to believe. In any case (if we must use commercial metaphors), would not a merger improve sales efficiency? It may be that in some parts of the world the real reason why we are distinct from other Christian groups is simply that we belong to a different social class, have different historical origins, or use a different set of social customs. If that is the case, let us be bold enough to admit it; it is a fact of no small theological significance in itself, and there would be no need to cast around for a distinctive theology that we could adopt to justify our separate existence.

If there is a properly theological reason why we should be concerned with the future of our traditions and anxious to preserve their integrity, it will be because of their wider value. Can it be that we have something to give, held in trust for the whole church and for the world, which we ought to discover and make more explicitly our own? Our question necessarily has ecumenical and global implications.

In answer to the question the Institute spent much of its time discussing John Wesley. In many ways the group on Wesley Studies made the running and other groups took up the theme. The central question then became, what does Wesley offer to the church today? Several answers were given. One was that the value lies in the man himself. One consequence of the Incarnation is that God continues to give himself to us through the lives of persons who have been formed by the Spirit of Christ. So the lives of the saints are a benefit to the church. The historical study of Wesley's life would have the value of setting before us the man in his genuine humanity, with both strengths and weaknesses, with the evidence of both grace and sin, as a testimony to the continuing work of Christ in human lives. This underlines the importance of the case made by the Wesley Studies group for a new study, embracing the whole of his life in its broadest historical context, using a proper critical edition of his works, and ignoring the glamorizing portrayals that most of us were brought up on. We need to be reminded that much of the image we have of Wesley is his own self-portrait, projected for the public through his published works. There is scope for the kind of psychological analysis Professor Fowler offered in his paper, and we need to be reminded that every historian writes within a context, so that what appears interesting and significant may depend on whether you are sitting in Oxford, Sao Paolo, or Budapest. More of that later.

As to the particular question of Wesley's thought, however, three principal answers were given. On the one hand it was observed in discussion that on various specific points, Wesley, like any other writer, has useful and stimulating things to say on issues of continuing interest. His

211

views on medicine in the *Primitive Physic* and the many opinions he expresses in the *Letters* were cited as examples. They are of value in themselves, not as parts of a larger system. At the other end of the scale, while it would not be possible to claim Wesley as a systematic theologian in the tradition of Aquinas or Calvin, he can be held up as an example of how to do theology: a people's theologian, working out what the truth of God must be in the light of what was happening in the lives of the Methodist people, looking for coherence rather than formal system, trying to state theology in simple terms, sharpening his ideas in controversy over the work of mission. Here the emphasis is on method, part of which will be what he based his theology on, the so-called quadrilateral of scripture, the ancient church, reason, and experience.

Between these alternatives is the view that regards Wesley as important because of certain broad themes in his thought. It was interesting to see how these emerged, developing in a sort of consensus. There was frequent reference to grace, especially prevenient grace, with its implications for the way we regard those who do not confess faith in Christ, and there was much stress on holiness as the essence of the work of God (being both a gift of grace at a moment in time and a matter of continual growth in grace), holiness as the expression of what it means to be fully human, and above all holiness as love, with its social implications, particularly identification with the poor. Another aspect, to which Professor Wainwright drew attention, was Wesley's particular combination of traditional doctrines, the "proportion of the faith."

It is surprising that more was not made of Wesley's emphasis on discipline and good order, his method-ism. Whatever may have been the psychological basis of the discipline he exercised over himself and the Methodists, it has theological significance in that it betrays the assumption that Christian living is life in community, in which we are accountable to and for one another. It would be valuable to explore in a future Institute the extent of this legacy today in different branches of Methodism and various parts of the world. If I am right in thinking that a love of order, with

212

centralized and regulated patterns of church government, still shows itself in all our traditions (witness our volumes of church discipline and constitutional practice), this is a contribution to the doctrine of the church.

But this approach raises a number of questions, for it is an inadequate answer to a question about the future of the Methodist traditions, still less adequate for a question about the future of Methodist churches. Wesley's writings are as accessible to non-Methodists as to Methodists; all that is needed is a good edition of his works. Historical study cannot be kept within the family; indeed some of the more important contributions have already come from outside it. If there is anything, therefore, which present-day Methodists have in trust for the world, it will be Wesley as mediated through our traditions—Wesley as he still lives in the life, thought, and activity of Methodists and others who look to him for their origins. That is the reason for Methodists to explore and reappropriate their heritage.

Our Methodist traditions are many and varied, and are the result of many influences beside John Wesley (the hymns of his brother Charles, for example, not really to be subsumed under his brother's thought in spite of the fact that they were published with John's editing and imprimatur. For most Methodists in the English-speaking world, they are the only first-hand contact with the writings of either brother). Professor Tamez drew attention to the eighteenth- and nineteenth-century Methodists in her paper, and cited their example for our current task of interpretation, but the Institute gave little attention to the nineteenth century except to decry its view of Wesley. Our manifold traditions deserve closer study. Disquiet was expressed for example over the report of the group on Ecclesiology and the Sacraments because its response to the WCC document was not felt to be broadly representative, and as we all know, there is often a gap between the official view of our tradition and what it actually is among the people of the church. The Wesleyan tradition has been watered down in all our churches over two hundred years.

The answer to this is not a mere revival of antiquity. We cannot and must not try to get back to him; that would be to deny all that God has given to the world in various movements, secular and religious, since his time. The twentieth century is not and cannot be the eighteenth. What we can and should do is to expose ourselves to Wesley afresh, so that as churches and as individuals we may be mediators through whom the gifts God gave us in Wesley can be shared with the rest of the world. As Professor Wainwright indicated in his paper, the Wesleyan tradition for our time has to be embodied in us. But that leads to the further question of Wesley's authority.

What authority should Wesley have for Methodists? It is clear that he does not simply lay down a form of orthodoxy to which we have to subscribe. Our various doctrinal standards do not require this, and in any case eighteenth-century answers will not do for twentieth-century questions. As Professor Tamez argued, we have to get away from quoting proof-texts and see the whole Wesley in his whole context and relate him to ourselves in our contexts, if we are to find in him any help for our own situation. An alternative is to regard his writings as an anthology of ideas from which we select what we already agree with, but this is merely to hijack him for our own cause. What then is (or should be) his authority? Professor Meeks introduced this problem at the beginning of the Institute, but we did not resolve it. The terms "mentor" and "teacher" were suggested, which are helpful in ruling out some alternatives, but an examination of the work of some of the groups might suggest that they are still operating with other assumptions. The temptation to resort to proof-texts taken out of context (and sometimes misquoted second-hand) is strong. More work needs to be done on this question.

It is of course only one aspect of the wider question of all authority in Christian theology, whether it be the authority of the Fathers, or of the Creeds, or even of the Scriptures. In each case we are looking for an understanding of authority, which will give definition and identity to the community that accepts it, provide inspiration and direction for the renewal of its thought, and yet allow it the freedom to be an authentic community of its own time. In each case there is the further question of the role of tradition in the interpretation of authoritative texts. Historic documents do not merely belong to the past; they live on in the life of the communities accepting their authority. But precisely because they are historic, earthed in a particular setting in the past, they cannot simply be assimilated to the present. They challenge our current understandings by their historical strangeness. Neither Wesley nor Luther (nor for that matter, Paul) can be treated as a ventriloquist's dummy for the utterance of our twentieth-century ideas, yet without their modern disciples they would remain, in an important sense, dumb. In each case, too, there is the tension between the work of the historical scholar or exegete and the present day heir of the tradition. Who better understands Benedict, the (possibly agnostic) historian or the monk who today lives according to the Rule? We are familiar with these questions in relation to the Bible but they apply to all theological authorities. Scripture in one sense remains a special case because its authority is primary, but I suspect that the answer will take a similar form in each case.

In the case of Methodism, however, there is a further complexity. Dr. Outler in his paper and the Wesley Studies group in their report stressed the importance of the whole Wesley in all his writings seen in their context and with all the development of his thought (although I presume that does not necessarily mean that the elder Wesley's thoughts were always better than his earlier ones). But many Methodist churches have official books of discipline or foundation deeds containing legal definitions of Methodist doctrinal standards. These often refer only to the first four volumes of the *Sermons*, the *Notes on the New Testament*, and perhaps the *Articles of Religion*. This is hardly the whole Wesley! In the practical application of authority in the life of the church, we are required to refer to a corpus of writings far more limited. There is a historical reason for this "canon" of writings, in some cases going back to Wesley's own specification. Is there also a theological justification, or ought we to be looking towards a revision of our official standards? What if this is not legally possible?

This discussion suggests that there is more work to be done on a number of fundamental questions. This was of course recognized, and each group produced a fairly extensive list of projects to be pursued in its own field. So far, I have tried to stress the particular need to broaden the examination to include our traditions as they have developed from Wesley. There are, however, other issues that arose and must count as unfinished business.

It became apparent in discussion that we were deeply divided on the subject of evangelism, which occupies a major part of the programme of the World Methodist Council. To some extent the differences ran along geographical lines but not entirely so. Fundamental to the debate is the legitimacy of hope and prayer for a world Christian awakening, and the relationship between evangelism designed, under God, to provoke that awakening, on the one hand, and on the other, two equally deeply held Christian convictions, the concern to respect the integrity of other faiths and the concern to see the righteousness of God embodied in a just social order. That debate is reflected in other pages of this volume and will continue. Here I simply press the need for caution when talking of global evangelism. Professor Wainwright in his paper drew attention to the dangers of Constantinianism (the alliance of church and state) and the consequences especially when the quality of religion declines. If we seriously talk of world or even national conversion, how are we to guard against the church swallowing up the state, only later to become secularized by it? Is it possible to build into our evangelism safeguards against the dangers of success? Indeed, we need a thorough critique of the concept of success in the life of the church. The view often seems to be held that "success" is a test of truth. If it works, it must be true; if people are converted in large numbers, the message must be right. There are grave dangers in thinking that, unless we are more than usually self-critical. "Woe to you, when all . . . speak well of you, for so their fathers did to the false prophets" (Luke 6:26).

What is success? As Wesley Ariarajah, among others, insisted, Wesley's concern was not simply for conversions but for scriptural holiness. This is much harder to measure and impossible to count as conversions may be counted. But it may take us nearer to the heart of the matter. Is the real test of the faithfulness of the church its diligence in evangelism, important as that is? Is it, to sharpen the question, evangelism that leads to conversions? Or is it readiness to go to the cross? One very common reading of Mark's gospel, after all, is to see it as a protest against superficial views of success and a recall to the way, not of popular support but of rejection and loneliness—the way of the cross. It would be a strange distortion of the gospel of Christ to depict a thousand conversions as success if thereby martyrdom counted as failure.

Conversion is, of course, an ambiguous word. For example, Ariarajah said in his paper that there is no such thing as conversion in the conventional sense because what occurs is only a movement from prevenient grace to justifying grace; we are talking about a new and different response to the God we already know. I doubt whether this view takes seriously enough the fact of sin—grace, in Wesley's mind, whether prevenient or justifying, can be resisted. The pathway to redemption is not just from one expression of grace to another but from resistance to grace to full trust and obedience. Even so this view is different from the idea of conversion as a shift from a world without Christ to a world with him. Professor Fowler, using the word *faith* in a more general sense, showed how a person with any world view, be it Christian, Jewish, or scientific humanist, may move from one stage of faith to another. He allowed in discussion that conversion is possible in the sense that we may move sideways, so to speak, from one world view to another. In Fowler's words, there may be "a reseating of the will, a redirection of the affections, a move to a new master story"—so a Muslim may become a Christian. But although the account he gave of John Wesley laid stress on the importance of Aldersgate Street, it did not give any clear portrayal of a conversion in that sense. As he acknowledged in the ensuing discussion, "the real question is how justification cuts across the naturalistic development."

These two examples illustrate the ambiguities and looseness of the word *conversion*, which in all our traditions must surely rank as one of the most frequently used words in the Methodist vocabulary. This is not surprising, since the word, and equivalents like *repent* and *return* have been used in widely different ways throughout Christian history from the Bible onwards. There would be value in a Methodist exploration of this issue and, in particular, of the usefulness of the term in the context of stages of development as well as of critical change, its legitimacy as a synonym for justification, and its appropriateness to John Wesley on May 24, 1738.

More work also needs to be done on Wesley's so-called "order of salvation" (the *ordo salutis*). What has the idea of stages of salvation in religious experience to say to us? Even if we succeed in correlating Wesley's stages with Professor Fowler's stages of faith, is the notion of definable steps in the Christian life (if these are seen as prescriptive and not merely descriptive) a helpful contribution to modern spirituality? The work of the group on Spirituality and Faith-development helpfully opened up new approaches to these issues, but we have only begun to look at the questions psychology poses, not just for Wesley's character but for his theology and pastoral methods, including questions about conscience and assurance (especially assurance of perfection). One of the most striking aspects of the *Plain Account of Christian Perfection* today is its psychological naivety. But the questions are not only psychological. Wesley's understanding of spiritual development also has to be assessed against the long tradition of Christian spiritual direction from the Desert Fathers onwards.

In retrospect there were two particular ways in which the Institute could have made better use of the opportunities it had, and it is appropriate for one of the organizers to point them out. One was our failure to make full use of the particular skills of members who were professional biblical scholars. The main themes of Wesley's theology are biblical, at least in his intention: grace, justification, sanctification. Yet our appreciation of these in their biblical expression has changed dramatically since his time. It would be a disservice to our times if, in restoring the original Wesley, we merely canonized his understanding of the Bible. We need parallel biblical studies to set alongside his treatment of these themes. Beyond this, however, is the problem of hermeneutics. We have referred to the question of tradition and interpretation, and the nature of authority already. There is a further more general point. Much was said at the Institute about interpreting Wesley right: the whole Wesley in context, interpreted in relation to our own context. That is a very sophisticated process, which demands above all a sense of the difference between two cultures in history. At the same time it was said that Wesley can be read by ordinary people. Certainly if he was a theologian for the common people we must not imprison him in our lecture-rooms and libraries. But how are the ordinary people to read him and not misinterpret him or be put off by his more conservative social attitudes? How indeed are they to read him at all in many parts of the world without translation, and if translation of all his extensive works is impracticable (and who apart from scholars will read them all?), what selection will authentically represent him? These are just the sort of problems biblical scholars face about the interpretation and ready availability of the far more ancient texts of Scripture. Some interaction between disciplines would have been helpful here.

Secondly, the Institute only partly fulfilled its avowed aim of making possible dialogue between specialists in different fields. The working groups were designed to make it possible to study limited subjects in depth, but it was hoped that there would also be intergroup dialogue, so that experts in each field would be exposed to the knowledge and criticism of those in other fields. This happened only to a limited extent. It may be that there was insufficient time both for the process of group integration and for real exchange between groups. However, the Institute would have been more fruitful if such integration had taken place.

Those who felt this lack most sharply were members of the Salvation and Justice group, especially representatives from Latin America, who felt that by their very preoccupation with certain questions to the exclusion of others, the majority of the Institute had failed to hear and be influenced by their insistence that the experience of the poor in their struggle for human dignity and social justice specifies the theological questions to be discussed, and makes possible a new creative insight into what the tradition holds in store (a criticism that may be apposite to the present paper, which has not attempted to summarize the whole Institute's work or be even-handed in its comments). Their insistence on the value of John Wesley for Latin American Methodists was striking, and perhaps to some more disillusioned Western representatives, surprising. There was certainly some misunderstanding. The report of the Salvation and Justice group sparked off a debate in which some questions of definition were clarified, but the use of the term *poverty* remained a stumbling-block. *Poverty* is notoriously difficult to define in any context, but the breadth of its meaning in theological discussion was not always realized. The poor comprise not only those who lack food, clothing, and shelter, but also those who, while they may have material possessions in some measure, are deprived of freedom, opportunity, and their fair share of power in the community.

The context in which we do our theological work is crucial and affects everyone. It explains perhaps why the subjects covered by some groups had greater appeal to representatives of some churches than others. Context also influenced our capacity to listen. Those who come from large churches, which in addition have traditionally acted as missionary agencies, perhaps find it more difficult to recognize the extent to which their own perception of the world and their appreciation of the Methodist tradition is conditioned by the setting in which they live. It is tempting to react to other views as deviations from the authentic tradition once passed on to their now wayward children. It does not help that these ecclesiastical relationships are often entangled with political relationships between the nations in which the churches are set. Nineteen eighty-two was the year of the Falklands war.

Various responses are possible. One is to react defensively, but with impeccable logic, and say that if theology is to be "contextual" and reflect the priorities determined by the setting where the theologian lives, then no one can decree that what is required by one setting must become mandatory for others whose context suggests other preoccupations. That would be to close the door to dialogue and deny the catholicity of the church. It may well be a truer response, more true indeed to the Methodist traditions derived from John Wesley, to see that Christian theology, if it is to be an exposition of God's response to the plight of the world, must always take account of the needs of the poor and the lost, and that insofar as he was a "theologian of the poor" John Wesley was a better theologian and more authentic Christian.

However that may be, it is hoped that the next Institute will be able to build upon the foundation laid in 1982, carry forward the exploration of our traditions on a broader front, and, being more representative of the diversity of those traditions, enable all the churches to appreciate more fully what our contribution to the future of the church universal might be.

List of Authors

S. Wesley Ariarajah

S. Wesley Ariarajah, an ordained minister of the Methodist Church of Sri Lanka, is Director of the subunit on Dialogue of the World Council of Churches with particular responsibility for Christian-Hindu/Buddhist relations. Educated at the University of Madras, the United Theological College Bangalore, Princeton University, and King's College, London, he was formerly lecturer in the History of Religions at the Theological College of Lanka, Sri Lanka.

Brian E. Beck

Brian E. Beck, Secretary of the British Methodist Conference, is an ordained minister, who has been engaged chiefly in theological education in Britain and with the Methodist Church in Kenya. Tutor in New Testament at Wesley House, Cambridge 1968-80, and Principal 1980-84, Beck is also co-chairperson, Oxford Institute of Methodist Theological Studies.

James W. Fowler

James W. Fowler, an ordained minister of the United Methodist Church, has taught at Harvard University and Boston College, and is currently Director of the Center for Faith Development at Emory University, Atlanta; Studies at Duke, Drew, and Harvard Universities; and author of *To See the Kingdom, Life Maps* (with Sam Keen), and *Stages of Faith*.

M. Douglas Meeks

M. Douglas Meeks, an ordained minister of the United Methodist Church, is Professor of Systematic Theology and Philosophy at Eden Theological Seminary, St Louis. Educated at Vanderbilt University, Southwestern at Memphis, Duke University, and Tübingen University, Meeks is the author of *Origins of the Theology of Hope* and editor of *On Human Dignity*, essays by Jürgen Moltmann, and also co-chairperson, Oxford Institute of Methodist Theological Studies.

Albert C. Outler

Albert C. Outler, an ordained minister of the United Methodist Church, is currently Research Professor of Religion at Texas Wesleyan College, Fort Worth, after having taught at Duke University, Yale University, Southern Methodist University, and Davidson College. He was trained at Wofford College, Emory University, and Yale University. Among his books are the Wesley volume in "A Library of Protestant Thought" and a four-volume critical edition of *Wesley's Sermons* (Abingdon Press, 1984-).

Elsa Tamez

Elsa Tamez, Professor of Biblical Studies at the Seminario Biblio Latinoamericano in San José, Costa Rica, is the author of *Diccionario Conciso Griego-Español del Nuevo Testamento, La Hora de la Vida*, and *The Bible of the Oppressed*. A native of Mexico, she has lived for thirteen years in Costa Rica where she completed theological studies at the Seminario Biblio Latinoamericano and studies in literature and linguistics at the National University of Costa Rica.

Geoffrey Wainwright

Geoffrey Wainwright, an ordained minister of the British Methodist Church, is Professor of Systematic Theology at Duke University. After studies at Cambridge, Geneva, and Rome, he taught in Yaoundé, Cameroon; Birmingham, England; and Union Theological Seminary, New York. His most recent books include *Doxology, Eucharist and Eschatology,* and *The Ecumenical Moment.*

David Lowes Watson

David Lowes Watson, an ordained minister of the United Methodist Church, is Director of Evangelism Ministries at the General Board of Discipleship of the United Methodist Church, Nashville, Tennessee, and recently was the occupant of the McCreless Chair of Evangelism at Perkins School of Theology, Southern Methodist University. A native of England, Watson was educated at Oxford University, Eden Theological Seminary, and Duke University. His book on the early Methodist class meeting and a program guide for covenant discipleship in the contemporary church are forthcoming.